The Short Oxford History of the British Isles

General Editor: Paul Langford

The Twelfth and Thirteenth Centuries

Edited by Barbara Harvey

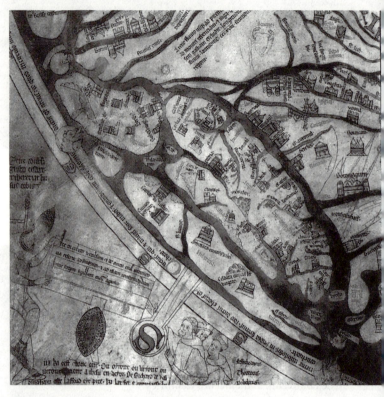

Figure 1 The British Isles as shown on the Hereford *Mappa Mundi*. The Hereford World Map was made at Lincoln, probably in the 1280s, but soon taken to Hereford. Richard of Holdingham, who tells us that he made the map, was either the designer or the craftsman who drew it. East is at the top of the map, and Jerusalem at the centre. In the north-west, England and Wales are an island, and Scotland is an island. Ireland is divided in two by the River Boyne.

The Short Oxford History
of the British Isles

General Editor: Paul Langford

The Twelfth and Thirteenth Centuries

1066–*c*.1280

Edited by Barbara Harvey

OXFORD
UNIVERSITY PRESS

OXFORD
UNIVERSITY PRESS

Great Clarendon Street, Oxford OX2 6DP

Oxford University Press is a department of the University of Oxford.
It furthers the University's objective of excellence in research, scholarship,
and education by publishing worldwide in

Oxford New York

Athens Auckland Bangkok Bogotá Buenos Aires Cape Town
Chennai Dar es Salaam Delhi Florence Hong Kong Istanbul Karachi
Kolkata Kuala Lumpur Madrid Melbourne Mexico City Mumbai Nairobi
Paris São Paulo Shanghai Singapore Taipei Tokyo Toronto Warsaw

with associated companies in Berlin Ibadan

Oxford is a registered trade mark of Oxford University Press
in the UK and in certain other countries

Published in the United States
by Oxford University Press Inc., New York

British Library Cataloguing in Publication Data

Data available

Library of Congress Cataloging in Publication Data

Data applied for

ISBN 0–19–873139–6 (pbk)
ISBN 0–19–873140–X (hbk)

1 3 5 7 9 10 8 6 4 2

Typeset in Minion
by RefineCatch Limited, Bungay, Suffolk
Printed in Great Britain by
T.J. International, Padstow, Cornwall

General Editor's Preface

It is a truism that historical writing is itself culturally determined, reflecting intellectual fashions, political preoccupations, and moral values at the time it is written. In the case of British history this has resulted in a great diversity of perspectives both on the content of what is narrated and the geopolitical framework in which it is placed. In the late twentieth century the process of redefinition has positively accelerated under the pressure of contemporary change. Some of it has come from within Britain during a period of recurrent racial tension in England and reviving nationalism in Scotland, Wales, and Northern Ireland. But much of it also comes from beyond. There has been a powerful surge of interest in the politics of national identity in response to the break-up of some of the world's great empires, both colonial and continental. The search for new sovereignties, not least in Europe itself, has contributed to a questioning of long-standing political boundaries. Such shifting of the tectonic plates of history is to be expected but for Britain especially, with what is perceived (not very accurately) to be a long period of relative stability lasting from the late seventeenth century to the mid-twentieth century, it has had a particular resonance.

Much controversy and still more confusion arise from the lack of clarity about the subject matter that figures in insular historiography. Historians of England are often accused of ignoring the history of Britain as a whole, while using the terms as if they are synonymous. Historians of Britain are similarly charged with taking Ireland's inclusion for granted without engaging directly with it. And for those who believe they are writing more specifically the history of Ireland, of Wales, or of Scotland, there is the unending tension between so-called metropolis and periphery, and the dilemmas offered by wider contexts, not only British and Irish but European and indeed extra-European. Some of these difficulties arise from the fluctuating fortunes and changing boundaries of the British state as organized from London. But even if the rulers of what is now called England had never taken an interest in dominion beyond its borders, the economic and cultural relationships between the various parts of the British Isles would still have generated many historiographical problems.

This series is based on the premise that whatever the complexities and ambiguities created by this state of affairs, it makes sense to offer an overview, conducted by leading scholars whose research is on the leading edge of their discipline. That overview extends to the whole of the British Isles. The expression is not uncontroversial, especially to many in Ireland, for whom the very word 'British' implies an unacceptable politics of dominion. Yet there is no other formulation that can encapsulate the shared experience of 'these islands', to use another term much employed in Ireland and increasingly heard in Britain, but rather unhelpful to other inhabitants of the planet.

In short we use the words 'British Isles' solely and simply as a geographical expression. No set agenda is implied. It would indeed be difficult to identify one that could stand scrutiny. What constitutes a concept such as 'British history' or 'four nations history', remains the subject of acute disagreement, and varies much depending on the period under discussion. The editors and contributors of this series have been asked only to convey the findings of the most authoritative scholarship, and to flavour them with their own interpretative originality and distinctiveness. In the process we hope to provide not only a stimulating digest of more than two thousand years of history, but also a sense of the intense vitality that continues to mark historical research into the past of all parts of Britain and Ireland.

Lincoln College
Oxford

PAUL LANGFORD

Acknowledgements

On behalf of all the contributors, I have the pleasure of thanking those who have helped in a variety of ways—each important, and many time-consuming—to bring this book to fruition. In particular we are grateful to Stuart Airlie, Dauvit Broun, Bruce Campbell, Barbara Crawford, Rees Davies, Piers Dixon, Archie Duncan, Joanna Innes, Michael Kennedy, Lucy Vinten Mattich, Richard Sharpe, J. Beverley Smith, and Matthew Strickland. We also thank most warmly Fiona Kinnear, Jo Stanbridge, Sarah Hyland, and Nik Payne, of Oxford University Press. As editor, I am also greatly indebted to my fellow-contributors, and to Paul Langford, the general editor of the series in which the book appears.

Barbara Harvey

2 January 2001

Contents

Conclusion   243
Barbara Harvey

List of Illustrations

List of Maps

Maps in the text

Map section

List of Contributors

DAVID BATES is Edwards Professor of Medieval History at the University of Glasgow. He has published widely on the history of Normandy, northern France, and Britain in the period from the tenth to the early thirteenth centuries, including *Normandy before 1066* (1982) and an edition of William the Conqueror's charters for the period from 1066 to 1087.

RICHARD BRITNELL is Professor of History in the University of Durham, specializing in economic and social history. He is the author of *The Commercialisation of English Society, 1000–1500* (1993). He has recently contributed to the first volume of *The Cambridge Urban History of Britain*, and is currently writing an economic history of medieval Britain.

ROBIN FRAME is Professor of History in the University of Durham. His publications include *Colonial Ireland, 1169–1369* (1981), *English Lordship in Ireland, 1318–1361* (1982), *The Political Development of the British Isles, 1100–1400* (1990), and *Ireland and Britain, 1170–1450* (1998).

BRIAN GOLDING is Reader in Medieval History in the University of Southampton. His publications include *Conquest and Colonisation: The Normans in Britain, 1066–1100* (1994), and *Gilbert of Sempringham and the Gilbertine Order, c.1130–c.1300* (1995). He is currently preparing an edition of the *Speculum Ecclesie* of Gerald of Wales.

BARBARA HARVEY was formerly a Fellow and Tutor at Somerville College, Oxford, where she taught Medieval History, and is now an Emeritus Fellow of the College. Her book, *Living and Dying in England, 1100–1540: The Monastic Experience* was joint winner of the Wolfson Prize for History in 1993.

HENRIETTA LEYSER is a Fellow of St Peter's College, Oxford. Her publications include *Hermits and the New Monasticism: A Study of Religious Communities in Western Europe, 1000–1150* (1984), and *Medieval Women: A Social History of Women in England, 450–1500* (1995).

HENRY SUMMERSON took his doctorate at Cambridge with a thesis on law enforcement in mid-thirteenth-century England, a field in which he has published several articles and an edition of the 1238 Devon crown pleas. He has also worked extensively on north-west England in the middle ages and later, publishing a two-volume history of medieval Carlisle in 1993. Since then, he has been a Research Editor with the *New Dictionary of National Biography* in Oxford.

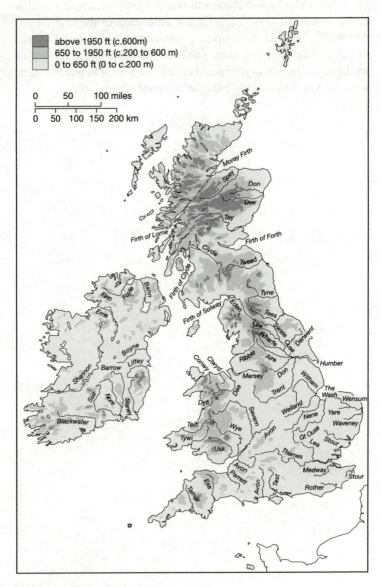

Map 1 The British Isles: physical features

Introduction

Barbara Harvey

The period

In the mid-eleventh century, Britain and Ireland had in common a position on the edge of the Continent of Europe, and much of Britain belonged, as Ireland did, to the Viking world. The Irish Sea was the effective centre of a maritime province extending from Norway to Dublin and embracing the Northern Isles and north and west Scotland, as well as wide territories bordering on the sea itself. Proximity, together with the many practical contacts already in existence, may have seemed to open up the possibility of a political relationship between Britain and Ireland, or at least between some parts of each, of a kind that must always have eluded the wider territories of the maritime province. What form that relationship would take, and, indeed, whether it would come into existence at all, were entirely doubtful matters. In sailing time, Galloway was the nearest point in Britain to Ireland. Writing towards the end of the twelfth century, but when conditions were probably little changed, Gerald of Wales noted that the sea narrowed between Galloway and Ulster to half a short day's sailing. For the actual conception of a political relationship we have to look further south, to England, where, from time to time, the kings of the late Anglo-Saxon period claimed a hegemony over other rulers in Britain, a claim extending even to rulers of the adjacent islands, including Ireland. In ecclesiastical affairs, the see of Canterbury claimed a comparable hegemony.

By the mid-eleventh century, however, the south of England was already turning away from the Viking world and towards countries in mainland Europe which no longer had any links with the latter. The

Norman Conquest ensured that this change of direction became effective for England as a whole, and tended to encourage a similar change in other parts of Britain. It gave fresh impetus to religious reforms already in progress in England itself but much better exemplified in the monasteries and cathedrals of Normandy, and especially at the Abbey of Bec-Hellouin. Lanfranc, whom William I chose for the see of Canterbury in 1170, had earlier been a monk at Bec, and prior there. As a result of the Conquest, new families, drawn from Normandy and a wider area of France, took possession of much of the land in England and the Marches of Wales, and later settled—though in this case by invitation—in substantial areas in the south of Scotland. Wherever this happened, the greatest among the new families became the political and social elite of the period. The new arrivals gave at least the final push, and often much more than this, to a transformation of lordship, the institution which, together with the family itself, did more than any other to shape the societies of this period. Early medieval models of lordship, based on the tribute and personal service rendered by dependants to their lords, were replaced by those characteristic of the high middle ages, when lords were in fact landlords and their dependants rent-paying tenants. It was the Anglicized descendants of the landowning families of Anglo-Norman England and the Marches of Wales who colonized much of central and southern Ireland in the second half of the twelfth century and greatly speeded the establishment of the new forms of lordship there. As events would show, however, their own numbers were too small, and those of the peasant immigrants who came in their wake too large, for the kind of fusion of peoples which had slowly emerged in England after 1066 to be achieved once again here. It is a long twelfth century that begins with the coming of the Normans to England in 1066. Yet there are important senses in which the history of the British Isles in the twelfth century does begin as far back as this.

Although many of the English lords who acquired lands in Ireland, including some of the greatest among them, spent much time there, the English in Ireland did not acquire a strong sense of their own identity in this period: they did so only in the fourteenth century. By contrast, the Gaelic inhabitants of Ireland and the Celtic inhabitants of Wales possessed, in each case, a highly developed sense of their identity as peoples and the inferiority of all incomers as 'foreigners'. In this period, however, a strong sense of national identity could exist without a matching political goal. It was in England, and not in the fragmented societies of Ireland and Wales, that a sense of national identity first became the mainspring of political action. From the end of the twelfth century, opposition to the employment of aliens in positions of influence in Church and state exemplified the new and more purposeful outlook. Yet despite some violent episodes in which aliens were victimized, the search in England for ways of expressing an identity in which so many confidently participated was for a long time essentially peaceful. The wars for which its kings sought, and sometimes obtained, aristocratic support were not yet national wars. But towards the end of the thirteenth century, political moods began to change, and not only in England. The rebellion of the Welsh, led by Llywelyn ap Gruffudd, against Edward I in 1282 marks a qualitative change which was not restricted, in the event, to Wales. In the new and more violent phase which now opened, to engage in armed conflict on an organized scale would often be the way of demonstrating a common identity or denying its claims when made by others, and political independence was, more often than previously, the goal. In this sense, the rebellion of 1282, which was soon followed by the beginning of the long drawn out Scottish War of Independence and the first premonitory rumblings of the Hundred Years War between England and France, seems to represent the watershed dividing the political life of the thirteenth century from that of the fourteenth. Accordingly, c.1280 has been chosen as the term for this book. Like the opening date the closing date will be interpreted flexibly.

The inhabitants

In the period 1066–1280, most of the inhabitants of the British Isles lived, not in towns, as they do at the present day, but in the countryside. The specialized activities of many townsmen and the marketplaces on which these were focused were indispensable to the economic growth which now occurred universally. With only a few notable exceptions, however, the towns themselves were small, and their populations often to be numbered in hundreds rather than thousands. All aggregate population figures for this period rest to some extent on conjecture; yet they are useful in indicating, very roughly, the orders of magnitude that we should have in mind. There are good reasons for believing that towards the end of the thirteenth century, when the early medieval growth in population was slowing down, England had c.6 million inhabitants. Circumstantial evidence suggests that the population of Scotland may normally have been in a ratio of c.1:6 in comparison to that of England. If so, we should envisage c.1 million here at this date; some estimates for Scotland, however, arrived at in other ways, are much lower. Figures of c.300,000 and c.1 million represent reasonable working hypotheses for, respectively, Wales and Ireland. By the late thirteenth century, towns were much more numerous than in the mid-eleventh and existed in many regions which previously had none; and the blank spaces on the urban map at the earlier date included the whole of Wales west of the central watershed (see Map C). Yet we can be confident that not more than 10 per cent of the total population of this later period lived in towns with a population exceeding 3,000, and that in many regions the proportion was much lower.

Most of the inhabitants of the countryside were, in a very general sense of the word, peasants. The minority, which included many of the clergy and all landowners who did not tend their own livestock or follow their own plough, had an influence out of proportion to its size, but peasants gave the societies of this period some of their most important and enduring characteristics. The fortunate among them owned land or occupied it as tenants, or belonged to families and households—in each case variously structured according to region—which did so. The less fortunate eked out a living by other means, and frequently by working for hire on other people's farms, large or small, or in the small-scale industrial concerns which were a common feature of the medieval countryside. Many led a hybrid existence as farmers who also engaged in by-employment of this kind, their holdings being too small to support their households; and wives and daughters as well as fathers and sons sometimes participated in such enterprises. Whatever their sources of livelihood, few, it appears, aimed higher in their economic life than to provide subsistence for themselves and their dependents—or, if they aimed higher, it was their fate to be often defeated. There are grounds for concluding that in England the proportion of the population existing at the very margin of subsistence was never less than one-third throughout this period, and the proportion elsewhere may have been as large. The so-called naked poor, the utterly indigent who lived entirely on alms, were from the beginning conspicuous in the countryside, and became so in the growing towns.

Yet economic life must always be seen in a social context. The societies which we have to consider were extremely diverse, but alike in believing, with few apparent dissentients, that much of the wealth made at their agrarian base should be passed, by various ways and means, up the social scale, to sustain privileged classes of rulers and lords in the enjoyment of the expensive lifestyles appropriate to their high status. Peasants were caught up to varying degrees in these arrangements, but few escaped their consequences altogether; and the payment of a tenth of all produce annually to the Church became a universal obligation in the course of this period, though one that was not always honoured in practice. Moreover, the typical peasant, like his lord, possessed a status to be affirmed by an appropriate level of material culture or imperilled if this was not sustained. Even in the subsistence economies we have to envisage, surpluses had, if possible, to be large enough to fulfil these obligations. How the wherewithal for these purposes was found depended on locality and region, on the presence or absence of organized markets and of money as a medium of exchange, and on other less important variables, all of which themselves tended to change in the course of the period. Subsistence itself was a variable, meaning for some households a bare sufficiency, but for others an existence well removed from the poverty line as we must understand the latter at this time; and since families experience life cycles, in which demands made on resources wax and wane according to the age and circumstances of their individual members, many households in this period moved between the two extremes which have been mentioned in the course of a single generation or two.

The natural environment

All peasants, however, had in common a dependence day by day on the natural environment—on terrain, soil, and vegetation, on climate and weather, and all the other resources which, together, made up the inescapable natural conditions of life. To a large extent townsmen shared this dependence, for medieval towns were intimately related to the neighbouring countryside, to which they looked for essential food supplies, for produce that could be sold in their markets, and for customers to purchase it. We should think of the environment as a changing and at times almost volatile thing. The process of change of concern to us began in the remoteness of geological time, when Britain and Ireland, each of which had been divided into two, became in each case a single island. But not until 10,000 BP or thereabouts did the latest ice-sheets melt and the islands begin to experience the warm conditions of the inter-glacial period which continues at the present day. More recently, and demonstrably from the Neolithic period onwards (4,000–2,000 BC; 5,950–3,950 BP), the process of change has been influenced by the very ways in which men and women have interacted with the environment on which they depend—by, for example, the boundaries they have chosen for their settlements, the woods they have felled and the woods they have spared. On the timescale we have to envisage for all these changes, a period extending only from the mid-eleventh century to the late thirteenth appears infinitesimal. Yet in the perspective of historical time, this period was an important one for the environment, and some of the changes were rapid. These are explained in part by technical innovation—by, for example, the invention of windmills—and by the more enterprising use of a number of techniques which had long been known but not previously much exploited. But they probably owed much more to demographic and economic developments, already touched on or to be discussed below—to a growth of population and a growth of markets, to an increasing use of money as a medium of exchange, and the flexibility in the use of resources which monetization of this kind conferred.

How, then did the natural environment change in the course of this period? Its history demands interdisciplinary forms of study, and many of the disciplines which contribute to this are relatively new. For chronology, however, we still depend largely on one of the historian's traditional employments, the study of written sources, and especially, in this context, the study of datable sources of this kind. These survive very unevenly. Thus from twelfth- and thirteenth-century Scotland, many charters survive but very few contemporary annals or chronicles; from Ireland and Wales, an abundance of annals and chronicles, but relatively few charters. Then again, if Domesday Book, fruit of the Domesday Survey of 1086, is not quite the complete record of landholding down to the last ox, cow, and pig that a contemporary observer believed it to be, it is nevertheless a unique record of rural life and agrarian practice at a defined moment in time. But only England and the Welsh borders were surveyed, and in practice much of the north of England is treated somewhat sketchily. Even so, the greatest difficulties arise, not from a scarcity of sources or their uneven survival, but from the huge differences we must allow for in the contemporary view of the environment of this period compared to our own view of it. We cannot hope to recapture that view in its entirety, but only to retrieve some of the pieces.

Terrain, soil, and land use

'Lowland', 'upland', and ' mountain' are not terms of art but words needing to be placed in a context before we can give them a precise meaning. In Britain, the 650 ft (c.200 m) contour serves very well to demarcate lowland from upland. In the north and west of the island, the greater part of the surface area lies above this contour, and much of this upland is sufficiently high or has slopes sufficiently steep to be described as mountainous (see Map 1). In the south and east, by contrast, most of the surface area lies below this contour, and none of it is mountainous. Ireland, however, is different again. Here, 75 per cent of the surface area lies below the 500 ft (c.150 m) contour. Yet this great expanse of lowland is almost ringed by the hills and mountains, most of which lie near the coast. The slopes of hills and mountains are affected by their use by man and beast, and by unassisted physical processes. Together, these factors will certainly have brought about significant changes in the form of many since the twelfth century or the thirteenth. But such changes are details in a larger canvas: painting with a broad brush, we can say that the uplands today show us the extent of the uplands of that earlier period.

The mountains, together with a distinctive configuration of coastlines and estuaries, encouraged regional differences in orientation and sometimes an apparently back-to-back stance on the part of neighbouring regions. In Scotland, the Highland Boundary Fault, running from Aberdeen to the Firth of Clyde, represents a fundamental geological division: indeed, it provides part of the evidence that Britain was once divided into two. To the north of it, the highest mountains in the island provide the source of rivers which flow either east to the North Sea or west to the Atlantic. These, together with a similar configuration in the Northern Highlands, tended to divide Scotland in this period into east- and west-facing segments. Similarly, England west of the Pennines looked west to Ireland; but England east of the Pennines looked east, and ultimately to Scandinavia. West of its steep central watershed, Wales looked towards Ireland, but on the east side across Offa's Dyke to Herefordshire and the English West Midlands. In Ireland, the central lowlands tend naturally towards south-east or north-west orientations, seemingly emphasized by the deep cut made by the River Shannon and by its wide estuary. Ireland west of that river looked towards the Atlantic. But the populous southern and eastern seaboards of Ireland looked east across the Irish Sea to Wales, and south to Cornwall and Devon—where 'waste' caused by raiders from Ireland is noted in Domesday Book—and ultimately to Brittany and Spain.

Both uplands and lowlands possess a variety of soils. However, the well drained or moderately well drained brown earths that are best suited to arable cultivation are common in the lowlands, especially in those lying under 300 ft (c.100 m), and the gleys and peats, the thin soils that are either poorly or excessively drained, tend to be characteristic of the uplands. The use of soils affects their texture and other properties, and in consequence most soils in existence at the present time may be described as man-made. Yet despite the changes we must allow for in the intervening period, we can probably assume that the broad contrast mentioned above was also present in the twelfth and thirteenth centuries. But marginal soils, so-called because they are particularly sensitive to changes in the demand for produce, existed in each of these broadly defined areas. Some of these were relatively poor but attracted the farmer and settler when population and demand increased to a critical level. The infield–outfield system, which allowed for part of the arable (the infield) to be cultivated continuously, though with an appropriate use of fallow, and part (the outfield) to be cultivated for a period but then rested entirely for several years, was common in such areas. Other soils, including many in the central English lowlands, were marginal in a different sense. These were of relatively good quality and well suited to arable cultivation, but suited also to pastoral husbandry. As, therefore, the market for agrarian produce expanded and commercially oriented agriculture became more common, these soils tended to be devoted now to the one, now to the other use, according to changes in demand and in the supply of labour. In the twelfth and thirteenth centuries, however, they were normally devoted to arable. Away from the margin, and whatever the demographic trend, we must allow in the uplands and lowlands alike for the subsistence farmer who grew the corn that he needed for the bread or the oatcakes belonging to his staple diet, and some winter feed for livestock, on soils that would never be considered for these purposes in a commercially oriented economy.

It is therefore only with important qualifications that we can speak of two ways of exploiting the land in this period, the one characteristic of the lowlands, the other of the uplands. Yet the contrast existed. Husbandry in the lowlands centred, characteristically, on the cultivation of arable. In the uplands, pastoralism was common; peasant livelihoods were obtained mainly by grazing cattle and sheep in the abundant pastures and pigs in the woodland, itself still extensive in parts of the upland; and cattle and sheep provided the cash crops of the seignorial demesnes and other large farms. In the uplands, it was unusual to attempt more than a single grain crop in the course of the year and the normal practice to sow this crop in spring. The chosen grains were normally oats and barley, the former being particularly well suited to poor soils and to the relatively short ripening periods to be anticipated in many such regions. On good lowland soils, however, both winter- and spring-sown grains could be fitted into the rotation courses, and wheat was extensively cultivated here, both as a commercial crop and as a bread corn for peasant consumption.

It is, however, of the nature of upland that it does at many points descend into the lowland. Where the two kinds of terrain were found in close proximity, mixed husbandry, allowing equal or nearly equal importance to arable crops and livestock, was common. Thus, the townships of the commote of Gafflogion, in the western extremity of Gwynedd, whose lands included uplands suited to grazing and lowlands to arable, were peopled by mixed farmers, as we can infer from taxation returns made in the 1290s. Their husbandry differed to a significant extent from the pastoralism practised in the heartland of Gwynedd and more resembled that of neighbouring, fertile, Anglesey. In Anglesey, wrote Gerald of Wales a century earlier, enough corn was grown to feed the rest of Wales, if crops should fail there. Yet in Anglesey, too, there were many mixed farmers at this date. In Yorkshire, where parts of the High Pennine Moors ran down to fertile lowlands in the Vale of York, the monks of Fountains Abbey took care to acquire both kinds of land for some of their granges: they could be mixed farmers here, if they wished.

Woodland and waste

In the late prehistoric period, pine woodland was extensive in the Scottish Highlands and the west of Ireland. In the twelfth and thirteenth centuries, however—as far as we know—little coniferous woodland, if any, existed in the British Isles. Oak and hazel were probably dominant, but with an intermixture of other species, including birch, alder—a tree of wetlands—ash and elm, which varied regionally. Little woodland was wild or trackless, but the existence of tracks does not imply that of signposts too, and much woodland may still have been inaccessible to strangers who did not know the locality in question. Where woods existed near undrained marsh or bog, a traveller's difficulties were enhanced. Yet the story, much embroidered, no doubt, by the time it reached Gerald of Wales, that in 1166 Diarmait Mac Murchadha made the woods near Ferns, which were on such a site, impenetrable to his enemies by scattering fallen trees and logs as obstacles, and digging pits and trenches in the level ground, would lose its point had there not been some tracks, and indeed tracks wide enough for men and horses, even here. At this time, woodland probably covered *c*.20 per cent of the whole superficial area of Ireland, and the comparable figure for Wales may have been even higher. In England, approximately one settlement in every two mentioned earlier in Domesday Book had woodland considered worthy of notice by the king's commissioners, and their record is demonstrably incomplete in this respect. In Scotland, although the Highlands had long since been disafforested on a grand scale, sufficient woodland remained in the Lowlands to provide the subject-matter of many prodigal grants by kings and lords to the new religious orders who established houses here in the twelfth century.

'Waste' is the term normally used in the present context to describe rough pasture which had not yet been appropriated for individual use, although it might be cultivated from time to time as an outfield by agreement among all those possessing common rights there. Much of the waste was not only rough but also wet, for, regionally, bog and marsh occurred as frequently in the waste as moorland and heath. In the central lowlands of Ireland, the former may have been much more extensive than the latter.

Woodland and waste were to some extent alternative resources. Thus, the inhabitants of the Norfolk Broadlands, like those of the more extensive lowlands of Scotland or central Ireland, had peat if they did not have wood for their fires. Without access to one or other, however, it was impossible to cook meals and keep warm, to build or repair dwellings, pasture animals, or heat the furnaces on which many industries relied, and town life itself would have been impracticable. Moreover, since trees could be felled and wetlands drained, these resources could provide a moving frontier for hus-bandry and settlement; and as population increased, so did the pressures to translate this possibility into action grow stronger. Yet if these were essentially economic resources, each, like population change itself, was greatly influenced by the social structure of the region and country in question. In particular, the strength of lord-ship, on the one hand, and the extent of free tenures, on the other, were important factors. Free tenants naturally wished to preserve the common rights in woodland and waste which were traditionally associated with their holdings and were essential to the proper func-tioning of the latter. The extent to which they were able to do so varied with region and period. Thus, the free tenants of south Wales could do little to protect their ancient rights of common against erosion at the hands of the English and Flemish immigrants who settled here in the late eleventh century. From the late twelfth century, however, free tenants in England were in a strong position, since they were permitted to litigate in defence of their rights in the royal courts.

As for the lords, by the late thirteenth century, many in all parts of the British Isles claimed the right to control access to woodland and waste, and in England lords made this claim throughout our period. But lords used such powers rather differently in the case of the two resources. In general, they seem to have done their best to preserve woodland from destruction, not least because much of it belonged to the so-called 'forest' where they were accustomed to hunt, but to have been very ready to permit and even to encourage settlement on the waste. They rightly perceived that if the waste were to be cleared and fenced, or drained and dyked, as appropriate, and brought into the demesne or leased to tenants, the gains would far exceed those of simply using it together with many other farmers as common pasture. The greatest colonists of all were the Cistercians, who engaged in commercial agriculture on a large scale in regions which had hitherto been marginal to agriculture and settlement and included extensive areas of waste. As colonists the Cistercians had profound effects on the landscapes of Wales, the north of England, and the south of Scotland, and no single group did more than they to bring about the considerable erosion of woodland as well as waste that occurred in the course of this period.

Climate and weather

These two words express different ways of looking at the same feature of the natural environment. By 'weather' we should understand the daily mixture of temperature, rainfall, and other variables experienced in a particular locality, and by 'climate' the general character of the mixture accumulating over longer periods of time and given these daily inputs. Climatic change occurs in cycles including extremes of climatic behaviour and evolving over periods so long that they cannot be measured in historical time, but only in the multi-millennia of geological time. But it also includes oscillations, or fluctuations, completed in periods which are short compared to these, and in some cases comprise only a few decades—the equivalent of a human lifespan or less. Weather varies seasonally within the year, and its seasonal behaviour, an accumulation of the daily mixture, varies from year to year: at the present day, winters tend to vary most and summers least. But weather, and therefore climate as well, also vary over horizontal distances and with height above sea level, and both are influenced by the nearness or otherwise of oceanic waters. Thus, Ireland, where the coastline is extensive in relation to the land mass it encloses, has a milder and more humid climate, with a narrower range of seasonal differences in temperature than, for example, many inland parts of England; in these inland parts, climate tends to be more extreme or 'continental'. Scotland, however, where the surrounding oceanic waters include the complex and variable waters of the north-east Atlantic, has a notably unstable climate. In the uplands and highlands in the British Isles considered as a whole, other variations occur: these regions have lower maximum temperatures in summer, and lower minimum temperatures in winter, than the lowlands; they also have heavier rainfall and a shorter growing period for vegetation than the latter. How many variations of these kinds do we catch sight of in the period 1066–1280, and in what kinds of sources do we catch sight of them?

For the middle ages, there are no meteorological data in the strict sense—no daily observations of temperature, rainfall, or wind-speed, the principal variants. We depend partly on information which, though gathered and processed for other purposes, provides circumstantial evidence about climate and weather. Thus, the width of the rings laid down annually by trees, which are sensitive to temperature and rainfall, may shed light on such behaviour in their locality; and deposits of pollen may do so in theirs by revealing changes over time in patterns of vegetation. Biological data of these kinds, lending themselves to systematic analysis, must carry special weight in the present context. But they are often hard to interpret because, like climate and weather themselves, they reflect the interaction of several variables which are not always distinguishable in the end result. Tree-ring chronologies, for example, are now extant from prehistoric periods to the present day, but the ring data for a particular year or sequence of years may leave it quite uncertain which of the possible variables was 'driving' the weather at that juncture. Harvest fluctuations, of which something is known in thirteenth-century England, possess a similar ambiguity. Normally, the weather exerted a greater immediate influence than any other factor on the quality of the harvest in a particular locality. Yet the manorial sources we rely on in the study of yields may not tell us which climatic variable was responsible for an abnormally good or bad harvest, if one occurred, or whether some factor of an entirely different kind operated in the year in question to produce such an effect. It is difficult to know what actually happened in the years of special interest to us.

Despite their evident subjectivity, narrative and literary sources still provide much of our information about climate and weather in the British Isles in the middle ages. But these must be carefully evaluated. Matthew Paris, a monk of St Albans and, after William of Malmesbury, the greatest historical writer of this period in England, normally included a description of the weather in the summary, or characterization, of each year which is a feature of his 'contemporary chronicle': this covers the period 1234–59, and from 1245 to the end, Matthew was writing only a year or two after the events he describes. Paris was unusual in showing an interest in the weather whatever it was like: most chroniclers who take any interest at all in weather or climate tend to highlight the exceptional and neglect the ordinary or average. Some, like the annalists of Inisfallen, may allude to these topics in tantalizingly indirect ways. 'A great yield of mast this year generally', the *Annals of Inisfallen* note in 1195, and similar entries follow in 1199 and 1200, when the fruit crops too are described as abundant.[1] Clearly, these are weather-related entries, but the historian would give much to be told about the weather itself in Ireland in these years.

Quite possibly—although the case cannot be put more strongly than this—climate in all parts of the British Isles was slightly warmer for much of this period than in the earlier middle ages, and the seasonal range of temperatures narrower in this period compared to the earlier one. A slow 'warming' process beginning in the ninth century may have underlain both these changes. By the end of the period, however, a deterioration was probably under way: *c.*1240, mean temperatures began to fall a little, and the seasonal range of temperatures to widen a little. If the changes at each end of the period were small, so too were those needed to exert a long-term influence on contemporary economies. Thus, a warming or cooling of less than one degree Celsius in maximum summer temperatures was fully capable of bringing about serious effects on agriculture in both Britain and Ireland; and changes of this order of magnitude may have been in process at either end of the period.

Whatever the degree of warming that occurred generally in northern Europe on the threshold of this period, the contrast between the mild climate of Ireland and the more 'continental' climate of England was evidently unaffected. 'This', wrote Gerald of Wales of Ireland towards the end of the twelfth century, 'is the most temperate of all countries', and he observed that, despite frequent rain even in summer, the weather in Ireland was never inclement and never extreme.[2] The contrast between upland and lowland climates, especially in the matter of rainfall, is implicit in other observations by Gerald. But he was not the only observant writer in our period. Writing in midland England early in the twelfth century, Henry, archdeacon of

---

[1] *Annals of Inisfallen* (*MS Rawlinson B.503*), ed. Seán Mac Airt (Dublin, 1951), 321, 327.

[2] Gerald of Wales, *History and Topography of Ireland*, trans. J. J. O'Meara (Harmondsworth, 1982), 53.

Huntingdon, betrays his surprise at the high rate of precipitation of rainfall in the uplands of the north and west. There are, he says, parts of England where 'the rain seems to rise up from the mountains and immediately fall on the plain'.[3]

Annual fluctuations in climate are well attested in thirteenth-century England, and we can assume that they were neither new at this time nor, as a climatic feature, confined to England. We are concerned at this point with fluctuations in the climate of, respectively, winter, spring, summer, and autumn from year to year. In the written sources, winter (Dec.–Feb. inclusive) and summer (Jun.–Aug.) are most frequently mentioned, and it is likely that to earn such notice they were in some respect unusual. However, a systematic analysis of the evidence by Astrid Olgivie and Graham Farmer suggests that winters in this century may have been as often below the norm in severity as above it, and summer rainfall, similarly, as often below as above the norm. Very cautiously, and using now the evidence of fluctuations in the quality of the harvest from year to year, we can say that southern England experienced as many 'good' years as 'bad' years in the thirteenth century. The best harvests seem to have followed dry autumns, hard winters, and dry summers, the worst ones, a wet autumn and winter, however dry or wet the following summer.

Bad years sometimes occurred in small clusters—a dire circumstance in subsistence economies where even one poor harvest might make it impossible to find all the seed corn that was needed for the next year. Thus, in 1110, the Anglo-Saxon Chronicle records storms, ruining crops, and a frost on 5 May which damaged fruit trees, and in the next year a long and severe winter and, again, later in the year, damage to crops. William of Newburgh tells us that the famine experienced in parts of France and England in 1197 was then actually in its fifth year. It is possible, indeed, likely that a long continued scarcity of this kind originated in a shorter run of bad weather, extending, perhaps, over two or three years. Some sixty years later, wet summers and harvest failures in two consecutive years, 1257 and 1258, brought about the deaths of very large numbers of indigent people: many died, we are told, in the streets. Despite these later

---

[3] Henry, Archdeacon of Huntingdon, *Historia Anglorum* (*History of the English People*), ed. and trans. D. Greenway (Oxford Medieval Texts; 1996), 23.

episodes, there were perhaps more climatically bad years in the late eleventh and early twelfth centuries than in the next hundred years or in the thirteenth century considered on its own. Yet in England, where the evidence, for all its shortcomings, is better than that surviving for any other part of the British Isles, the period as a whole was not, it appears, characterized by marked fluctuations in climate. Nor do such fluctuations as occurred fit into a cyclical pattern, as some have suggested might be the case: on the contrary, England in these years had a climatic stability that anyone looking back from the early fourteenth century would have envied.

Commerce

Travel for a private purpose, to visit a shrine, seek out a teacher or a patron, or look for a better livelihood than one could hope for by staying at home, was a feature of life throughout the middle ages, in and from the British Isles as elsewhere. In the period discussed in this book, but especially in Ireland and the north and west of Britain, many lords received renders in kind from their clients and tenants, who sometimes travelled considerable distances with livestock on the hoof and more awkward renders like barrels of mead or eggs by the hundred. To those who travelled for these traditional reasons, we must add some new faces in the twelfth and thirteenth centuries: royal servants, for example, travelling to keep one end of the Angevin realm in touch with another; justices on eyre; clergy bound for Rome, on business at the papal curia; and legates coming from Rome to hold councils, visit monasteries, or even to pacify a realm, as Ottobuono Fieschi came to England in 1265.

Commerce made different demands on systems of communication from any so far touched on, including a demand for more elaborate arrangements at the quayside. Long-distance trade was small-scale throughout this period, but important on account of its ripple effects throughout the economy as a whole. By the late eleventh century, it was already indispensable to the way of life of many households of the better sort, an incentive to accumulate capital, and a means of dispersing the latter through a widening network of merchants and markets. The Viking traders of Dublin, whose clients included high kings of Ireland, imported Welsh slaves through the port of Chester and wines from Poitou, and no doubt other luxury products from this and other sources; and we know that they exported marten skins at this time to Chester and Rouen. 'What would Ireland be worth without the goods that come in by sea from England?', wrote William of Malmesbury patriotically a generation or two later.[4] Now, the wines were as much in demand as ever, the slave trade in decline, and Bristol beginning to replace Chester in the Anglo-Irish trade. Later in the century, when Diarmait Mac Murchadha and Strongbow besieged Wexford, a ship from Britain, laden with wheat and wine intended for the market, was the one ship anchored in the harbour which the besiegers did not immediately set on fire but attempted to capture. By the early thirteenth century, moreover, if not from an earlier date, monasteries in the south of Scotland were shipping grain for their own needs from Irish ports.

Nor was it only on these western seaboards that traders were active. It is likely, although the point cannot be proved, that Anglo-Scottish trade had already fallen into the pattern which only later sources actually reveal: this trade, though extremely varied, was dominated by English exports of grain to Scotland and Scottish exports of livestock on the hoof, or barrelled meat, to England. Exports of wool from England to Flanders, which had become a regular feature of English trade in the late eleventh century, took off to reach an altogether different level in the twelfth. In the latter century, a new political link between England and Aquitaine facilitated English imports of wine from Gascony, and exports to Gascony of grain and other products, including tin from mines in Devon and Cornwall. Towards the end of the twelfth century, stone from Caen was used for the rebuilding of Canterbury Cathedral, and in the mid-thirteenth century freestone from Caen was used for mouldings and carvings in Westminster Abbey. Trade with Scandinavia, source of abundant timbers, furs, and fish, and providing a market for grain and cloth, among other commodities, did not disappear in this widening of commercial enterprise and cultural perspectives. On the contrary, it may have increased in volume in these centuries, even from the Irish ports

---

[4] William of Malmesbury, *Gesta Regum Anglorum* (*History of the English Kings*), i, ed. R. A. B. Mynors, R. Thomson, and M. Winterbottom (Oxford Medieval Texts; 1998), 739.

which the Vikings had raised to greatness much earlier, partly on the basis of this trade; but it sank in relative importance.

Like long-distance trade, regional and local trade developed at an uneven pace in different parts of the British Isles. Some exchanges of a kind must have existed from a very early date. No household, for example, could exist without a supply of salt, the essential preservative for meat and dairy produce. Yet many lived far from brine springs and salt pans and, unless given salt—as many religious houses were by their benefactors—must have purchased it. Organized markets, however, developed later than these basic exchanges: later in Scotland than in England, where many existed by the late eleventh century, and later in Wales and Ireland than in either of the former. Whenever it occurred, the development of markets of this kind affected, not only the frequency with which many ordinary people used the highways and trackways, and the waterways, of their region, but also the directions in which they needed to go, and the distances travelled. Although many markets were founded by lords in the hopes that the profits would swell the incomes they received from their estates, marketing patterns rarely coincided with patterns of estate ownership: indeed, perhaps only in parts of English Ireland, where such arrangements were more secure than any other available at the time, did this happen. By the thirteenth century, many people whose predecessors had rarely needed to travel, except to fulfil an obligation in some other part of their lord's estate, now frequented markets chosen entirely for their convenience, irrespective of the geography of landownership. The journeys now were sometimes longer, sometimes shorter than previously, but they had a different orientation. How far, then, did the means of travelling and transporting goods prove adequate to all these changing demands?

Communications

Hard evidence about medieval ships derives mainly from wrecks, of which all too few have so far been recovered. Artistic evidence, on which we must often rely, may take liberties with its subject and be a poor guide to the chronology of actual change. It can only be hoped that the ensuing short account does not have similar shortcomings.

The best ships built anywhere in the British Isles in this period were probably those built in Ireland, and in the first half of the thirteenth century a number of galleys were built here for John and Henry III. But galleys at this time were warships, and large ones. For the carrying trade in northern waters, including the Irish Sea, we should envisage a great variety of vessels but a preponderance of small ones. By the thirteenth century, many may have been cogs. These were clinker-built—that is, with timbers overlapping and not laid flush—with flat bottom, straight stem and stern posts, a stern rudder and a single sail. However, hulks may still have been widely used as sea-going vessels. These had rounded hulls and strakes gathered into the upper end of the latter and not, as in a cog, ending at the stem and stern posts. It is of interest that the manuscript known as 'The Leaves of Becket', which dates from the period 1220 x 1240 and probably copies a lost work of Matthew Paris, shows Thomas Becket arriving at Sandwich, on his return from exile in 1170, in a hulk. It has a single sail and a starboard rudder and perhaps tells us what kind of vessel was still common in English waters in the early thirteenth century. As for size, the tonnage of ships in this period was reckoned literally in terms of capacity to carry tuns, or casks, of wine, each containing c.250 gallons, whatever the nature of the cargo. Arrangements for the king's prise, or right to take one tun below market price from cargoes of 10 to 19 tuns, but two from cargoes of 20 tuns or more, suggest that some ships with a capacity under 20 tuns may have been used in the Anglo-Gascon wine trade; by the thirteenth century, this trade now dominated imports of wine into England. Ships exceeding 100 tuns were rare in this trade in the thirteenth century. Passengers could probably be taken in a carrying vessel of any size, but a relatively large one was needed to take their horses as well. Gerald of Wales, needing on one occasion to cross the English Channel on the first stage of a journey to Rome, looked first along the Essex coast near Tendring, and finding no ship there large enough to take his horses, resolved to cross the Thames and make his way to Sandwich, where some ships from Flanders were said to be waiting for the right wind. But he had no expectation that even these would take his horses, and in the end he hired his own ship.

In estuaries and on the major inland waterways, many boats built for the purpose of carrying goods and passengers operated, and more did so at the end of this period than at the beginning. Some of these would be described today as barges, a term confined at the time to sea-going vessels. Few, if any, in private service would have been as large as two that were built in 1282, one at Winchelsea and the other at Romney, for Edward I's use in north Wales, but the cost of these— £46. 14s. 10d. and £30. 1s. 1d. respectively—may indicate the order of magnitude of the outlay needed to obtain a purpose-built barge. Even the lower of the two sums would have kept a knight and his household comfortably for a year at this date. In the thirteenth century, large boats, known as shouts, were used for carrying heavy loads on the Thames between Henley and London, and on the Lea, a tributary of the Thames. The shout excavated at Blackfriars, London, in 1970 was built c.1400, but its carrying capacity of 7.5 tonnes may be applicable to earlier boats of this kind. On the Thames and other large and busy waterways, a professional carrying service developed. Large landowners, however, making regular use of these waterways tended to have their own boats. In 1291 the abbot of Westminster, who used the Thames from Laleham to Westminster to carry goods for his household to and from some of his manors in the Home Counties and West Midlands, found it necessary to replace his existing boat with a new one. The new boat was built at Laleham by carpenters and locksmiths, and the materials which they used included 150 planks, presumably of oak, 900 rivets, and 900 nails, of which 500 were of wood and evidently treenails used for the frame. Flock was used for caulking, and 50 yards of cloth of an unspecified kind for the single sail. The total cost was £7. 5s.—less than the cost of a royal barge, but enough to keep a small household of this period in considerable comfort for more than a year.[5]

Given the high cost of a purpose-built vessel, it seems likely that many boats carrying goods and passengers on inland waterways were simply fishing boats whose owners turned an honest penny from time to time in this way, or simply obliged friends and neighbours without charging them. In the less monetized economy of native Wales in the twelfth century, coracle owners may have performed a comparable function, for Gerald of Wales tells us that these small boats, which, to his surprise, were round or triangular and covered with skins, were used for fishing or to cross rivers.

[5] Westminster Abbey Muniments 27110 (cited by kind permission of the Dean and Chapter of Westminster).

Water transport was cheaper than transport by road for heavy goods, such as stone and grain, and the logs which Thames shouts often carried for citizens of London to use in their houses. In his great *History of Agriculture and Prices*, Thorold Rogers estimated that the cost of the former in England in the thirteenth and fourteenth centuries may have been only one-sixth the cost of the latter. More recent studies have confirmed the existence of a very large differential and illustrated the importance of rivers as well as seas in this context. The thriving trade between Wales and south-west England, in which the Severn estuary played a vital part, was mainly of heavy goods: the Welsh sent hides, leather, wool, and fish to English markets from Tenby, Carmarthen, and Kidwelly, via Bristol and imported iron, coal, and timber from the Forest of Dean, and on occasion other English commodities. The cheapness and importance of water transport at the time explains the location of some of the earliest Scottish burghs to appear. Thus, Roxburgh stood at the junction of the Teviot and the Tweed, and Perth at a fordable point of the Tay, from which there was access by river to the sea.

Yet in England, after the mid-twelfth century, water traffic on inland waterways failed to grow with the remarkable growth of inland trade which now took place. For this, several reasons can be suggested. Transport by water, whether by sea or river, was even more unpredictable than transport by road, and waiting for the boat to go or the wind to change was a preliminary that might take some time. Such an inconvenience no doubt became the less tolerable the less heavy the load and smaller the cost advantage of having the patience to accept the delay. Some long stretches of navigable river could in fact be used only in winter, when the water was high; and fish weirs placed by riparian landowners could impede progress at any time of the year. Given these hazards, the improvement in the quality of many bridges which occurred from the late twelfth century onwards, as stone began to replace wood as the common material, may have helped to tilt the balance of advantage towards road transport: stone bridges were safer for horses and carts than the wooden bridges they replaced, which often lacked guide-rails. But the main reason why the inland waterways fell somewhat behind in England at this juncture was probably that a great many of the new towns and markets, whose growth is a feature of this period, were not near enough to navigable rivers to make water transport viable for them.

Many earlier foundations of this kind were deliberately sited near such rivers, but these, on the whole, were not.

Roads in medieval Britain often followed the line of Roman roads for substantial distances. Moreover, the representation on the Gough Map of five main highways radiating from London to, respectively, Exeter and beyond, Bristol, St Davids, and—in two cases—Carlisle, has a 'Roman' feel about it, since the actual Roman system of roads radiated from London. This map was made in the fourteenth century but illustrates a system which, in its basic outlines, was probably in existence much earlier. Roman roads, however, were made to facilitate the direct movement of armies and other personnel to and from towns and fortified places. Medieval roads, by contrast, served primarily the needs of those who were travelling relatively short distances. As routes to distant places, they were often rather indirect, and, as though to draw attention to the break with the Roman past, sometimes ran parallel to Roman roads but did not use the latter. Yet the distinction frequently drawn between a highway (*magna via*) and lesser ways, sometimes in England and in Scotland called 'public' or 'common' ways, represents a distinction between the main roads, which covered long distances, and secondary ones, each of which did no more than link two towns or settlements of the larger kind. In Scotland, moreover, David I occasionally referred to highways as royal ways (*vie regie*), and by the late thirteenth century they were so called in English Ireland. In England, offences committed on major highways were the more serious because the latter were the king's highways.

Some of the mountain passes in use in this period were engineered. Moreover, town authorities occasionally spent money on the upkeep of approach roads, and, more frequently, on that of streets within their walls. With these exceptions, it is unlikely that highways or common ways were engineered anywhere in the British Isles or normally given any kind of artificial surface. Like the trackways and paths that many people were obliged to use for their journeys, highways and common ways were made and kept open largely by use. Verges, however, which provided ideal cover for thieves if the trees and bushes were allowed to grow near the actual road, were almost as important to a successful journey as the road surface itself. In England, throughout this period, the task of keeping the verges of highways clear was probably regarded in official circles as one for the neighbouring landowners, and, indeed, to some extent discharged by them as part of an ill-defined 'royal service' originating in the late Anglo-Saxon period. If so, the Statute of Winchester (1285) had a basis in custom. This required landowners, with the assistance of the neighbourhood, to widen the verges of highways leading from one market town to another by levelling all trees with undergrowth, hedges, and ditches to a width of 200 ft (c.60 m) on either side. Yet it is only sensible to assume that throughout this period the verges of many highways in England were uncleared. On these roads, no doubt, travellers often felt as insecure as Gerald of Wales did on the highway from Dublin to Waterford: there, he complains, the woods came so near that one would hardly have the opportunity to draw a weapon if attacked. Alton Pass, in Hampshire, which had become a notorious haunt of robbers by the end of our period, ran through woods which provided abundant cover for their purposes.

How wide were the actual roads, as distinct from their verges? A legal compilation made in England in the early twelfth century prescribes a width for highways under the king's protection: they were to be wide enough for two wagons to pass, two herdsmen to make their goads just touch, and sixteen armed knights to ride abreast. Rather a squeeze for the knights, we may think, but a fighting knight of this period was much less splendidly mounted and equipped than many knights were later to be. Drove roads, used by those driving animals to and from seasonal pastures, could not have served their purpose had they not been very wide, since these journeys might take several days, and ground vegetation would be needed at the edges for grazing on the way. Some which have been traced in the wapentake of Elloe, in Lincolnshire, were apparently 100 ft (c.30 m) wide. Trackways serving a more limited purpose were evidently much narrower. Roger de Mowbray's gift to the monks of Fountains Abbey, in 1174 or 1175, of part of his forest of Nidderdale (Yorks.) included the right to make a new 'way' 30 ft (c.9 m) wide where it should be most convenient for them to do so. Thirty feet perhaps represented a good width for a beaten trackway in these parts.

In general, travel and the transport of goods were easier in England than elsewhere in the British Isles. The critical minimum level of population needed to keep roads and trackways in use occurred more widely here than elsewhere. Monasteries as well as towns were magnets for the traveller in the widest sense of the word and for this reason left deep marks on road and trackway systems. At the beginning of our period, England had fewer monasteries, square mile for square mile, than Ireland; but throughout the period, it probably had more towns than any other part of the British Isles. Mile for mile, the uplands of England had fewer stretches of roads and trackways impassable to wheeled traffic than the uplands elsewhere, and no barrier to communications quite as daunting as the central watershed of Wales, much less the northern edge of the Highland Boundary Fault. Moreover, the rulers of England took a high view of their role in relation to roads, and to those who travelled on them, that is not often in evidence elsewhere. Stephen was the least effective of all the kings of England in this period, and it is easy to believe the anonymous author of the *Gesta Stephani* (*The Deeds of Stephen*) when he says that highway robberies increased during the reign. Yet at the very end of the reign, the monks of Athelney Abbey, in Somerset, considered it necessary to obtain the king's permission to divert an ancient way in order to make a watercourse through the moor near their monastery. Even in this reign, vestiges of a unitary control over the road system and access to it survived. In Ireland, an official view of what constituted acceptable roads existed by the end of this period, if not at a considerably earlier date, and is enshrined in the first major collection of Irish parliamentary legislation, made in 1297: roads were to be of sufficient width and clear of briars and trees, whether standing or lying. However, in Ireland as in Wales, the fragmentation of authority and the endemic violence made it extremely hard to achieve a standard, even when this was agreed, and for travellers there was a consistently high level of insecurity.

The speed of road travel depended on a number of variables, of which the most important was the intention of the traveller: was it to arrive as quickly as possible or to dawdle a little on the way? Next in importance, however, was the actual mode of travel: mounted, or on foot, with or without a retinue, and so on. The elite, whose journey times tend to be the only ones recorded, never travelled alone, although they sometimes sent their heavy baggage ahead with an advance party, whose job it was to open up the house or prepare hired accommodation, and themselves travelled light and quickly some days later. This practice may help to explain how it was that Henry II could cover as much ground as he did in a day: he travelled, as Walter Map tells us, by stages that were unbearably long, as though a post.

Travelling as a post—that is, using relays of horses—a small party could probably average forty miles or more a day on good roads, depending on the season; and Map's remark is one piece of evidence we have that a post system and the hostelries on which it depended, existed on some English highways by this date. Those who used their own horses travelled more slowly, since it was necessary to rest the horses at intervals, but many of them would have had a target in mind. This was the 'day's stage' which is sometimes mentioned casually in sources of the period, as though everyone knew the distance involved. Needless to say, the actual day's stage varied with the terrain—a point clearly made in the works of Gerald of Wales, who regarded a day's stage as twenty-five miles in Wales but as many as forty in Ireland. But the stage also varied with the other circumstances of the traveller. In the thirteenth and fourteenth centuries, a royal messenger in England, who used his own horse and travelled alone, was probably expected to cover about thirty miles in a normal day. But the speed of those travelling with packhorses for the baggage would be that of the servants walking beside the horses. Even when the going was good, this is not likely to have exceeded twenty miles a day.

How much could a packhorse carry? This depended, of course, on the horse and the skill with which the goods were packaged and secured; but there were norms. In his *History of the English People*, Henry of Huntingdon notes that a horse's normal load was approximately one sester, or quarter—that is, eight bushels—of grain. Grain was not as heavy, bushel for bushel, in the middle ages as it subsequently became, and if Henry had wheat in mind, the load he mentions probably weighed between 380 and 400 lbs (*c*.170 and *c*.180 kg); but a quarter of oats would have been considerably lighter. In practice, less than a quarter of grain seems often to have been expected of a packhorse: say four to eight bushels per load as the norm, but the heavier the grain the fewer the bushels; and it was recognized that some commodities, including salt, were heavier, bushel for bushel, than grain. The monks of Kelso, who used a measure known as the boll instead of the bushel, required tenants at Redden, in Roxburghshire, if doing carrying service with a horse in summer, to carry three bolls of grain each time from Berwick-on-Tweed to the monastery, or two bolls of salt, or one and a half of coal. In winter, although the prescribed loads were lighter, similar proportions were observed. A one-horse cart could carry much more than a packhorse but travelled more slowly. It could also carry much more than a one-ox cart, and except on heavy soils it travelled faster than the latter.

Though still little used for ploughing, horses were increasingly used for hauling on large and small farms alike in the course of this period, and not only in England, where the evidence for this development is most abundant. Thus, taxation returns at the end of the century show that the typical household in the commote of Gafflogion and parts of Anglesey owned a horse and two oxen as well as cattle and sheep—the horse presumably for hauling, and the oxen for the plough. For many farmers carting was, indeed, a form of by-employment as well as a normal part of agrarian life: given the opportunity, they hired themselves out as carters when they were not busy on the farm, and some heroic feats are recorded. In 1277–80, during the building of Vale Royal Abbey, in Cheshire, at Edward I's expense, thousands of cartloads of stone were carried to the site from quarries five or six miles away. The work was done mainly by one-horse carts, hired locally, and some of these made two journeys a day, involving, on the days in question, a total distance of twenty miles and more with loads that were probably as heavy as any normally transported in one-horse carts. Cessation of the work during August and September, the harvest months, seems to show that these were indeed farm horses and carts. In London and some other English towns, a more elaborate system is recorded. This offered a wide choice of vehicles and a long-distance service to those in need of it. Even at the end of May 1265, as the war between Simon de Montfort and the supporters of Henry III moved to its climax, Eleanor de Montfort found it possible to send two casks of wine from London to her husband at Kenilworth in carts hired for the purpose.

Twenty miles a day, or ten miles there and back, and at the end of the day in question perhaps a quarter of grain had been moved by each packhorse and three quarters by each horse and cart; more, of course, by a two- or four-horse wagon. A quarter of grain, if the grain was wheat, would probably make from 400 to 450 lbs (c.180 to c.205 kg) of bread, the exact amount depending on the coarseness of the flour extracted from the grain and the temperature of the oven; and a quarter of grain would make c.60 gallons of best ale and twice as much of weaker kinds. By no means everyone broke bread or drank ale every day, but many people of high status, including many who maintained large households, consumed these staple foods on a considerable scale, together with meat or fish, and sometimes dairy produce as well. Some of those who did not drink ale sometimes drank mead, a drink which was no lighter to transport.

Together, these figures remind us of the huge expenditure of labour on transport required by every large-scale enterprise of this period, from provisioning a noble household to building a church, or fighting a war. For such enterprises to succeed, moreover, the carts and packhorses involved had to survive the journey unscathed, and, in many cases, before the packhorses and the carts took over, ships had to make landfall with their cargoes, and ports be open to enable them to do so: we can assume, for example, that the goods carted from Berwick-on-Tweed for the monks of Kelso had first been shipped there. We know that these and other features of the systems of communication in use in this period often faltered and sometimes petered out altogther. In April 1172, Henry II, as we learn from Gerald of Wales, crossed from Wexford to St Davids in half a day: he embarked at dawn and arrived at noon. But Gerald also tells us that during the previous winter it had been virtually impossible to cross in the opposite direction, from Wales to Ireland. Perhaps he exaggerates; but his description, in another place, of the Irish Sea as 'nearly always tempestuous' carries conviction. Piracy was a universal feature of sea and estuarine travel. Fords and ferries were notoriously unsafe. Yet these might provide the only form of passage for horses and carts across an important river, if the bridge in existence was constructed of wood and not stone. Even in the thirteenth century, substantial areas, including the central Highlands of Scotland and parts of the southern uplands, probably had no actual roads.

Communications in this period were often hazardous and always unpredictable. Even so, we should not reduce their history to a set of anecdotes, tempting though it sometimes is to do so. By the thirteenth century, large areas of the British Isles, including much of south Scotland, the lowlands of Wales, and the south and east of Ireland, as well as most of England, had a sufficient basic provision of roads and trackways, and we can say of rather smaller areas that networks of the same existed in them. The amount of traffic of all kinds which these carried is in general impressive. The natural environment did much to perpetuate the shortcomings of these modest systems, and much also to ensure that the former were more strongly represented in some regions than in others. But it can rarely be isolated as a factor in the development of communications: it is nearly always found in association with other factors, in complicated ways that are now hard to disentangle. Levels of population, for example, played a crucial role in the development of roads and trackways; so, too, standards of law and order and political structures. Considered in this wider context, how strong an influence did the environment exert on life in Britain and Ireland in the twelfth and thirteenth centuries? The following pages will, it is hoped, suggest answers to this question and others of comparable importance.

Figure 2 The castle and town of Carrickfergus *c.*1560.

Conquest and settlement

Robin Frame

During this period all the countries of the British Isles were affected by conquests and colonization. To some extent these may be regarded as flowing, however indirectly, from the victory of Duke William of Normandy at Hastings in October 1066. But they also need to be viewed in a European setting, and not merely because the political link between England and Normandy inaugurated by the Norman Conquest continued to affect Britain and Ireland for several generations. The archipelago was just one of the areas exploited by the French-speaking aristocracy rooted in the former Roman province of Gaul, whose expansion, at its height during the late eleventh and twelfth centuries, also led to the creation of principalities and lordships in the western and eastern Mediterranean. Occasionally an individual career provides a reminder of the broader scene: William Pantulf, founder of the line of barons of Wem in Shropshire, had been in the circle of Robert Guiscard in southern Italy. The growth of population that marked these centuries is also significant. It prompted an enlargement of the area of land under cultivation and offered opportunities for entrepreneurial lordship. These trends, which peaked in England in the second half of the thirteenth century, had obvious implications for the extension of Anglo-Norman activity into Wales and Ireland.

The experiences of England, Wales, Scotland, and Ireland reveal sharp contrasts, though perhaps no sharper than those between the regions of which each country was composed. Differences arose from many sources. Among the more significant were physical geography and communications, the structure of the pre-existing societies, the changing contexts—economic and cultural as much as political—across more than two centuries, and the degree of involvement and control by kings. It is, in short, misleading to conceive of a single, uniform military and colonizing movement that spread ever wider across the archipelago. Perhaps inevitably, this chapter stresses certain features that the various areas had in common—the intrusion of new ruling groups, the establishment of similar institutions of lordship, and the complete or partial dispossession of existing elites. It does, however, touch upon at least some of the characteristics that distinguish individual phases and zones of conquest and settlement.

The period begins and ends with two fairly clear-cut conquests: of England by William I and his followers, and of north Wales, the one part of Britain south of the Tweed and the Solway that had remained resistant to English power during the thirteenth century, by Edward I. Midway between them, another, less conclusive, series of conquests began. In 1169–70 Anglo-Norman lords, recruited by Diarmait Mac Murchadha the exiled king of Leinster, sailed from south Wales to Ireland. Starting as mercenaries, they soon threatened to dominate the south-east of the island. In 1171 Henry II followed them to Ireland. He seems to have been prompted chiefly by the need to discipline them, but in doing so he made real both a claim to English over-lordship that went back to the Anglo-Saxon period and a more recent papal grant obtained in 1155 on the initiative of the church of Canterbury. By about 1250 English control had expanded to embrace, with differing degrees of firmness, about three-quarters of Ireland. Conquest in Ireland had much in common with the earlier Norman expansion into south and mid-Wales, which had proceeded simultaneously with the conquest of England itself. This too had been the work of aggressive lords who by the late 1090s had estab-lished outposts as far west as Pembroke, and (more temporarily) Aberystwyth and Bangor. As in Ireland, royal influence had some-times been asserted after the event. Other similarities between the two conquests included their regional, spasmodic character and their vulnerability to reversal, particularly on the extremities.

The term 'conquest' may seem less appropriate to the settlement of Anglo-Normans across much of Scotland south of the Highland line, which took place by invitation of the Scottish kings. In contemporary usage, however, the word *conquestum* did not necessarily imply military force. When, around 1195, Thomas de Verdon and Hugh de Lacy, men prominent in the occupation of eastern Ireland, agreed as part of a marriage arrangement between their families to share equally 'what they can conquer in the land of war', the meaning is scarcely ambiguous.[1] But when an Anglo-Norman lord in his charter speaks of *meum conquestum*, the best translation is usually 'my acquisition'. Even in Ireland and Wales, the sword was not the sole weapon. William de Burgh (d. 1205) married a daughter of Domnall Ua Briain, king of Thomond (d. 1194). Thereafter he consolidated his gains in Limerick and Tipperary partly through alliances with his Irish brothers-in-law, who were quarrelling over the succession to their father. Those gains, moreover, originated in grants from the crown: William had arrived in Ireland with the future King John in 1185. In Scotland, except on the outer edges of colonization such as Galloway or Moray, the emphasis was certainly more on patronage and infiltration through marriage than upon the sword. But acquisitiveness was not absent; where Anglo-Norman settlement took place, it involved some dispossession or loss of status for members of the existing aristocracy and ministerial class. Behind this lay the threat of force: it was the power of the Scottish kings, to which their Anglo-Norman entourage contributed, that enabled them to arrange transfers of property and muffle overt conflict. Their role had something in common with that played by King William and his representatives in southern England during the protracted readjustments of property and status that followed the battle of Hastings. What happened in Scotland was a point on a continuum that ran from peaceful settlement to violent seizure, rather than a wholly different experience.

During the thirteenth century Scotland saw a further development which had some characteristics of a conquest, as the kings increased their power in the west and north. This is symbolized by the 1266 Treaty of Perth, by which Norway ceded its rights over the Western Isles to Alexander III, in return for an annual payment. The agreement followed a generation or more during which the influence of the Scottish court, operating through ecclesiastical and noble networks as much as armed force, had penetrated regions such as Argyll and Caithness. The absorption of the Western Highlands and Isles

---

[1] *Calendar of the Gormanston Register*, ed. J. Mills and M. J. McEnery (Dublin, 1916), 144 (calendar), 192–3 (text).

differs in crucial respects from Edward I's conquests in Wales. The latter were a logistical *tour de force* involving vast resources, consolidated by a remarkable feat of administrative remodelling: the former rested upon excluding an alternative focus of allegiance for the aristocratic kins of the west, and drawing them into a closer relationship with the Scottish court. But the two processes had an important feature in common: both reflected the growth of royal power across the two centuries. The conquest of 1066 was unusual for its time in the degree of central control exercised over it: this sprang from, on the one hand, Duke William's position at the head of a coherent group of predatory aristocrats, and, on the other, the exceptional administrative unity of England south of the Trent. The royal direction of the events of 1266 and 1282, by contrast, seems wholly typical of the later thirteenth century.

The personnel and dynamics of conquest

The most obvious characteristic common to the entire period was the acquisition by an aristocracy, whose ultimate origins lay in Normandy and adjacent parts of northern France, of land, lordship, and cultural dominance across most of Britain and Ireland. Even in north Wales the king shared his gains with his nobles. Edward reserved for himself the heartlands of Llywelyn ap Gruffudd's principality, in Snowdonia and Anglesey. East of the River Conwy, however, new lordships emerged, such as Denbigh, Ruthin, and Chirkland. Among the beneficiaries were Henry de Lacy, earl of Lincoln, and Roger Mortimer of Chirk, from families whose members had participated in the conquests in the Welsh March two centuries before. Likewise in western Scotland, Alexander III's successes permitted further gains by the Stewart family, whose ancestors had been among the incomers of the twelfth century.

The conquest of England, of which the occupation of the Welsh marches is best regarded as part, was fundamental to all later acts of appropriation. This may seem platitudinous, but it is worth stressing for two reasons. Links between England and Gaul were ancient, and a close relationship with Normandy went back to 1002, when Ethelred II married Emma, the daughter of Count Richard I. Edward the

Confessor, their son, spent his early life in exile in Normandy. Not surprisingly, his reign saw a significant continental presence, both lay and ecclesiastical, in his court circle. Pointers to the future may already be discerned—in Edward's use of Norman military men on the Welsh frontier, and in the northward flight of the Normans Osbern Pentecost and Hugh to Macbeth in 1052. Personal names suggest, moreover, that before 1066 southern and eastern England had seen more settlement from northern France than can be explained merely by the presence of Normans in the Confessor's entourage. But despite this habit of interaction, William's victory at Hastings, and the ensuing forfeiture by 1070 of the bulk of the Anglo-Saxon higher aristocracy, changed things utterly, opening England to a swift and conclusive race for land and power. This in turn shaped what happened in the rest of the British Isles. There seems to have been at most a thin trickle of men directly from northern France into Scotland, and there is little evidence of migration directly from the Continent to Ireland. To that extent the custom by which Scottish and Irish historians have peopled their pages with 'Normans' is misleading. England, with Wales, was the source from which tributaries of manpower flowed further north and west.

Already by the time of the Domesday Survey (1086) migration to England from Normandy and adjacent provinces was largely complete, though this does not mean that all England was firmly within the newcomers' grasp: their presence in the far north was limited to footholds at Durham and Newcastle, while Cumbria lay within the orbit of Malcolm Canmore, the Scottish king. The rapidity with which this new area of enterprise filled up owed much to certain dynamics of aristocratic expansion, which were to show themselves everywhere. The chief of these was the habit of instant devolution, for control and exploitation could be achieved only by passing responsibility downwards. In England, the Conquest was presided over by William and a group of about a dozen powerful associates, headed by his half-brothers, Odo, bishop of Bayeux, and Robert, count of Mortain. They supervised and took part in a rapid and often provisional apportioning of what were at first not so much landed estates as military commands and spheres of influence. A leading figure could quickly find himself with widespread interests and various roles. William fitz Osbern (d. 1071), a ducal kinsman and household steward, was placed in charge of the Isle of Wight, the ancient royal centre of Winchester, and Hereford, from where he took the title of earl. Lords such as fitz Osbern were in turn focuses for the aspirations of members of their own kin, members of families who held lands of them (or were simply their neighbours) in Normandy, and men who adhered to them in England. The speed with which a leading lord could acquire widely dispersed interests, and the implications of such acquisitions for others, is apparent in the case of Roger de Montgomery (d. 1094), vicomte of the Hiémois, who crossed to England when King William returned from Normandy late in 1067. Roger gained Arundel, one of several key bridgeheads on the south coast, and by 1071 was also established on the Welsh frontier at Shrewsbury. Close to this royal centre he built a castle at Hen Domen, which took the name Montgomery from his chief Norman lordship. Rapidly castles and lands were allotted to sub-tenants. The beneficiaries included men who were his tenants in Normandy: Warin the Bald, the sheriff of Shropshire, at Oswestry; Picot de Sai at Clun; and Corbet, whose origins in the Pays de Caux were to give his castle and lordship the name 'Caus'. They in turn had dependants and associates who became involved in the defence and settlement of their emerging baronies. In this way, a region was occupied and reorganized through the households and webs of connection that surrounded greater and lesser lords.

Also of critical importance was the family. It is too simple to say that Norman society practised primogeniture, but it shared the tendency throughout northern France towards a narrowing of the lineage for the purposes of succession. From this sprang the phenomenon of the *juvenes*, young—sometimes in fact not so young—men who lacked land commensurate with their aristocratic birth. The opening up of Britain as an area of exploitation eased for a time pressures of this sort upon the Norman aristocracy. The Montgomeries again exemplify the point, in characteristically exaggerated form. Roger, by establishing a presence on both sides of the Channel, created possibilities of advancement for the next generation. Initially his eldest son, Hugh, succeeded him as earl of Shrewsbury. Robert 'of Bellême', the second son, received the bulk of the paternal inheritance in Normandy, together with his mother's lands in Maine, from which he took his name. When Hugh was killed in north Wales in 1098, Robert reintegrated his father's lands. Two younger sons also had spectacular careers. Roger 'the Poitevin' acquired interests in Poitou through marriage to the daughter of the count of La Marche, while the patronage of the Norman kings gave him extensive lordships in the north of England, where at one stage he held what was to become Lancashire together with parts of the Lake District. Arnulf participated in his father's campaigns into Wales, becoming lord of Dyfed, where he built a castle at Pembroke; royal favour brought him Holderness in east Yorkshire. Just before the entire kin lost its British interests in 1102–3 through supporting Robert of Normandy against Henry I, Arnulf concluded an alliance with Muirchertach Ua Briain, the most powerful king in Ireland, whose daughter he married. The fall of the Montgomeries may have postponed the political involvement in Ireland that was to lead to conquests two generations later. The history of the family shows the speed with which a powerful kin could spread itself across a wide geographical area, and also the way in which such expansion drew in others, intensifying the Norman grip upon core districts, and form-ing local landowning societies that were to prove less vulnerable to the turn of fortune's wheel than their political masters.

A smaller wave of immigration accompanied Henry I's seizure and consolidation of power. At the time of William Rufus's unexpected death in 1100, Henry held the county of the Cotentin, the lordship of Domfront, and other interests in Lower Normandy, towards the Breton frontier. Men from that region benefited from his success in England. Henry also cultivated an alliance with the count of Flanders and made heavy use of Flemish troops; the appearance of Flemish settlers in Britain in the early twelfth century was probably the result of this link. The role of Henry's men is particularly obvious in two areas. They took part in the remodelling of south Wales and the March that followed the fall of the Montgomeries. For instance, the Breton Alan fitz Flaad became lord of Oswestry, and was a key figure in the establishment of a direct royal presence around Shrewsbury. Pembroke, so recently a centre of resistance with dangerous overseas ties, was organized as a shire. Flemish settlements there, of which we first hear in 1107, may have been organized by royal agents. Yet Henry's 'new March' also confirms the importance of immigration during the two decades after 1066. The scope for newcomers had been created only by the forfeiture of established interests; and the beneficiaries included, besides Henry's men, families such as the de Clares that were already present in Britain.

Henry's circle was also influential in the north, where the situation was different. After William's 'harrying of the North' in response to the resistance in 1069–70, Norman settlement had proceeded in Yorkshire. But in the far north the critical period began as late as 1092, when Rufus established Carlisle as a royal base, building a castle and encouraging settlement. This challenged Scottish influence in Cumbria and may have provoked Malcolm's fatal campaign of the following year. After 1093, Malcolm's sons became dependent on Norman support. The development of Carlisle, which became the seat of a bishop under Henry I, and of new castles and lordships in Cumbria, helped to shield the lowlands of Durham and Northumberland from Scottish raids, which could come from west as well as east of the Pennines. The reshaping of the region did not stop at the Tweed or the Solway. A prominent member of Henry's circle was his brother-in-law, David, the youngest son of King Malcolm. During the reigns of his elder brothers, Edgar and Alexander I, David remained mostly at Henry's court. Around 1113, he received a windfall, in the form of the marriage of Maud de Senlis, heiress of lands in the east midlands, which made him earl of Huntingdon. Shortly afterwards, King Alexander granted him lordship over much of southern Scotland. Upon his succession to the kingship in 1124 David retained his English estates and close ties with Henry. In these circumstances, Norman settlement in the north of England and southern Scotland may be viewed as part of a single process, in which members of Henry's circle were prominent. An example of the processes at work is provided by Robert de Brus, whose family came from Brix in Lower Normandy. Robert was established, probably early in Henry's reign, as a landowner in Cleveland, with interests also north of the Tees in Hartness. One of David's first recorded acts as king was to grant him Annandale, just north of the Solway (see Figure 4). Brus was thus a frontier baron in two senses: holding an important position in a region where Henry's government did not yet operate intensively; and, from David's perspective, an ally with resources and connections who from his castles at Annan and Lochmaben could reinforce royal authority in the south-west, facing the semi-regal native lordship of Galloway. Another of David's men was Walter fitz Alan, a younger son of Alan fitz Flaad. Walter's eldest brother, Jordan, remained in Brittany, the second, William, received Oswestry, leaving Walter with only some scraps of land in Shropshire. From David, however, he

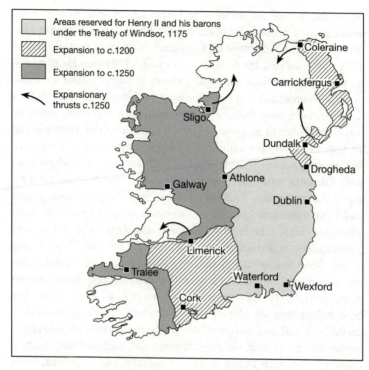

Map 2 The main stages of English expansion into Ireland

received the office of household steward, together with extensive holdings in southern Scotland, including the Clydeside lordships of Renfrew and Paisley, on the northern fringes of Galloway and Carrick.

The extension of the Anglo-Norman aristocracy into Ireland reveals a similar mixture of regionally specific and broader influences (see Map 2). The former are apparent in the contrast between the regions lying, roughly, north and south of Dublin. During the years after 1177 John de Courcy conquered Ulaidh, the area of modern Down and Antrim, establishing in effect a principality where he struck halfpence and farthings, some with his own names on the obverse and the name and crozier of St Patrick on the reverse. His wish to celebrate, and perhaps exploit, the Patrician associations of the area was probably encouraged by the Irish bishop of Down, with whom he formed an alliance, and who joined with him and the archbishop of Armagh in requesting Jocelin of Furness to write a life of the saint. As recounted by Gerald of Wales, and embellished by Tudor antiquarians, his deeds have a maverick flavour. He is said to have broken away from the royal garrison at Dublin with a few companions in order to carve out a lordship for himself. The fact that his main ties were long thought to have been with Somerset, where he was a benefactor of Stogursey priory, has added to the impression of an individual venture with little strategic or geographical logic. In fact, there is reason to link him less with south-west England than with Cumbria, where his maternal grandmother, Alice de Rumilly, was a major heiress. Analysis of those to whom he made grants and who witnessed his charters shows a preponderance of men associated with Cheshire, Lancashire, Cumbria, and south-west Scotland. His ecclesiastical patronage reveals the same bias, taking in the Benedictines of Chester, the Augustinians of Carlisle, and the Cistercian houses of Furness (Lancashire) and Holmcultram (Cumberland). In this setting, de Courcy's activities seem less improbable; they developed out of existing interactions—ecclesiastical, political, and commercial—within the north Irish Sea region. Similar ties are evident south of Carlingford Lough in Uriel (Louth), where families such as the Audleys, Dowdalls, and Copelands from north-west England figure prominently.

The better known conquest and settlement of southern Ireland, on the other hand, drew more upon south Wales and the west country. Pembrokeshire was strongly represented, for example by Gerald of Wales's maternal and paternal kins, the Geraldines (FitzGeralds) and the Barrys of Manorbier. Within the smaller world of early colonial Ireland, the Geraldine lineage revealed a capacity for acquisitive ramification worthy of the Montgomeries or the descendants of Alan fitz Flaad. Several sons of Maurice fitz Gerald (d. 1176), who participated in the first expeditions, did well for themselves. The eldest, William, who retained lands in south Wales, founded the line of barons of Naas in eastern Kildare. Gerald made gains in western Kildare and was ancestor of the barons of Offaly and earls of Kildare. Thomas, from whom the lords and earls of Desmond descended, took part in the extension of colonization into west Munster during the 1190s and early 1200s. Other sons and kinsmen of Maurice acquired substantial sub-tenancies across south Leinster and Munster, founding lines such as the lords of Kerry and the knights of Glin. Among settler families of both the first and the second rank, 'Cambro-Norman' and native Welsh names are common. This gives point to the depiction in the early thirteenth-century verse chronicle of the invasion, known as *The Song of Dermot and the Earl*, of men going into battle with the cry 'St David' on their lips. There are also many names, such as Deveneis and de Exeter, that associate men with the wider catchment area. A similar emphasis is visible in the geographical distribution of the toponymics recorded in the lists of admissions to the Dublin guild merchant, which begin as early as *c.*1190 (see Map D).

Conquest and settlement, thus regarded, resembled a series of stepping-stones. The society of south-west England and south Wales, which was expanding into southern Ireland, itself still showed the marks of colonizing activity, which was in some cases quite recent. There were Pembroke families, such as the fitz Martins, whose origins are traceable on the southern shore of the Bristol Channel. The occupation of Glamorgan seems to have been launched from Gloucestershire and involved crossings by water to the initial lordship centre at Cardiff. Ireland was far from an unknown land; trading ties between Dublin and Waterford and Bristol and other south-western ports were well established. Movement to Ireland, initially perhaps in the military entourage of one's lord, must have seemed a variation on a familiar theme. For Pembrokeshire men such as Godebert de Rupe (Roche) and Maurice de Prendergast, whose ancestors had migrated' from Flanders to Wales little more than half a century earlier, it may not have seemed a particularly dramatic variation. The image of successive leaps is confirmed by one of the last pieces of expansion that was primarily aristocratic rather than royal in its direction, the conquest of Connacht by Richard, the son of William de Burgh, during the 1220s and 1230s. The platform from which he thrust north and west beyond the Shannon was his existing cluster of lordships in Limerick and Tipperary. Those to whom he distributed sub-tenancies were members of families such as the Cogans, Berminghams, Butlers, and Geraldines, already settled in Leinster and Munster.

For all the importance of proximity, ease of communications, and local networks of kinship and lordship, expansion cannot be understood purely within regional contexts. The wider scene constantly intrudes. In part this reflects the far-flung interests of leading participants. David I may have introduced settlers such as Robert de Brus and William de Somerville from Yorkshire, but the tenure of the earldom of Huntingdon by the Scottish royal house for most of the period 1113–1237 drew men from the east midlands into Scotland, notably the Morville family, who acquired lordships in Lothian and Strathclyde, together with the office of Constable of Scotland. Walter fitz Alan's links with Oswestry brought in men with a Shropshire background, who are thought to have included the ancestors of William Wallace, as sub-tenants on the Stewart lordships. David's close ties with Henry I probably led to the planting of Flemish soldiers around Lanark and also in Moray, after a rising there in 1130. Similarly eclectic recruitment occurred in Leinster, where the early phases of settlement in 1170–76 were directed by its first lord, Richard fitz Gilbert de Clare ('Strongbow'), lord of Strigoil in south-east Wales and claimant to the earldom of Pembroke, who married the daughter of Diarmait Mac Murchadha. Strongbow endowed the Geraldines and others from south Wales. But as a member of a leading Anglo-Norman baronial house he was no provincial figure; he had estates in many counties of southern and eastern England, and also across the Channel. Among those he specially favoured were families such as Bloet, Ridelisford, de Quency, and Boisrohard, who were connected with him as tenants or allies in England and perhaps Normandy. Other newcomers of varied backgrounds were drawn to Leinster by his son-in-law and successor, William Marshal, earl of Pembroke (d. 1219), who spent several years in Ireland during John's reign.

Above and alongside the interests of such major nobles lay the pervasive influence of the crown, whose capacity to plant (and to uproot) individuals, and to fix the limits of their ambitions, was as marked in Ireland as in Wales. The de Burghs' position in Connacht rested on a grant by John to William de Burgh, made during the 1190s. It was not fully realized until a generation later, when Richard de Burgh served as justiciar of Ireland (1228–32) and had the backing of his powerful uncle, Hubert de Burgh, the justiciar of England, and after Hubert's fall in 1232 of Henry III himself. The de Burghs did not belong to the western nexus. Their ties were with the royal household, and their background was in East Anglia. These characteristics were shared by another settler lord who first appeared in Ireland during John's 1185 expedition, Theobald Walter, ancestor of the Butler lords and earls of Ormond, who acquired extensive lordships in Munster and Leinster. Theobald was a brother of Hubert Walter, the future archbishop of Canterbury and justiciar and chancellor of England. His Suffolk links were probably responsible for the appearance of the Cantwells, from Kentwell, as a knightly lineage in Kilkenny. Ireland thus received both an overspill of land-hungry men from the frontier regions of Wales and Cumbria, and a significant injection of the upwardly mobile from court and administrative circles. Despite Gerald of Wales's vaunting of the military skills of his marcher kinsfolk, the record suggests that the swords of the second group were just as sharp, and their eye for land and profit at least as keen.

An older historiographical tradition portrayed twelfth-century kings of England as having 'failed' to subjugate Wales, because their infrequent expeditions did not result in a conquest of the sort that took place under Edward I. Likewise, Henry II has been criticized for the limited results of his Irish expedition of 1171–2, which created only short-term balances, whether among the settler lords or between them and the Irish kings. That a different scenario was conceivable in the late twelfth century is clear from Gerald of Wales, who devotes chapters to strategic advice about how each country might be subjugated. It has often been pointed out that Gerald's prescriptions for Wales bear a striking resemblance to Edward I's eventual approach in the campaign of 1282–3. Edward's success has been linked to an enlargement during the intervening period of the practical capabilities of the English state. But in view of the massive deployment of funds and manpower for the defence of Normandy and Anjou by Richard I and John, and the strategic grasp shown by the former, it is rash to conclude that north Wales could not have been conquered at an earlier stage. The simple fact is that the aims of English kings— including Edward I himself in his first Welsh war of 1276–7—were more limited. What they required was recognition of their lordship, from marchers and Welsh kings alike, and the restoration of stability. These were achieved through occasional military displays and through constant diplomacy. By that measure, Henry II's intervention in Ireland also achieved its aims. He earmarked the rich and strategically important Viking ports of Dublin and Waterford and their hinterlands for himself, prescribed spheres of influence for settler lords, and received fealty from most of the Irish kings and bishops. Nor were the six months he spent in Ireland a short time when set against the movements of a peripatetic ruler who was in

France for more than two-thirds of his reign. Successful management of the frontiers involved exacting submissions, constructing and maintaining points of influence, and creating favourable coalitions. It is not realistic to look for definitive political settlements on the ragged edges of an assemblage of provinces that sprawled from the Cheviots and the Shannon to the Vexin and the Pyrenees.

Royal expeditions might have clear defensive purposes, as in the case of the early Norman kings' campaigns against Malcolm Canmore. In Wales and Ireland the agents of instability were as likely to be aristocratic factions as native rulers. Alliances between the two—as formed by the sons of Roger de Montgomery in Wales or by Strongbow in Ireland—might appear threatening and require special measures to confirm the king's authority. These in turn led to the creation of new royal bases and even the rudiments of administration: the construction of Newcastle upon Tyne in 1080, Rufus's castle at Carlisle, Henry I's centres at Montgomery, Carmarthen, and Pembroke, and Henry II's control of the southern Irish ports shared something of the same rationale. Ideas of cultural superiority and of a 'civilizing mission' in relation to the other peoples of the archipelago were certainly present in court circles. But in practice, as at other periods, perceptions of its own security drew the central power outwards—leaving us with the irony of an expanding English royal authority in the hands of rulers who only intermittently promoted an expansionist drive, and who were rarely present in the areas where conquest and settlement were taking place. It should not be concluded from this that Norman and Plantagenet kings were reluctant to see the orbit of their influence enlarged. Materialistic cost-benefit analysis may have been alien to them, but they were well aware of the uses of new territories. These included future revenues: treasure from Ireland as well as England was deployed by John for the defence of Normandy and Anjou. More significant perhaps, was the scope to reward those close to them. In that respect, despite periodic tensions between individual kings and lords, the interests of crown and aristocracy were in harmony.

The effects of the continental orientation of the monarchy upon the entire British Isles are plainly visible. Wales and Ireland participated in overseas ventures. Welsh leaders served Henry I in France and at least from the time of Henry II Welsh footsoldiers, recruited chiefly by marchers but occasionally by native lords, formed the basis of the infantry in many royal armies. Magnates and troops from Ireland took part in continental expeditions during the thirteenth century; both Richard de Burgh and the heir to the Geraldine lordship of Offaly died on Henry III's 1242–3 campaign in Poitou and Gascony. The presence of contingents from the different countries of the archipelago—even though the main participants may have been culturally indistinguishable from the aristocracy of England or Normandy—enhanced the king's standing by symbolizing his position as a quasi-imperial overlord. Although Malcolm IV contributed to Henry II's glory by serving on the Toulouse expedition of 1159, and was dubbed a knight in reward, Scotland's role was different, though equally revealing. It is customary to date Franco-Scottish cooperation (the 'Auld Alliance') to the treaty made at Paris in 1295, which set the scene for the intertwining of the Anglo-Scottish and Anglo-French wars of the later middle ages. In fact, negotiations between the Scots and the Capetians can be traced at least as early as the 1160s. While it is true that Owain Gwynedd (d. 1170) and Llywelyn ab Iorwerth also had transient diplomatic contacts with French kings, these had no material results. By contrast, when Alexander II invaded northern England and occupied Carlisle in 1216–17, while the future Louis VIII and his baronial allies were campaigning in the south, the Plantagenet dynasty probably faced a greater external threat than it was to encounter again before the 1380s.

Settlement and institutions

The spread of new elites, together with the authority of their royal overlords, across much of the British Isles brought with it characteristic expressions of power and forms of organization. These are often labelled 'feudalism', a term that, in the dominant English historiographical tradition, has led to over-concentration on the quotas of military service that by the twelfth century accompanied land-tenure among the ruling groups. For present purposes the less abstract term 'lordship' may be more useful. It is possible to pick out features that were in some degree common to all the areas subject to conquest and settlement during these centuries. Across much of Britain and Ireland, the newcomers built castles and made arrangements to garrison and support them. Aristocrats and kings, with a view to economic advantage, gave the privileges associated with borough status to favoured communities, often associated with castles. Everywhere, occupation of territory involved lords and their men in complex tenurial hierarchies. In the upper reaches of society, with which we are primarily concerned, lordship carried entitlements such as military service, rents, counsel, wardship, and jurisdictional rights: these were the institutional accompaniments of the devolution of land and power. A brief description such as this inevitably highlights the lowest common denominators, masking change over time, variations of status, and regional differences.

Castles, for instance, differed, not just in scale and morphology, but also in function and significance according to their location and the context in which they were built. Earth and timber fortifications were hastily erected, whether in motte-and-bailey or in ringwork form, in new areas during the eleventh and twelfth centuries. Mostly they were the work of aristocrats and their leading sub-tenants. From 1066 onwards, they often belong to the process of conquest as incoming lords sought to create sufficient security to take a grip on territory and on the renders and services of the local population; they might be abandoned, reconstructed in stone, or occupied for generations. The vast masonry castles, built during and after Edward I's conquest of north Wales, often like Conway and Caernarfon with integral walled boroughs, belong to a different world: they are testimony to a planned enterprise undertaken by one of the most organized states of medieval Europe. Castles might represent new centres of power and a fresh orientation of lordship, as seems to have been the case at Carrickfergus (Antrim), where John de Courcy began a stone fortress with a massive square keep, designed to dominate both the surrounding lowlands and the approaches to Belfast Lough. On the other hand, they often involved the remodelling of existing fortified centres, which themselves varied enormously in their setting and function. At one extreme was the ruthless clearance in the years after 1066 of sites for castles within established Anglo-Saxon royal *burhs*, some of which, like Lincoln or London itself, were by north European standards major trading towns. At the other were the Marshal fortress on the rock of Dunamase (Laois) or the de Bermingham castle at Dunmore (Galway), each of which replaced the *dún*, or raised fort, of an Irish dynast. Nor were castles always the work of Anglo-Normans.

Where conquest was contested, native lords might build similar structures. Many mottes in later twelfth-century Galloway were the work of the lords of Galloway, as they sought to resist the advance of the Scottish kings and their Anglo-Norman circle. Cardigan, originally built by the de Clares, was at the same period occupied and reconstructed by Rhys ap Gruffudd (d. 1197), the ruler of south Wales, with whom Henry II came to terms.

Differences are equally apparent when boroughs are considered. Many borough charters enhanced the privileges of communities now resident at long-established trading centres, including of course royal *burhs* of the Anglo-Saxon period. Ancient Scottish royal centres such as Stirling and Perth no doubt had settlements with some trading function long before they are described as royal burghs in the charters of David I. Other boroughs, however, were new ventures, in Wales and Ireland often associated with conquest castles and promoted as part of a seignorial drive to exploit a developing lordship (see Map 8). Brecon, founded by Bernard of Neufmarché after 1093 on a carefully chosen strategic site at the confluence of the rivers Honddu and Usk, remained a small garrison town whose history was inseparable from that of the adjacent castle. In 1194 Walter de Lacy, lord of Meath, granted a charter to Drogheda, towards the mouth of the River Boyne, developing a planned town which proved successful in channelling the trade of the Boyne valley. The Marshals founded New Ross (Wexford), at the confluence of the rivers Barrow and Nore, a few miles above the royal city of Waterford, provoking decades of commercial competition between the two centres. In places the absence of radical subsequent change in a landscape makes it easy to visualize the logic of seignorial activity. At Alnwick, dominating the valley of the River Aln in the agricultural lowlands of eastern Northumberland, during the twelfth century the de Vescy family fostered a borough beside their great castle, together with a seaport three miles away at Alnmouth, on the river-estuary. Alongside such examples of greater or lesser success, there were scores of small communities, especially in Ireland and Wales, which had borough status but never became more than tiny rural settlements.

Similarities in the institutional forms of lordship disguise huge differences in scale, organization, and political context. At the risk of considerable oversimplification, a distinction may be made between very local units of lordship, roughly on the village scale, and much more extensive zones of authority, which might bring many square miles within a single structure. Both forms are to be found across much of Britain. The former was more common in southern and midland England, where the lands and rights of a major Norman proprietor were often made up of clusters of manors (or portions of manors), scattered across many counties, and thus intermingled with those of other great lords and lesser landowners. In the north of England, in much of southern Scotland, and above all in the Welsh Marches, the latter was more prominent. The reasons for such differences have generated much debate, and cannot be pursued here. Explanations based upon stark alternatives—whether the supposed contrast between pre-existing Anglo-Saxon and Celtic forms of organization, or the deliberate decisions taken by conquerors, often for strategic reasons—are unduly reductionist. In every region they entered, the newcomers worked with what they found, but at the same time showed a capacity to make choices and to revise existing arrangements.

In the aftermath of 1066, the south and midlands were of course absorbed first. In this region, where the nucleated village was common and royal power was at its most intensive, the incomers often received land in smallish lots, perhaps in tranches as individual Anglo-Saxon thegns were expropriated. Even here, however, quite different arrangements could be made, and sometimes the impact of security requirements seems clear. On the south coast, Sussex was parcelled out in blocks which formed extensive, compact lordships or 'castleries' such as Arundel, Pevensey, or Bramber. A similar pattern can be seen in the south-west, where William I faced resistance at Exeter in 1068, and where interference from Ireland, to which Harold's sons had fled, was possible: Totnes in south Devon is an example of a consolidated lordship dependent on a major castle. As Norman power moved northwards after the crisis of 1069–70, it entered regions where the linking of lowland mixed farming and upland pasture had favoured extensive units that drew dispersed settlements within a single estate structure. Even so, strategic considerations shaped the emergence of large, compact lordships which often, as in the Welsh Marches and in Strathclyde, took their names from their chief castles. Pontefract, granted to Ilbert de Lacy, was a castlery dominating the old Roman road leading north. Richmond in north Yorkshire, held by the Breton count Alan Rufus, was critically placed in relation both to north–south communications and to movements across the Pennines. These lordships appear to have been deliberately assembled and did not simply replicate existing tenurial arrangements. Further west, great lordships such as Kendal and Annandale may possibly preserve the tribute-districts of the former kingdom of Strathclyde, which had spanned the Solway. In parts of Wales and the March grants were expressed in terms of commotes and groups of commotes, reflecting pre-existing territorial units.

Investigation of conquest and settlement in the regions of Ireland is still at an early stage; questions of continuity and change remain patchily investigated. But it seems probable that the pattern had much in common with that in northern and western Britain. This has been masked by a quirk of vocabulary. Irish scholars have tended to adopt the terminology of the fourteenth-century clerks who composed rentals and valuations of estates, using the term 'manor' to describe what were by any standards very extensive lordships. Southern Ireland, for example, contained 'manors' such as Gowran (Kilkenny), Thurles (Tipperary), and Castleconnell (Limerick), focused on magnate castles, which in their extent and structure were more akin to the smaller lordships of the Welsh Marches than to the manorial villages of southern and midland England (see Map 3). Further west, 'manors' were even larger: the de Burgh manor of Loughrea, named for their castle on the Shannon, covered much of the later County Galway, and included the port of Galway itself.

Early grants by the crown in Ireland were often expressed in terms of existing kingdoms, and might be provincial, or semi-provincial, in scale, as in the cases of Leinster, Meath, Connacht, Thomond, and Desmond. Magnates in turn often made grants that reflected the districts occupied by Irish sub-kings, as the crown itself did in north Munster, which was not handed over to a single lord. This practice does not mean that the lordships of the newcomers should be regarded as native kingships in Anglo-Norman hands. The zones of influence of Irish rulers, like those of their Welsh counterparts, were fluid; power was measured more in allegiances and tributes than in stable control of land. In frontier districts this continued to be the case: the earldom of Ulster contained colonized districts in the low-land areas east of the River Bann but also involved potential lordship over upland zones and over extensive territories to the west of the river, just as the lordship of Glamorgan included at different periods

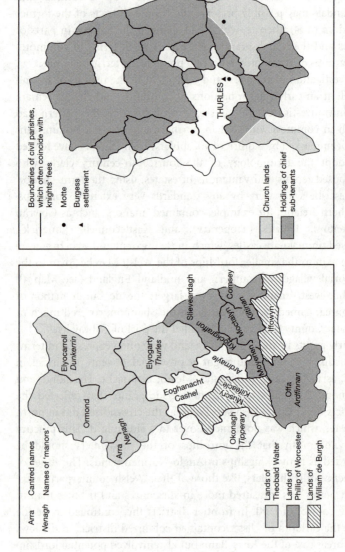

Map 3 i. Cantreds and cantredal 'manors' in Tipperary, late twelfth century; ii. Subinfeudation of the cantred of Elyogarty or 'manor' of Thurles, late thirteenth century.

Arra   Cantred names
Nenagh   Names of 'manors'

Boundaries of civil parishes,
which often coincide with
knights' fees
● Motte
▲ Burgess settlement

Church lands
Holdings of chief sub-tenants

THURLES

Elyocarroll *Dunkerrin*
Ormond
Arra *Nenagh*
Elyogarty *Thurles*
Eoghanacht Cashel
Slieveardagh
Comsey
Kilnan
Mocarky
Knockgraffon
Moyester
Ardmayle
Muscr *Killeagle*
Okonagh *Tipperary*
Offa *Ardfinnan*
Iffowyn

Lands of Theobald Walter
Lands of Phillip of Worcester
Lands of William de Burgh

more, or less, of the larger area of the Welsh kingdom of Morgannwg from which Glamorgan took its name. Where conquest was fairly complete, however, lordships and their sub-divisions had a stability and territorial definition unknown in earlier times. Castle building, the creation of sub-tenures, the formation of parishes, the marking out of burgess settlements, all signalled a shift towards more settled and regular forms of control and exploitation. Equally important was the appearance of a settled hierarchy of authority. The sub-tenants of a lordship held defined lands and rights on similar terms from the same lord, whose court, which they had an obligation to attend, regulated their disputes. Over and above them lay the power of the king and his courts. As well as defining and protecting its own lands and rights, the crown determined boundaries and jurisdictions, and settled any disputed successions. Ireland, more than England, was a world of large, fairly compact units of lordship; but it was one where spheres of influence were no longer determined primarily by warfare and local alliances.

Land was useless without people. In England, and indeed Scotland, there is no doubt that the vast bulk of the population was indigenous; Norman settlement was primarily an aristocratic affair. In Wales and—particularly—Ireland, on the other hand, conquest was accompanied by considerable immigration by peasants and craftsmen. This distinction between countries requires some qualification. Everywhere, incoming lords and their military followers had family members, dependants, and servants, who sought property, occupations, and often no doubt brides. The chronicler Orderic Vitalis, for example, was a son of Odelerius, chaplain to Roger de Montgomery at Shrewsbury, who married an Englishwoman. Existing links, which were drawing settlers from the Continent to England, were intensified by the Conquest. Winchester and Battle seem to have had substantial French elements in their populations; Flemish immigrants can be traced in Berwick and other royal burghs of twelfth-century Scotland. Such immigration was not separate from, let alone at odds with, the strategies of lords and kings, whose households were the main centres of consumption in this society. The Beaumont twins, Waleran, count of Meulan (d. 1166) and Robert, earl of Leicester (d. 1168), were considerable entrepreneurs, with agents active in the wine and grain trades. But, although some towns may have had sizeable foreign groups among their burgesses, across England and southern Scotland essentially the rents and services of an existing rural population were redirected to sustain a new ruling class.

Settlement in Wales and Ireland had an additional dimension. In Ireland, south and east of a line running roughly from Dundalk to Limerick and Cork, there seems to have been substantial immigration, which was probably at its height between *c.*1170 and *c.*1220. It is true that charters and other records of this period mention colonizing activity only occasionally and mostly obliquely. There is no equivalent of the references in continental sources to the work of seignorial agents who marked out settlements and organized the movement of people in frontier areas of Germany or Spain. Evidence comes mostly from estate surveys and legal records which survive from the late thirteenth century onwards, showing the presence of thousands of lesser free tenants, farmers, burgesses, cottiers, and others who had non-Irish names and English legal status. Some historians have suspected that many of these were in reality Irish who had anglicized themselves. Certainly there were some Irishmen who sought advantage by taking English names, only to be exposed by the courts; but such camouflage itself testifies to the strength of a settler society to whose styles it was worth conforming. Other things too warn against undue scepticism: the close match between the period of likely immigration and that when the occupation of land in England was reaching its peak; the prevalence of Welsh as well as English names across the south; and the persistence of a sense of ethnic distinctiveness in such communities amidst the Gaelic recovery of the later medieval period. Burgess status was probably used as a bait to encourage settlers; lords are unlikely to have conceded it to communities composed primarily of native Irish. From 1260–1 we have the names of seventeen burgesses of Pallas Grean (Limerick), who acted as pledges for a collective amercement owed by their community: John le Lung, William Widie, Roger Bastard, Robert Turgis, Richard Payn, William Deveneis, Walter Andrew, Hugh Hert, Walter Cachepol, John Gascoyng, Thomas Ponnys, John the Worthchiche, Thomas 'fiz au feure', John Payn, William le Flemeng, David Dunning, and Roger Hert.[2] It is reasonable to suppose that many of these were the sons or grandsons of men who had migrated to Ireland just before or after 1200, perhaps with the

---

[2] Royal Irish Academy, MS 12 D9, fo. 111 (transcript of Irish pipe roll, 45 Henry 111).

encouragement of Geoffrey fitz Robert, the first lord of Grean, a Wiltshire knight of William Marshal.

The reasons for the plantations that accompanied conquest in Ireland and Wales can only be surmised. W. L. Warren suggested that exploitation of the possibilities eastern and southern Ireland offered for the production of grain—especially the wheat crop that was prized by Anglo-Norman lords—could not be achieved with native labour. This idea, with its unintentional echo of Gerald of Wales's condescending observations about the pastoralism and 'laziness' of the Welsh and Irish, has not found full acceptance. Mixed farming was normal in both countries. Nevertheless, it seems likely that a combination of the ready availability of manpower in England and the pastoral emphasis of rural life in Ireland and Wales created favourable conditions for immigration, which were capitalized upon by landowners intent upon developing new lands and maximizing profits. Possibly too, manpower was less than abundant. Some royal grants licensing lords to occupy lands contain prohibitions against filching (Irish) *nativi* from the king's demesnes; and the writ *de nativo capiendo*, by which a lord could recover his fugitive villeins, was one of the first English legal procedures traceable in Ireland. Security, in countries which remained incompletely subdued, may also have been a consideration. The conquest of north Wales, documented in a way that earlier settlements are not, shows the deliberate recruitment of settlers for Edward I's boroughs, and the displacement of native communities in favour of immigrants by new lords in areas such as the Clwyd valley.

Since conquests and settlements took place over a long period and in differing political contexts, it is scarcely surprising that the institutional results were not uniform. While the Welsh Marches and Ireland both saw protracted aristocratic conquests, the early date of the intrusions into Wales produced lordships with a diversity of custom and a measure of jurisdictional independence unknown in their Irish counterparts. The key period in Ireland (*c.*1170–*c.*1240) coincided exactly with that when the law of the king's courts was achieving definition. So, paradoxically, the more distant dominion, though equally turbulent, was brought into close conformity with England. By the time of the conquest of north Wales, English government was sufficiently defined and self-conscious for Edward I in the Statute of Rhuddlan (1284) to equip his new principality at a stroke with what amounted to a written constitution. A related contrast is that Welsh marcher lords, unlike tenants-in-chief in England and Ireland, did not owe fixed quotas of military service to the crown (though their own tenants came to owe such quotas to them, sometimes in the form of castle-guard). Explicit, written definition of quotas was a feature of the twelfth century, reaching full development in the 1166 Inquest of Fees, a detailed inventory of the knight service due from England. This was the climate in which Henry II required a hundred knights from Leinster, fifty from Meath, and thirty each from the two grantees of Desmond. The charters of twelfth-century Scottish kings likewise record the precise services owed by the lords to whom they made grants.

Knight service, however, was not the only or most important accompaniment of royal lordship. More significant was the right to the wardship and marriage of minors and heiresses who held directly of the king. By the later twelfth century this was particularly valuable since the crown had established its claim to have custody of the entire inheritance even if the bulk of it was held of intermediate lords. This gave kings access to a vast store of patronage: they could traffic in wardships and marriages, making them available to court and household figures. These rights, moreover, applied across all the king's insular dominions: in that crucial sense what has been described as 'the lordship of England' *included* the conquered parts of Wales and Ireland. Upon the death of Walter de Lacy in 1241 his two granddaughters became heiresses to his lands and lordships in England, the Welsh Marches, and Ireland. Each had a share in all three areas, and the elder girl was married successively to members of Henry III's Savoyard court circle, Peter de Geneva (d. 1249) and Geoffrey de Joinville (d. 1314). By the thirteenth century the Scottish kings exercised similar authority within their kingdom, giving them a strong influence over the transmission of land and lordship. The spread of the Anglo-Norman ruling class, in an age when royal government was developing fast, shaped the articulation of power in crucial ways.

The fate of native elites

Conquest and settlement created casualties. Across much of the British Isles, the indigenous ruling groups in varying degrees suffered loss of land, office, and status. Their experience differed from country to country. The conquest of England involved a virtually clean sweep of the Anglo-Saxon aristocracy. In Scotland, by contrast, old and new elements existed side by side as subjects of the king, and gradually blended. Wales and Ireland present a third pattern. Both came to be shared by rival elites, though relations between them at local level were by no means consistently hostile. For much of the thirteenth century, the newcomers were more securely placed in Ireland than in Wales. However, Edward I's wars gave the English the upper hand in Wales, whereas Ireland was to remain debatable ground. This brief outline ignores many complications, of which the most straightforward is regional variation. Displacement of Anglo-Saxon landowners was less complete in northern England than in the south. Scotland north and west of the Highland line was largely insulated from conquest and settlement, though not from cultural influences. Despite Norman military incursions during the late eleventh century, Gwynedd remained in Welsh hands until 1282; south-east Wales, by contrast, was permanently removed from the control of Welsh lords at the same period. Similar sharp differences existed between north-west and south-east Ireland. In both Wales and Ireland, however, many areas lay in between such extremes, and were shared in a patchwork fashion largely dictated by local topography.

On the morrow of the battle of Hastings England presented a paradox. William I claimed the kingship as legitimate successor to Edward the Confessor; he was crowned according to the established English rite, and ruled as 'king of the English'. The logic of this posture was that the Anglo-Saxon ruling class should become his subjects, rather than suffering dispossession. There was tension between this presumption of continuity and the expectation of enrichment on the part of those who participated in the 1066 expedition or crossed the Channel during the months that followed. The contradiction was resolved, messily and sometimes violently, by the progressive forfeiture within less than a decade of the upper levels of

English landowning society. This was assisted by the fact that the group of Anglo-Saxon earls was exceptionally narrow, being dominated by the immensely wealthy kins of Godwine (the family of King Harold) and Leofric. The Godwinsons and their associates fell through their act of 'rebellion' in resisting William in 1066; this at once released lands and offices for redistribution, and created a need for them to be occupied. The speed with which William fitz Osbern was established at Hereford reflects the fact that Harold had been earl there and the area was full of his dependants, who might form dangerous alliances with the Welsh. Even so, after William's coronation the political hierarchy still included important English lords, notably the earls Edwin of Mercia and Morcar of Northumbria, of the house of Leofric. It was not until the crisis created by risings in south-western, eastern, and northern England, accompanied by invasions from Scotland and Scandinavia, during the years 1068–72 that a substantial remnant of the former ruling class lost its position. By 1072 only one native earl, Waltheof, the son of Siward of Northumberland, was still in place. Waltheof was executed in 1076 for alleged complicity in a rising. By then the official emphasis on continuity had long ceased to be reflected in the personnel at the summit of society. Domesday Book shows that by 1086 the vast majority of the hundred or so king's thegns, who formed the other main element of the lay ruling class, had also been displaced.

Below that level, it is probable that there was much greater continuity, though we face the predictable problem that the evidence reveals little about the middling ranks of society. In addition, the cultural dominance of the newcomers ensured that native families would give their children continental names, making ethnic origins difficult to pinpoint. Nevertheless, particularly in the west and north, there is clear evidence of survival among the lesser ministerial element—men of the sort who might serve as subordinates to the sheriff, or figure as king's huntsmen or foresters. The domestic and recreational side of Henry I's own court was run partly by men and women of native origin. Occasionally a family of English ancestry could carve a more imposing niche for itself in the new world, as in the case of the descendants of Eadnoth the Staller (d. 1068), who aligned himself with the Normans. Although most of Eadnoth's lands seem to have passed to the earls of Chester, his son Harding retained parts of them. Harding's own younger son, known as Robert of Bristol, benefited from the patronage of Henry II, who granted him the lordship of Berkeley. Robert, who helped to fund Strongbow's invasion of Ireland, was the founder of a leading baronial family.

Rebirth after the fashion of the Berkeleys is far from typical. But the Norman elite who dominated the court and exercised lordship locally shaded off into a broader society of small landowners and functionaries who were of English, or mixed, descent. With some well-known exceptions, the Norman aristocracy did not contract marriages with the English, but many of the knights, serjeants, and servants who accompanied them to England did do so. The passage of property from English to Norman families may sometimes have been negotiated partly through marriage. It would be wishful thinking to regard this as evidence of affectionate reconciliation between the two groups: particular women may have been treated as heiresses, sometimes at the expense of their male kin, because this was to the advantage of the incomers. Even in Ireland, where women did not inherit or transmit claims to land and lordship, Diarmait Mac Murchadha and Strongbow could promote Strongbow's bride, Diarmait's daughter Aoife, as heiress of Leinster, because it suited them to do so; the losers were Diarmait's brother, nephew, and cousins. Thus, there was in England a wider constituency with whom the official stress upon continuity and legitimacy had resonance. This may help to explain why Henry I, having seized the throne in 1100 and provoked a conflict with the supporters of Robert of Normandy, chose to marry Edith, the sister of the king of Scots, and niece of Edgar Atheling, the Confessor's nephew. Later writers were to echo the Anglo-Saxon Chronicle in stressing her descent from 'the rightful royal house of England'.

The endowment of the Anglo-Normans in southern Scotland was a far more protracted and patchy affair; its implications for the existing elites varied greatly from place to place. The almost complete absence of chronicle evidence, so valuable in providing glimpses of the catastrophic side of the settlement process in England, may leave the impression that Scotland was freer from friction and violence than was in fact the case. But there is nothing to suggest widespread upheaval. Although William the Lion (1165–1214) and his predecessors were said by an English chronicler to have preferred 'Frenchmen' to native Scots, the kings of Scots were neither able nor disposed to turn their backs on the provincial lords and thanes. The witness-lists of their charters confirm that Anglo-Normans were pre-eminent in court circles, but show native earls continuing to appear as witnesses, with precedence over the incomers, who in the twelfth century lacked comital titles. Nor were conflicts within the kingdom polarized along national lines. William's periodic campaigns against rivals based in the north were backed by figures such as Lachlan (later known as Roland) of Galloway and Farquhar Mac Taggart of Ross. The native lords, as well as having their own rivalries, were of varied origin; they ranged from the Anglian earls of Dunbar, descended from the former Northumbrian ruling house once based at Bamburgh, to the Gaelic-Scandinavian descendants of Somerled (d. 1164), who were powerful in Argyll. Old and new elements possibly had more to unite than divide them: their shared noble status, attachment to the same royal court, and an interest in patronizing the fashionable religious orders. Applying simplified ethnic labels is not the best means of understanding Scottish aristocratic society.

By the late thirteenth century, when royal lordship had come to involve most of Scotland, much integration had occurred. One vehicle of this was intermarriage, with its consequences for the transmission of property and office. Ness son of William, lord of Leuchars in Fife in the mid-twelfth century, was probably the son of an Anglo-Norman father and a Scottish heiress. Roland of Galloway (d. 1200), whose grandfather, Fergus, may have married an illegitimate daughter of Henry I, took as his bride Helen de Morville, who brought his descendants extensive property in eastern Scotland and in England, together with the office of Constable. Given the initial reluctance of Anglo-Norman lords to marry their daughters—all of whom were potentially heiresses—to men from an alien cultural group, the marriage is as suggestive as Roland's adoption of a French name. During the thirteenth century, when the king's courts applied rules of inheritance identical to those used in England, earldoms began to pass to lineages of Anglo-Norman origin. Around 1212 William Comyn acquired Buchan by marriage; and before the death of Alexander III in 1286 earldoms and great lordships beyond the areas of the original Anglo-Norman settlements had come to the heirs of Robert de Brus and the Stewart descendants of Walter fitz Alan, among others. For the royal house, its link with the Scottish past was no propaganda tactic; kings played a critical part in mediating the interactions between native and Anglo-Norman society.

The position in Wales and Ireland was very different. Royal authority normally operated from a distance and remained essentially
external to the native world. This did not preclude alliances. In
1081 William the Conqueror went on a pilgrimage expedition to St
Davids, where Rhys ap Tewdwr, the king of Deheubarth, submitted
to him, inaugurating a link that lasted until Rhys's death in 1093.
William's aim was no doubt to create stability in a region perilously
close to the sea lanes to Ireland where Norman lords might outrun
his control. In 1175 Henry II negotiated an agreement at Windsor with
emissaries from Ruaidrí Ua Conchobair, king of Connacht and
high king of Ireland. The text offers an insight into the thinking of
the parties which is absent in the laconic chronicle accounts of the
Conqueror's time. Ruaidrí recognized Henry's overlordship, promised tribute, and accepted that Meath, Leinster, and the hinterland of
Waterford were now the sphere of the king and his barons. In return
Henry would back Ruaidrí as superior lord over the Irish kings of the
rest of the island, and would protect him against Anglo-Norman
incursions. John and Henry III, too, made frequent deals with kings
and princes in north and south Wales, and in western Ireland. Native
rulers were pieces on the political chessboard, alongside Anglo-
Norman lords; their internecine quarrels and fear of baronial expansion could be exploited in order to provide useful allies, not least at
times when the crown itself wished to set limits to the ambitions of
particular aristocratic interests. But these, often transient, alliances do
not alter the fact that the interests of English kings were more likely to
be aligned with their own people. In neither country did they cultivate links with the native past of the sort that existed naturally in
Scotland and were consciously exploited in relation to England itself.
Wales lacked a single regnal tradition that might have been taken
over; during the thirteenth century Llywelyn the Great and his successors were struggling to construct one. In Ireland provincial
dynasties competed for a high kingship that retained something of
the character of a cyclical paramount chieftaincy. Moreover, the
English invaded Ireland in a climate of ecclesiastical reform and
moral disapproval that was not conducive to appropriating the
native past. Gerald of Wales's accounts of Wales and Ireland present the indigenous inhabitants as culturally distinct from the English
and French; their virtues, which he acknowledged, were those
commonly found among the inhabitants of what a later age would

call 'underdeveloped' countries. Ironically, the most notable employment of native traditions came at the very end of the period, when Edward I, to symbolize his conquest, laid up the insignia associated with Llywelyn ap Gruffudd's principality in Westminster Abbey.

These questions of perceptions and high politics must be set in the more mundane context of conquest and settlement on the ground, which was spasmodic, patchy, and incomplete. The assimilation of native lords into Anglo-Norman society was rare. In Ireland, the clearest example is provided by the descendants of Mac Gilla Mo Cholmóc, ruler of the territory immediately south of the city of Dublin. His grandson, who appears in early thirteenth-century records as 'John fitz Dermot', was married to an Anglo-Norman woman, and held his lands by knight service. By the late thirteenth century John's successors were indistinguishable from the settler gentry of County Dublin, with whom they shared in its defence against raids by the Irish of Wicklow. Normally, however, Welsh and Irish lords remained in intermittently hostile occupation of those parts of their former territories that lay beyond the areas settled and directly governed by the new rulers.

The capacity of rival aristocratic societies to coexist in this way raises questions about their structure and resources. For the Anglo-Normans, the key areas were the lowlands, often coastal or riverine, that were suitable for arable farming. Exclusion from these was serious for the ousted dynasties, which lost access to the manpower and produce of rich areas of tillage and grazing. However, the pastoral character of rural life in native Wales and Ireland (and indeed in upland Galloway) allowed room for manoeuvre. Hilly, wooded, and marshy regions, marginal from a settler point of view, were capable of functioning as core areas of native lordship. Indeed significant older and newer centres of Welsh and Irish culture and ecclesiastical organization—Strata Florida, Bangor, Glendalough, Clonmacnois— were within or on the fringes of such areas. The Anglo-Norman advance did not leave them untouched. In Ireland, the mountainous see of Glendalough was at least superficially absorbed by the archdiocese of Dublin. In the boggy midlands lordships were sketched out around such fortified centres as Dunamase (Laois) and Geashill (Offaly). But settlement there remained light and control fragile; by the 1270s there are signs that such ventures had constituted over-extension.

At propitious moments the wealth and standing of native lords could be revived through attacks on settled areas. This happened in Wales during Stephen's reign, which saw the energies of marcher lords drawn eastwards by the Anglo-Norman civil war; Henry II stabilized the marches but was unable to restore the favourable conditions of Henry I's time. Ireland's distance from the political centre made it rather less sensitive to the vicissitudes of high politics. Nevertheless, in the north and west, where the balance of advantage remained uncertain, native lords could be presented with opportunities by minorities and political mishaps that afflicted magnate families. The apogee of the career of Aodh Méith Ó Néill of Tír Eogain (west Ulster) coincided with a period (1210–27) when the north of Ireland was affected by the forfeiture of Hugh de Lacy, earl of Ulster, who had quarrelled with King John.

Relationships between the leaders of the two aristocratic groups were largely personal and political. In both countries, the new regional powers exploited the succession disputes that afflicted native dynasties, among whom primogeniture was not practised and the Church's rules on marriage, divorce, and bastardy made slow headway. The profusion of kings' sons and grandsons, all liable to regard themselves as disinherited, made allies and clients easy to find. Cadwaladr, the brother and intermittent rival of Owain Gwynedd, for instance, is more than once found in alliance with marcher lords against him; in 1157 he participated in Henry II's expedition to north Wales. Links of this sort were normal, not exceptional. The expansion of Anglo-Norman lords in Ireland took place through alliances with Irishmen whom it is anachronistic to label renegades or traitors. Indeed native manpower played a large part in the conquests in both countries. This is apparent in 1171 in Ireland, when Strongbow succeeded Diarmait Mac Murchadha and established his dominance in Leinster through plundering raids on which he was accompanied by Irish allies. In thirteenth-century Wales the Marshals, de Clares, and others formed links with native lords, not least the many descendants of Rhys ap Gruffudd, who were vying for land and status. In 1219, in the aftermath of Llywelyn the Great's southwards expansion, Rhys's son Rhys Gryg married a daughter of Gilbert de Clare, earl of Gloucester. Two years later Rhys Gryg's nephew Rhys Ieuanc, angered by the favour shown by Llywelyn to another of his uncles, Maelgwn ap Rhys, joined William Marshal II, earl of Pembroke, who was trying to counter Llywelyn's influence.

Normally such relationships are glimpsed fleetingly in chronicles, but occasionally documentary evidence survives. In 1268 Walter de Burgh, earl of Ulster and lord of Connacht, subjected Aodh Buidhe Ó Néill, to whom he had given a kinswoman in marriage, to a written bond, after an act of disobedience. Aodh was to pay a fine of 3,500 cows in instalments, to surrender a son together with three kinsmen of his vassal lords as hostages, to maintain his wife honourably, and to accept that he might be replaced in the kingship if he failed to observe these terms. Holding hostages—something that happened in Anglo-French society only at times of crisis when normal conventions had broken down—was usual among the Welsh and Irish. It symbolizes the fact that magnates were interacting with a world where lordship still amounted to a ceaseless competition for allegiances across territory where walled towns were absent and major fortresses remained few. Gerald of Wales's moralizing remarks about the 'fickleness' and 'faithlessness' of the Welsh and Irish may be read as comments on societies where power could shift with bewildering speed and which lacked the stable pyramid of authority that could guarantee rights and predictable successions.

Thus described, interactions may appear to be between separate societies, which touched only through individual arrangements made between their leaders. There is some truth in this: magnates worked through native lords who, they hoped, might serve as agents of stability and as conduits through which resources—of military manpower as much as livestock or cash—might be extracted. Relationships did, however, extend beyond the personal and immediate. In south Wales, lesser Welsh lords were accommodated within the structures of marcher lordships without being wholly assimilated. Glamorgan, for example, had three parts: a core area around Cardiff, organized along the lines of a shire; subsidiary lordships such as Talyfan, Coety, and Margam held by major sub-tenants or ecclesiastical institutions; and upland zones such as Afan and Senghennydd, which were occupied by Welsh dynasties (see Map 4). All the satellite areas enjoyed some immunity from the lord's officers, but major matters from the entire lordship lay within his purview. His courts would apply either the local variant of March law or Welsh custom, depending upon the nature of the case and the identity of those involved. In Ireland a variety of practical arrangements existed. Rents were owed to magnates or the crown by native kings and lords in return for recognition

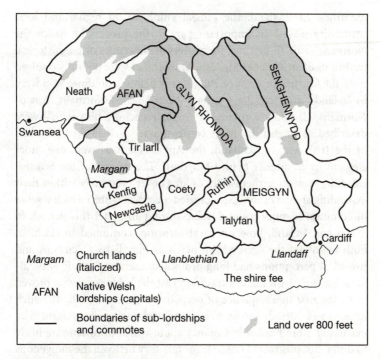

Map 4 The lordship of Glamorgan in the thirteenth century

of their retention of parts of their former territories. In the northwest these were usually expressed in cattle, in the south-west in either cattle or cash. The lords of native Ulster owed the earl of Ulster renders to support specific numbers of garrison troops in peacetime. The Irish who bordered on the de Verdon lordships owed rents in money, cattle, and squirrel-skins at the castles of Roche (Louth) and Loughsewdy (Westmeath). Across the midlands there are references to obligations to military service, free if a local campaign allowed Irish leaders to return home at night, but at the lord's expense if he wished to take them further afield. Some of these arrangements may represent colonial impositions, others the continuation or adaptation of tributes and services owed to pre-conquest overlords. By such means native lords were formally linked to, but not fully integrated with, settler society.

These contrasting experiences were crucial for the shaping of identities. In England, the official emphasis on regnal and legal continuity played an important part in the process by which the Normans came to perceive themselves as inheritors of the historical traditions of an ancient kingdom. Ambiguities were not fully resolved until the fourteenth century. But already before 1200 those who went to Ireland—and who have usually been labelled Normans, Anglo-Normans, Cambro-Normans, or Anglo-French by historians—were described as English by most contemporary writers on both sides of the Irish Sea. In Scotland, the Anglo-Normans were one more element in an already hybrid kingdom. The success of the Scottish rulers in presenting themselves as kings over everybody within their expanding sphere of influence created a context within which a sense of common identity could develop during and after this period. In Wales and Ireland, however, rival identities continued to clash. In both countries the *literati* who acted as guardians of custom and historical perceptions had long promoted a sense of ethnic and cultural identity; Irish literary tradition cast the Vikings as what proved to be the first in a sequence of perpetual 'foreigners'. Whether such notions were already too set to respond to changing circumstances by becoming more flexible is a matter about which historians are likely to differ. But protracted contests for territory between the indigenous elites and an intruding aristocracy backed by a monarchy that had no stake in the Welsh or Irish past were hardly fertile ground for the construction of alternative, more capacious, myths. Nor did the fact that Welsh and Irish women were not heiresses in the Anglo-Norman sense make intermarriage the solvent that it proved to be in Scotland. The aristocracy that became English in England and Scottish in Scotland showed a propensity to assume, or retain, an English identity in Wales and Ireland. The consequences were profound.

Together, the developments surveyed in this chapter amount to a fundamental redrawing, not merely of the lines of influence and authority within the archipelago, but also between the British Isles and the outside world. It is often said that 1066 marked the removal of England from a Scandinavian orbit and the beginning of a close association with northern France. There is some exaggeration in this. Ties between southern and eastern England and the nearer Continent were very old, and had remained strong during the tenth and eleventh centuries. Nevertheless, the reign of William I saw both the successful repulsion of Scandinavian assaults in the north and the beginning of enduring political ties between England and France, which had implications for Britain and Ireland as a whole. The marriages of the Scottish kings—who between the 1070s and the 1280s took every one of their eight brides from England or the Continent— are a symptom of this. The other major shift involved communications and power around the Irish Sea. In the eleventh century the western waterways were the scene of trade, diplomacy, and war, in which dynasties, many of mixed Celtic and Scandinavian descent, competed and allied (see Map A). The power of a ruler in north Wales could depend on troops from Dublin, whose Scandinavian dynasty had links with the Manx kings and ultimately with Norway, but might itself be subject to the overlordship of an Irish ruler of Leinster or Munster. The appearance of the Normans, whether in west Wales in the 1090s or in Ireland in the late 1160s, might well have been followed by their absorption into this Irish Sea world, so perpetuating an east–west division in the politics of Britain. The power of the English monarchy, and later of the Scottish kings, prevented this, and brought about crucial transformations (see Map B). The establishment of English control in southern and eastern Ireland was especially radical in its effects. Native Wales was now caught between two blocks of English power, as the contribution of men, money, and supplies from Ireland to the Welsh campaigns of Henry III and Edward I showed. The north Irish Sea region was never so firmly absorbed, partly because the outbreak of the Anglo-Scottish wars in the 1290s interrupted the process. Nevertheless, in 1266 Scottish royal power had excluded Scandinavian political influence and was predominant on the western seaboard from the Hebrides to the Isle of Man. In 1282 English administrative systems were about to be extended to Anglesey and Meirionydd (see Map 5). Western Britain and Ireland had been drawn within the orbits of kings based in the south and east of England and Scotland; the extent and depth of their control would have amazed William the Conqueror and Malcolm Canmore.

Tenth-century rulers such as Athelstan and Edgar, who campaigned beyond the Humber and had fleets operating on the Irish Sea, had created impressive overlordships. But it was in this later period that the equivalents of their ealdormen, earls, and thegns were planted from Pembroke to Kerry, Galway, and north Antrim; and that

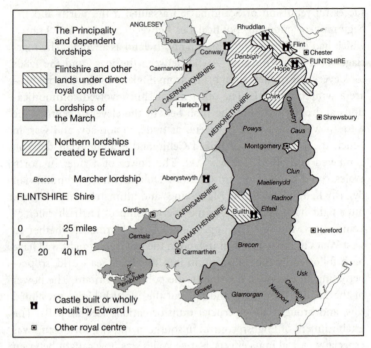

Map 5 Wales after Edward I's conquest

administrative systems developed which gathered regular revenues and routinely offered royal justice from Penzance to Carmarthen and Carlisle, and from Waterford to Cork, Athlone, and Dundalk. The Scottish Kenneths, Constantines, and Malcolms of the tenth and eleventh centuries had long reigns and possibly a longer reach than the exiguous sources reveal. Yet in Scotland too it was in the twelfth and thirteenth centuries that aristocrats from Galloway and the Hebrides to Ross and Sutherland responded to a single political centre, and the custom of the king's courts came to regulate the lives and property of the upper class. In fundamental ways, conquest and colonization had reshaped most regions of the archipelago, together with the interactions between them.

Figure 3 Westminster Hall. Along with the White Tower of London, Westminster Hall which was built for King William II is the finest surviving example of the great buildings erected in England under the Norman kings. At the time of its construction, it was probably the largest hall in Europe. It and the neighbouring abbey, which had been refounded by Edward the Confessor, formed a typical combination of the religious and the secular at a major royal residence. The original roof was probably supported by wooden pillars. The one which can be seen nowadays was built for Richard II.

Kingship, government, and political life to *c.*1160

David Bates

The size and diversity of the British Isles are a factor of great importance for the history of kingship, government, and political life in the
islands in this period. The world is likely to have looked very different, dependent on whether one was based in, say, Winchester, Dublin,
Roxburgh, or Kirkwall (See Map 6). It is nonetheless certain that
Duke William of Normandy's victory at Hastings sent shock waves
throughout the British Isles. Although their intensity had diminished
almost to nothing by the time they reached the regions most distant
from the epicentre, their political impact throughout England, on the
princes of Wales and on the kings of Scots, was powerful and disturb-
ing. While the consequences of the Conquest were undeniably significant, there is a lot to be said for the view that on a long-term
perspective native traditions proved to be extremely resilient. As far
as the British Isles as a whole were concerned, the Norman Conquest
was after all just the last of a sequence of conquests and settlements,
of which the most recent was the relatively short-lived conquest by
the Danish kings Sven Forkbeard (d. 1014) and Cnut, king of England
from 1016 to 1035, which provided England with her rulers for less
than thirty years (1013–1042). William the Conqueror's victories over
the armies of the Danish king Sven Estrithsson in the 1060s and early
1070s and the failure of Sven's eventual successor Cnut IV's projected
expedition in 1085–6 brought to an end the prospect of a North Sea

Map 6 The kingdoms of the British Isles to 1160, with places mentioned in the text of Chapter 2

empire of the kind that the earlier Cnut and his sons had ruled. Although this is a turning-point of very great importance in the history of southern Britain, the continued existence throughout the period of Norse settlements in Dublin, the Isle of Man, and the Western and Northern Isles kept some of the old contacts between the British Isles and Scandinavia in existence.

The violence of the Normans and French is a regular and potent theme in the contemporary sources (especially in Wales). This was part of a technical and tactical superiority over the native peoples of Britain enjoyed by the new Norman kings of England that had profound effects on politics everywhere. Although a similar superiority had arguably been enjoyed by the pre-1066 English kings, the newcomers, to a greater or lesser degree, forced the Welsh, Scots, and other peoples of Britain even more on to the defensive, while at the same time provoking a significant level of imitation in, for example, castle building. Although Ireland was at this stage largely beyond the aristocratic diaspora which had such an impact elsewhere, its extensive economic, ecclesiastical, and political links with the west of Britain meant that it was significantly affected. It is nonetheless important to keep in mind the implications of the Conqueror's claim that he was Edward the Confessor's designated heir. This not only had consequences for the way in which England was ruled, but was equally important for the rest of Britain because of the supremacy over all the British peoples which the Norman kings believed that they had inherited from their English predecessors. Although their power within Britain was such that the Welsh chronicler who wrote *Brut y Tywysogyon* stated that Henry I had brought the whole island of Britain under his authority, there were in practice significant limitations to their claims and their power which were in part conditioned by their British heritage. Acknowledgement of supremacy, rather than conquest, was the kings' objective. The intensification of contacts between England and northern France which resulted from the union of Normandy and England under a single ruling family, and the existence of the cross-Channel landholdings of the aristocratic elite, had a significant impact on both politics and government both in England and to a lesser extent throughout the British Isles. This was so because of the rulers' frequent absences, the heavy taxation required to finance campaigns in France, and the wars fought over the succession in Normandy and England. Nonetheless, within the British Isles the main theme of the whole chapter is undoubtedly England's power in relation to its neighbours.

The Norwegian king Magnus Barelegs's expedition of 1098 regularized Norwegian claims to overlordship in the north and west of the British Isles which were not finally extinguished in the Northern Isles until the fifteenth century. Although the agreement which he supposedly made with Edgar, king of Scots, drawing a demarcation line between the mainland and the Isles as the spheres of both kings' power, established a *modus vivendi* between them, King Magnus's intervention cannot in truth be seen as much more than a short-term disruption of a northern and western British political world in which British- and Irish-based local dynasties vied for power and control. In spite of references to the Norse of Dublin as 'the foreigners of Dublin' in contemporary sources, the Norse settlements in Dublin, Wexford, and elsewhere had to a considerable degree become integrated into their Irish and British context; their military strength, and in particular their ships, tended no longer to be an independent political force, but to be at the disposal of Irish kings striving to expand their power both within Ireland and across the Irish Sea. After Magnus Barelegs's death in 1103, the Isle of Man and the Western Isles were as often as not under the rule of Gofraid Méránach (Godred Crovan) (d. 1095) and his descendants. From about 1130, Somerled (d. 1164) dominated not only the Isles, but also much of Argyll. Galloway, a Gaelic kingdom, where Fergus rose to pre-eminence in the 1130s, remained largely outside the direct control of the Scottish kings and appears to have been quite closely associated with the rulers of the Isle of Man. Radical change in this situation came only after the English penetration of Ireland and the expansion northwards and westwards of the power of the Scottish kings in the later twelfth and thirteenth centuries.

The narrative riches of the twelfth-century 'golden age' of Norman and English historical writing, as well as the mass of record sources, permit insights into the norms of politics and power. William of Poitiers (writing shortly before 1077) provides a marvellous exemplar of the construction of a case for political legitimacy and Orderic Vitalis, in the first half of the twelfth century, a reflective moral critique thereon. Orderic is excellent for political narrative and for the role of the military household of kings and lords. Historians such as William of Malmesbury and, later, William of Newburgh, also suggest that contemporaries were very aware of the great differences between the English kingdom and the rest of the British Isles. Their frequent denunciation of Welsh, Scots, Irish, and others as barbarians derived in part from identifiable differences in political culture. Specific concerns were the savagery with which all of these peoples waged war and the extensive killing and enslavement of non-combatants—the Scots and Galwegians were thought particularly reprehensible in this respect—and the slaughter of rivals during their numerous succession disputes which characterized above all Irish and Welsh politics. Welsh, Scottish, and Irish sources, although much less numerous, can on occasion supply the other side of the coin in terms of resentment and ethnic aspiration. Awareness of difference did not, however, obstruct the existence and the development in peaceful times of an enormous range of political, economic, cultural, and ecclesiastical contacts throughout the British Isles. Politics was multilayered, internalized within each of the numerous kingdoms, yet also involving all of them in complex interactive relationships.

Kingship

Although all kings seemingly passed through a ritual inauguration— the evidence is less clear-cut for Wales than elsewhere—only the English kings were anointed with holy oil in the style of the main western European monarchies. A strong sense of the traditional ran through all these rituals, with the English ceremony retaining a basic character which had been established in the tenth century and the Scottish and Irish apparently retaining elements of their earlier pagan forms in spite of the regular presence of churchmen at royal inaugurations. In line with the Norman regime's emphasis on legitimacy, William the Conqueror, even though the actual *ordo* may have been relatively new, was crowned in Westminster Abbey according to English rites. David I, although apparently desirous of a more obviously Christian ceremony, went through a traditional Scottish enthronement at Scone. Although the so-called Anonymous of York/Rouen, in contentious circumstances, could claim that the coronation placed the English king on the same level as a priest, sacrality played little part in the propagation of kingship anywhere in Britain. When a jester gazed at a resplendently dressed William the Conqueror and announced that he saw God, the king did agree to Archbishop Lanfranc's suggestion that the fool be flogged. That it was Lanfranc who made the suggestion may indicate that William was not greatly concerned to punish the blasphemy. William Rufus, although much more conventionally religious than is often thought, is most unlikely to have had truck with sentiments about the religious nature of the royal office. Inauguration rituals were more important for marking the moment when a man became king than for their sacrality. Henry I, Stephen, and Malcolm IV, with rivals to contend with, were crowned quickly. The Empress Mathilda, who was never crowned, was known as *domina Anglorum* rather than *regina*. Homage and fealty performed by the great men after the coronation were arguably of greater practical importance than the ceremony itself.

All kings lived an itinerant and public lifestyle. Once more emphasizing continuity with perceived Anglo-Saxon tradition, William the Conqueror, when his cross-Channel commitments made it possible, celebrated Easter at Winchester, Whitsun at Westminster, and Christmas at Gloucester, a pattern which he apparently believed his predecessors had also followed. Charters confirmed on these occasions show the mass political weight of the kingdom gathered, and the one great royal hall of this period to survive, William Rufus's Westminster Hall, illustrates magnificently the scale and dignity of these occasions (see Figure 3). Archaeological and documentary evidence together show beyond doubt that the Norman kings of England built larger and more spectacular buildings than their predecessors; monumentality may indeed be a form of triumphalism. This style of kingship, in a lot of respects still resonant of the much older culture of the king and his warriors gathered in the royal hall, on vastly differing scales prevailed throughout the British Isles; in Gwynedd, for example, Gruffudd ap Cynan (1095–1137) 'always built his courts and held his feasts honourably'. A religious dimension was also usually present, typified through the chanting of the Anglo-Norman *Laudes Regiae* and the churches which stood alongside most kings' residences; while on different scales the abbeys of Westminster and Dunfermline and 'Cormac's chapel' at Cashel (see Figure 11) epitomize this pattern, it is again notable that Gruffudd ap Cynan is said to have constructed churches at each of his chief courts. Even for the most powerful, however, kingship was normally a less grand and formal business. William the Conqueror, for example, is described making a grant 'while sitting on his carpet at Bénouville' (probably Bénouville near Caen), and numerous other gifts were made at the hunting-lodges which the universal kingly passion for hunting necessitated. Hunting, like the army, was in any case an extension of normal political intercourse and business.

The court and the royal entourage were the great centres of power. Within them, alongside the king, the queen was a figure of central importance. From England and Scotland, the *Laudes* and the inauguration rituals, patterns of charter attestations and the extra-ordinary Life of St Margaret show queens sharing in their husband's power, organizing patronage and playing the traditional female roles of counsellor and peace-maker. With the exception of Adeliza of Louvain, all English queens at some point substituted for their husbands; they might on such occasions be surrounded by their husband's trusted advisers, but it was the queen alone who could formally exercise kingly power. In the case of Mathilda of Boulogne, Stephen's queen, the role extended as far as leadership in war. If queenship can legitimately be regarded as an office, then a king's closest kindred were also crucially important. At times sharing in a king's power or acting on his behalf, as in the case of the Conqueror's half-brother, Bishop Odo of Bayeux, Henry I's son William, or David I's son Earl Henry, they were manifestly raised to a status above the rest of the aristocracy. The witness-lists of charters convey the impression that sons, even when adult, were often in their father's company. Disputes about the terms of collaboration within the kindred were frequent and could on occasion lead to conflict, as, most famously, between William the Conqueror and his son Robert Curthose over the latter's role in the duchy of Normandy and between Henry I and the Empress Mathilda over territorial provision for herself and her husband. Both these disputes contributed to the outbreak of prolonged wars after the patriarch's death. So important was the collaboration of the close family group that the image of family cooperation was retained even in times of stress; both William Rufus and Robert Curthose and Henry I and Robert on occasion displayed their separate roles in England and Normandy as a *condominium* over both.

Generosity was everywhere recognized as a kingly virtue and what was seen as a good quality in William Rufus was, for instance, likewise identified in Bleddyn ap Cynfyn and his son Cadwgan ap Bleddyn, kings of Powys. This generosity was the oil which articulated the military households crucial to all royal power. While brilliant detective work has demonstrated the tentacular characteristics of the Anglo-Norman royal *familia* (i.e. military household), which resembled a standing army, and could divide and disperse at the king's bidding through Normandy and England into a garrison to defend a castle or form a special strike force, its equivalents elsewhere were of similarly central importance. The contrasts of scale were of course immense, with William Rufus and Henry I able to recruit warriors from all over Europe. Yet Welsh, Scottish, and Irish kings all had households which to a greater or lesser extent resembled the Carolingian model prevalent in England and western Europe; the portrayal in the surviving life of Gruffudd ap Cynan of his court and that of David I's entourage by Ailred of Rievaulx exude the same military and cultural ambience as Orderic Vitalis's accounts of the *familia* of the Norman kings of England. In 1078 the destruction of Rhys ab Owain of Deheubarth's *teulu* (i.e. *familia*) was followed shortly afterwards by his death.

The royal court was also a centre of literary patronage. The medium varied, from the bardic poets who entertained Welsh and Irish kings to the Latin poets who wrote verse for the Anglo-Norman court. The poetry and literature was often a mirror of how the king and the aristocracy who surrounded him liked to think of themselves. Much that was read and sung celebrated prowess in war and the glorious deeds of ancestors. Yet, through his queen, Henry I could be involved as a patron of William of Malmesbury's *Gesta Regum Anglorum*, which sought to inform the Normans about their English predecessors. Geoffrey of Monmouth's *History of the Kings of Britain*, which would have satisfied both Welsh and Anglo-Norman audiences, also received English courtly patronage. If, in comparing Gaimar's description of 'the love affairs and the courting, the hunting and the drinking, the festivities and the pomp and ceremony, the acts of generosity and the displays of wealth, the entourage of noble and valiant knights that the king maintained, and the generous presents that he distributed' at the court of Henry I with the recurrent themes of war and feasting in bardic poetry, we detect a contrast between the new chivalric world of the twelfth century and older sets of values, then we are dwelling above all on the greater wealth of the English court and its closer connections with the Continent.[1]

Government

In terms of governmental organization, the contrast between England and the rest of Britain was in many respects enormous. The making of Domesday Book and the Exchequer procedures illuminated by the single surviving Pipe Roll of Henry I's reign, as well as the continuous sequence of Pipe Rolls from the start of Henry II's, have justifiably been seen as evidence of probably the most organizationally developed monarchy of contemporary Europe. Within the British Isles only Scotland from David I's time onwards even remotely compares. Very few charters survive from Wales and Ireland, despite their strong, long-standing literary traditions. Yet it would be wrong to think that there was always an immense conceptual chasm between England and elsewhere. Kingship and aristocracy were present everywhere, and the ethos and power of both in considerable degree derived from a similar and related Germanic and Celtic past. Despite the undoubted power of the English shires and hundreds and of Scottish kingship, institutions were everywhere by later standards relatively undeveloped, kings were itinerant, and their capacity to communicate with their subjects limited. The English documentation, which is vastly greater in quantity than that surviving from anywhere else, has been the basis for sophisticated studies of revenue, justice, and patronage which are impossible elsewhere. In terms of taxation in particular, it also illuminates the undeniably overwhelming military and financial power of the English state in relation to its British neighbours, even though these resources at this time were almost exclusively deployed in the defence of their French possessions. The period as a whole is notable for a steady intensification of governmental activity. Everywhere kings' power intruded more often into the local affairs of their kingdoms and literate modes of recording property transactions became everywhere much more common (see Figure 4).

---

[1] Geffrei Gaimar, *L'Estoire des Engleis*, ed. A. Gell (Anglo-Norman Text Soc., xiv–xvi, 1960), lines 6505–10.

Figure 4 Writ-charter of David I granting forest in Annandale to Robert de Brus (Public Record Office, London, DL 25/L/78). The grant dates from between 1150 and 1153 and is a specific grant of forest rights within a large region granted to Robert in all probability in 1124. The charter illustrates the installation of the Bruce family in Scotland and also shows how literate business spread to the Scottish kingdom in David I's reign. Although it is not certain that this document was written by a scribe of the Scottish royal chancery, its diplomatic form does show very clearly how David's regime imitated English practice.

Royal and aristocratic power was exercised through a multitude of personal networks. Their complexity is well illustrated by the career of Hugh de Port, a tenant of the Conqueror's half-brother, Bishop Odo of Bayeux, in Normandy and England. Probably sheriff of Kent and subsequently sheriff of Hampshire, Hugh held land of the two great Winchester churches, the Old and New Minsters, and in 1088 took part in the proscription of rebels, including his former lord and patron Bishop Odo, who had sided with Robert Curthose's ambitions to take the English kingdom from his brother William Rufus. In such a scenario lordship and loyalty are relative terms and hierarchy and status have little meaning. The ultimate determinant of Hugh's and many others' careers was the magnetic attraction of the royal court and the opportunities that it provided in terms of office and marriage. The courts of the aristocracy were lesser microcosms of kingship's immense power. This mobility has led to the history of English government and society being analysed in terms of the rise of 'new men', whose *raison d'être* was more administrative than that of the established aristocracy, and who constituted a new kind of more specialized royal servant. Scottish history has fed off this model as well, with analysis of David I's and his successors' imports from England also raising the dimension of ethnicity. Most recent scholarship has, however, resisted the lure of Orderic Vitalis's famous denunciation of men 'raised from the dust' by Henry I and instead rightly seen Anglo-Norman political society in much more conservative terms. While the modern tendency to distinguish between magnates and *curiales* has some merit, everywhere, just as for many centuries before and after, serious political power lay with a small very wealthy elite, into which newcomers might rise through royal favour from a lower aristocratic level. Just as William I and his successors were surrounded on great occasions by the great cross-Channel magnates, so were David I's and Malcolm IV's courts attended at the equivalent times by the great earls, the great majority of whom were of Gaelic descent. This does not, however, imply either that aristocratic society anywhere in the British Isles was static, or that government was not an agent of social and political change. English and to a lesser extent Scottish aristocratic society were indeed notably fluid in the aftermath of the *bouleversement* of 1066. While the dramatic history of the Bigods who rose from minor Norman landowner to earl in two generations supplies a particularly startling example,

Eustace fitz John's acquisition of vast lands in northern England in Henry I's reign and Hugh de Moreville's similar rise in David I's Scotland exemplify so many other careers.

All kings drew resources from demesne estates and received regular food-rents, services, and payments in money or kind. All, such as the Scottish *cáin* and *conveth*, were ancient and customary. In this area the differences between England, with its well-developed silver coinage minted under royal control, and Ireland, where coins which imitated the English pattern had been minted in Dublin from the late tenth century, Scotland, where minting was only introduced under David I, and Wales, where there was no native coinage, are very great. The English tax known as Danegeld, as well as the various other levies referred to as gelds, which had been created in the tenth century to pay off Danish attacks, and which had been kept by Cnut as a means to extort money from his new subjects, was unique, not just in the British Isles, but throughout western Europe. It remained a very profitable tax throughout Henry I's reign, declined under Stephen, and proved politically untenable for Henry II after 1161–2. It is of course undeniable that the Exchequer, initiated in England under Henry I, represents a more advanced type of financial procedure than anything existing elsewhere in the British Isles. The capacity to collect debts in stages and to use exemption from taxation as a form of patronage shows both its sophistication and that royal generosity had become cold and calculating. It would, however, be wrong to see the Exchequer's inception as anything other than evolutionary. Since it was largely responsible for the same forms of revenue and expenditure that had existed before 1066, it is hard to believe that some rather simpler sort of system of accounting had not existed in Anglo-Saxon England.

The making of Domesday Book in England is *sui generis*, not just for the British Isles, but for Europe as a whole. A record of resources and tenure, it provides information on the rest of Britain's history by including references to parts of Wales and to tributes paid by the Welsh kings. The relative weakness of its information for much of northern England brings out the southern-English-based character of the English monarchy. For its time an effort of unique intensity, it highlights the demands that the king could make on the local communities of shire and hundred, and brings sharply into focus the importance of these local communities as repositories of local knowledge. It was undoubtedly executed at remarkable speed, since the order to undertake the survey was made at Christmas 1085 and the initial returns reached William before he left England for Normandy in the autumn of 1086. It is now, however, thought certain that the manuscript which we know as Great Domesday Book was completed during the first years of William II's reign, rather than before William I's death. This reappraisal of the speed of production eliminates any notion that it was an unsuccessful whim of the Conqueror's: its purpose was serious and it was part of the normal process of government. Making sense more as a survey of resources than of tenure, it is erratic as a record of disputes and of both landholders below the level of tenants-in-chief in 1086 and at all levels in 1066. Its demonstrable dependence on records whose origins lie before 1066 and on the collective memory of shire and hundred makes it a powerful testimony to the resources of the late Anglo-Saxon state.

For all its deficiencies as a record of land tenure, Domesday Book remains a remarkable record of how English land was redistributed after 1086. Its complexities are such, however, that there has been controversy as to whether land passed from a specific Anglo-Saxon landholder to a specific Frenchman according to well-understood principles, or whether these principles were so often overriden as to make the Norman Conquest a 'tenurial revolution' as well as the occasion of the annihilation in a personal sense of the upper reaches of the Anglo-Saxon aristocracy. The multitude of local disputes which the survey reports are a further complication. The majority of current opinion puts the emphasis on legal continuity as the prevailing factor, while acknowledging that the king might well choose to redistribute estates strategically; such tenurial reorganization is most evident in the compact castellanries of northern England, the Sussex rapes, and the earldoms on the Welsh border. It is also recognized that the situation is complicated by the jurisdictional and tenurial factors associated with soke, succession to a specified *antecessor* and land held on loan, and that, although the aggressive and often illegal seizure of estates was an inevitable feature of the Conquest, both lands and disputes could be transferred from an English landholder to his post-Conquest successor. Impressed as we should be by Domesday Book, we should not fall into the trap of thinking it either an objective or a non-political survey. With a primary interest in royal rights, it inevitably puts the emphasis on royal power and on a hierarchy culminating in the king. The reality, applicable to all contemporary societies, is a world where the memory of local communities was the predominant guardian of order, where many of those responsible for maintaining local order (epitomized in this case by the Domesday jurors) had connections with powerful lords, and where royal officials sought to manipulate circumstances to their own advantage. The decisive importance of royal power when it was wielded shows a continuity of power from the Anglo-Saxon past, but the very infrequent references to such royal interventions, either written or oral, demonstrate that they had little part to play in the life of largely self-regulating communities.

Increasing royal involvement and regulation of affairs in the localities is a theme everywhere. The immense disparities of documentary survival are once more an obstacle to a clear perspective, yet there are unmistakable signs throughout the British Isles that the ancient and deeply entrenched kingly responsibility for law and justice was being slowly transformed. From the Welsh and Irish *cantrefi*, to the Scottish shires and the English hundreds, as already emphasized, local communities were the repositories of memory and the regulators of local justice. Although the law text known as *Glanvill* might opine in late twelfth-century England that each shire and lordship had its own customs, law had long been inexorably associated with kings, as the Anglo-Saxon law codes and the reputed Laws of the tenth-century king of Dyfed, Hywel Dda, testify. Kingly legislation was infrequent and done only with the requisite consultation, but it is known not just from such obvious candidates as William the Conqueror, but also from, for example, Bleddyn ap Cynfyn of Powys, and the edicts of several Irish kings. Henry I's itinerant justices and David I's new sheriffs and justices exemplify the increasingly vigorous kingship of the twelfth century, yet the facts that Henry's justices were chosen largely from the administrative personnel prominent at the Exchequer and that the geographical scope of David's new officials was relatively limited, remind us that we are not dealing with the legal professionals of later generations or major changes to the existing structure, but with men who were fundamentally royal enforcers with the responsibility of seeing that the king's will was done. Although in England the Norman Conquest was seemingly a break in the continuum of localized memory which prevailed elsewhere, the kings denied its significance by reiterating that the laws of England were the *laga Edwardi*, the laws of Edward the Confessor's day. Changes, such as the introduction of trial by battle or the *murdrum* fine, were changes to the existing *corpus*. While Norman/French settlement in Scotland started a trickle of legal change, the survival of the *brithem* or *iudex* into the thirteenth century exemplifies the numerous strands of native survival.

Modern reinterpretations of the term 'feudalism' and of its meaning of necessity require reappraisals of the relationship to kingship and government. Where the English kings' capacity to demand knight service from their own aristocracy was once seen as one of the lynch-pins of their power, so now it is generally seen as no more than one of a multiplicity of links and obligations between king and aristocracy. In particular, if the proliferation of new terminology at whose heart is the word *feudum* is to be interpreted primarily as a linguistic change, rather than a social change of fundamental importance, then the perceived scale of social and political change must be reduced. England, with, as ever, much the most plentiful documentation, provides a mirror for development elsewhere. If, for example, we accept, as surely we must, that household troops were the mainstay of most armies, that Anglo-Saxon lords led their followers into battle, and that these followers held their lands in return for providing this and other services, then by implication we must think of lords elsewhere in the British Isles doing something similar. The suggestion has already been made for Ireland. It is also one which must be taken seriously for Scotland, especially as the new terminology is strikingly rare in charters of David I and Malcolm IV, and because the army which David led to the Battle of the Standard appears to have consisted wholly of household troops and Galwegian and Scottish levies.

In England, the general character of the framework of lordship over land is best grasped in Henry I's so-called Coronation Charter; above all, in the case of such matters as reliefs, wardship, and control over tenants' marriages. Although the Charter's prescriptions are couched in general terms, they must reflect debate about acceptable norms of power as well as a search for balance between individual opportunity in, for example, a case where a large cash offer might secure marriage to a wealthy heiress, and a widespread concern about exploitation and oppression. In English historiography, a lord's power to do justice to his (and occasionally her) tenants has on occasion been seen as a barrier to, and a weakening of, royal authority. The antithesis between feudal and statist historiographies, so influential in France, has on occasion been applied rather thoughtlessly to England. Without underestimating the aggression inherent in medieval aristocratic power, it is important to emphasize that in England various forms of aristocratic control over local jurisdiction, such as, for example, hundred courts and soke jurisdiction, long predate 1066 and remained very important after the appearance of a common law. Seignorial courts were functionally necessary to regulate affairs between lords and tenants. The period witnessed increasing, albeit still infrequent, royal interventions in the localities to overturn unacceptable verdicts in local courts, to hear particularly difficult cases through a representative, and on occasion to support a tenant in a case against a lord. In England and Scotland, even though lordship as understood by Normans and French differed somewhat from previous times, the overriding emphasis on kingship's overriding responsibility for law and order ensured that royal authority was never seriously compromised after 1066. We are not, however, dealing with institutionally overlapping jurisdictions in a modern sense, but with different mechanisms whereby law and communal activity were articulated. In this scenario, power is constructed and constrained through dialogue and custom.

Politics

The culture of politics

By the twelfth century, England and much of southern and central Scotland differed from Wales, Ireland, and the rest of Scotland in being under the rule of single, as opposed to multiple, kingship. These two were differentiated from the rest by a reasonably clear pattern of unique lineal succession and by a substantial territorial base which supplied the kings with a relatively stable flow of material wealth. This said, the drama of William the Conqueror's last days at the priory of Saint-Gervase of Rouen and the subsequent long succession dispute between his three surviving sons are merely one version of a story repeated countless times in different legal contexts, involving, for example, the brother and sons of Malcolm III after 1093, Rhys ap Tewdwr (d. 1093) of Deheubarth's violent elimination of kinsmen who might threaten his succession, and Muirchertach Ua Briain of Munster's elimination of his brothers after the death of their father Toirrdelbach in 1086.

Disputes of this kind, emanating from different individual or collective perceptions of where right lay within rules of succession which were, in theory at least, relatively well defined, were the stuff of politics everywhere. Irish and Welsh tended to be more complex and bloody than Scottish and English. Their significance was at times no more than regional, but there were in practice very few occasions when outsiders did not join in to try to extract benefit or influence events. Such succession disputes could affect the balance of politics throughout the British Isles, as they of course had done in 1066, and when the long civil war in England and Normandy between Stephen and the Empress Mathilda gave David I of Scotland the opportunity to take over the most northerly counties of England, the Welsh to recover much territory taken from them since 1066, and the Irish Church to free itself from the primacy of the archbishopric of Canterbury. And in war, every dog might have its day; the Welsh did after all defeat an Anglo-Norman army in a pitched battle north of Cardigan in 1136.

Honour, status, and property were crucial political issues. Only occasionally can we discern the alliances and factions which must have existed at court and the manoeuvres which ensured relative prominence for some and relative obscurity for others. The land disputes between Odo of Bayeux and Archbishop Lanfranc in the Conqueror's day and the well-known rivalry at court between the Beaumonts and Earl Robert of Gloucester in King Stephen's early years provide outstanding examples from England. The revolt of the earls in Scotland in 1160 after Malcolm IV's return from Toulouse could well have resulted from a sense of exclusion from the court of a king with a strong sense of his responsibilities towards his English lord. Property and position were divisive issues about which aristocratic memory was long. Just as kingly relatives throughout Britain and Ireland waited their moment to launch a well-remembered and long-nurtured claim, so too did the aristocracy of Anglo-Norman England bide their time for a favourable opportunity. The Marmions and William de Beauchamp contended for Tamworth during the civil war between Stephen and Mathilda because both were descended from daughters of the brother of a long deceased tenant; the explosion during the civil war after 1135 was fuelled by a multitude of disputes of this kind. Kings' deaths were often followed by violent attempts to reverse resented acts of patronage in favour of one individual at the expense of another. War broke out in Warwickshire immediately after Henry I's death between Roger, earl of Warwick, and Geofrey II de Clinton. A well-negotiated marriage alliance and territorial settlement ensured that this erstwhile dispute played no apparent part in the politics of the civil war. The sons of Malcolm Mac Heth (probably the son of Heth, Earl of Ross, who seems to have forfeited his earldom under David I) and Somerled, the ruler of Argyll, rose against Malcolm IV in 1154 soon after David I's death.

Conflict within the ruling kindred or challenges to it from another kindred inexorably divided the aristocracies of every part of Britain and Ireland. In situations such as the risings in England in favour of Robert Curthose in 1088 and 1101, the subsequent support for Curthose's son William Clito in Normandy against Henry I, and the long conflict which developed after 1135, the most powerful cross-Channel magnates had to choose sides, or risk charges of disloyalty to their king or duke. Choice of sides could be determined by a considerable variety of factors, such as regional and familial ties and even loyalties formed in France and exported to England. Individuals' revolts against kings were probably motivated by a sense of infringed honour; this would certainly apply to those rebels in England of 1075 and 1095, such as Earl Roger of Hereford and Earl Robert of Northumberland, and it probably explains the revolt against Malcolm IV in 1160. Although punishment for the defeated could be severe, with, for example, Bishop Odo of Bayeux in 1088 and Robert de Bellême and his brothers in 1102 losing their lands and Malcolm Mac Heth possibly being imprisoned for a long time after 1134, in England and Scotland, at least the majority of rebels usually negotiated a settlement before the situation became too serious. In the Anglo-Norman world politics and warfare were subject to a wide range of conventions which were usually, but not always observed. Thus, for example, although there were exceptions, a vassal who followed his lord into rebellion usually escaped punishment. A garrison which surrendered on terms when its lord could not bring relief was normally treated honourably as a mechanism for political reintegration. In situations of either military stalemate or where the stakes involved in a pitched battle were too high, the aristocracy could take on a mediating role; the most obvious examples from Anglo-Norman history occurred in 1101 and at Wallingford in 1153, when the great lords prevented, respectively, Robert Curthose and Henry I, and Stephen and the future Henry II, from fighting decisive battles. The nobles of Gwynedd are also known to have negotiated a settlement between Owain Gwynedd and his brother in 1144 and Cellach, abbot of Armagh, arranged several truces in the years after 1100 between Muirchertach Ua Briain and Domnall Mac Lochlainn.

A major difference in the political cultures of the different parts of the British Isles lay in the treatment of defeated political opponents. The unfortunate Robert Curthose was imprisoned for the rest of his life after being defeated by Henry I at the Battle of Tinchebrai, and individuals such as William the Conqueror and Robert de Bellême acquired deserved reputations for treating prisoners cruelly. Some members of the Anglo-Norman aristocracy were treated badly or killed in cold blood during the war between Stephen and Mathilda. Succession conflicts in Wales and Ireland were nonetheless much bloodier, with, for example, Diarmait Mac Murchadha killing or blinding seventeen members of the royal families of Leinster in 1141. Scottish politics were characterized by a mixture of leniency and savagery; the latter is much more evident in Gaelic Galloway than in the regions directly under the control of the Scottish kings. Why this contrast in political behaviour should have existed is a matter for speculation. It may be explicable in terms of a code of manners or in terms of the economics of power. In England and, to a degree, Scotland, warfare was about the control of large areas of territory and the objective was occupation. Elsewhere, where smaller amounts of land were at issue, killing one's opponents was the only way to prevail. The conduct of war as a means to achieve a political objective was also seen by contemporaries as differing in different parts of the British Isles. While all showed very little respect for the peasantry and devastated the countryside as a deliberate stratagem, the Scots and Galwegians were in particular accused of seizing slaves and raping women; the descriptions of David I's army's advance into northern England in the late 1130s were particularly lurid, although it is at least worth noting that David replaced the horses of the garrison of Wark-on-Tweed in 1138 because they had had to eat their own.

Succession crises and struggles for hegemony

Although Wales and Ireland remained lands under the rule of a multiplicity of kings and princes throughout the period, the sort of unification by force which had created the kingdoms of the English and the Scots in the tenth and eleventh centuries was not entirely out of the question there. In Wales, however, the hegemony over the other kingdoms and principalities achieved by Gruffudd ap Llywelyn, king of Gwynedd (1039–63), had been destroyed by English intervention and any recurrence was prevented both by inter-princely conflict and Norman/French intrusion. In Ireland, a succession of kings from the time of Brian Bóruma (d. 1014) of Munster contended for overall control and the title of high-king. In the early twelfth century Muirchertach Ua Briain, who controlled Munster, Leinster, the Norse settlements on the coast and was powerful in Meath, and Domnall Mac Lochlainn of the northern dynasty of the Cenél nEógain expanded the practice of incorporating smaller kingdoms into the larger ones. The politics of kingly succession were in any event a consistent theme everywhere. While custom put the accent on the indivisibility of kingdoms—the Welsh laws are indeed notably articulate on the subject—conflicts within the kindred and outside intervention were universally disruptive.

Itself a profound succession crisis, the Norman Conquest not only exported the uncertainties of the pre-1066 Norman ducal succession into the politics of the British Isles, it added the problem of deciding whether or not the two distinct territories of Normandy and England should be treated as a single unit. While fortuitous circumstances, such as Robert Curthose's absence on the First Crusade at the time of William Rufus's accidental death, provided a context for success, William I, William II, Henry I, and Henry II all ultimately prevailed by force and by persuading a sufficiently large proportion of the aristocracy to support them. The death of Henry I's son William in 1120 in the wreck of the White Ship and the king's failure to father more sons raised the question whether a woman might rule. Although both aristocratic succession practices and near-contemporary—if rather fraught—royal successions in Jerusalem and Castile suggest that there should not have been any theoretical obstacles to female rule, the political culture of northern France was in practice an unpromising one. The Empress Mathilda's prospects were further damaged in advance by quarrels with her father and by his unwillingness to provide her and her husband with an adequate territorial base. In consequence, her cause never acquired sufficient momentum.

Scottish kingship was in contrast relatively stable after the conflicts of the 1090s, when Malcolm III's sons only prevailed against their uncle Donald Bàn with William Rufus's military support. These relatively smooth successions are perhaps surprising since the classic possibilities for instability existed with a number of the kings (Duncan II, Edgar, Alexander I, and Malcolm IV) dying without male heirs to succeed them, David I being succeeded by a young grandson, and because tension between the brothers in the cases, for example, of Alexander and the future David I, and Malcolm IV and the future William the Lion, is well attested. David I's anticipatory association of his son Henry is often regarded as the importation of a Capetian custom into Scotland, an interesting reflection of the widening horizons of the Scottish monarchy. No contemporary source explains this new stability. Remarkable biological luck may well have been a factor, with William fitz Duncan's death a couple of years earlier meaning, for example, that there was no obvious alternative to Malcolm IV at David I's death. Although there was serious trouble in David I's early years, the relative absence of military intervention after a king's death by the rulers of Moray, a kindred which had provided a successful eleventh-century king in Macbeth, can probably be explained by the new Norman/French military elite of the Scottish kings rallying around each successive king. Intervention from England, or the prospect thereof, may also have been a factor. In general, monarchies where real or potential conflict was largely confined within the issue of a deceased king were more stable than the others. In Scotland, these circumstances appear to have crystallized in the first half of the twelfth century.

Succession disputes in Wales and Ireland usually involved a larger number of kin. Over the past thirty years, scholars have clarified that conflicts invariably involved individuals and lineages related by blood to previous kings competing for control over well-established kingdoms. It appears too, in Wales, for example, that although the three chief kingdoms of Gwynedd, Powys, and Deheubarth were obviously predominant, individuals of kingly status might on occasion emerge briefly in control of smaller territories which might temporarily acquire the name of kingdom. The rulers of Morgannwg are known to have ceased to refer to themselves as kings soon after 1066, but resumed the title briefly after 1135. Politics had a hot-house quality, as kings and claimants made and broke alliances designed to advance their cause. The advance of Rhys ap Tewdwr of Deheubarth involved the deaths of three cousins and the defeat in 1081 at the Battle of Mynydd Carn of Caradog ap Gruffudd ap Rhydderch, who was the descendant of a common kingly ancestor who had died in 988. Rhys was himself temporarily expelled in 1088 by an invasion from Powys and was killed in 1093 by the Normans inhabiting Brycheiniog, after which his kingdom was overrun. Powys after the death of Madog ap Maredudd in 1160 was the subject of a war involving a nephew (who was the son of an elder brother who had predeceased Madog's father), a brother, and his three surviving sons. Since no one was strong enough to overcome the others, this conflict led to the permanent dismemberment of the kingdom. Such a volatile society was bound to be relatively unstable, yet it was also a world in which a ruthless strong man might flourish. Rhys ap Tewdwr of Deheubarth was one of these, Gruffudd ap Cynan of Gwynedd (d. 1137) of Gwynedd another, and his son Owain Gwynedd (d. 1170) a third. In Gwynedd the relatively lower levels of disruption from outside and dynastic disturbance must have contributed to the emergence of the strong principality in the thirteenth century.

In Ireland, these struggles for hegemony are symbolized by the quest for the 'high kingship'. As in Wales, politics were increasingly dominated by a small number of kingdoms. In the same fashion, although there was a pattern whereby a powerful ruler tried to pass on power to his close kindred—and in the case of Toirrdelbach and Muirchertach Ua Briain actually succeeded in doing so—contenders for kingship frequently emerged out of a much wider range of kin. As everywhere, charisma and military skill counted for a great deal. The predominant pattern is for a successful king's power to fade in old age and for kingly pre-eminence to pass to the ruler of one of the other kingdoms. Thus, after 1114, Muirchertach Ua Briain of Munster was succeeded as the most powerful king by Toirrdelbach Ua Conchobair of Connacht. A further element is the growing symbolic importance of Dublin, which anyone aspiring to high kingship set out to seize. It is possible that one of the Irish kingdoms might ultimately have established a more permanent hegemony, but for the common pattern whereby a worsted claimant sought outside aid. Muirchertach

Ua Briain of Munster succumbed in the early twelfth century to the temptations presented by the technical military superiority of the Normans and French on the mainland and used troops supplied by the Norman earl of Pembroke. Diarmait Mac Murchadha's actions in seeking the aid directly from Henry II in 1166–7 were to have much more far-reaching consequences.

The politics of the British Isles and northern France

It was Gerald of Wales in the later twelfth century who provided the earliest known expression of the idea regularly repeated by historians since, that the conquest of 1066 was greatly assisted by the temporary weakness of the French principalities which surrounded Normandy (see Map 7). The rapid re-emergence of the county of Anjou and the Capetian monarchy, both disrupted by minorities in 1066, made life exceptionally difficult for William the Conqueror in the last decade of his life. The longer perspective supplied by Normandy's pre-1066 history suggests that these rivalries were vexatious enough without the added complication of the quarrels within the Anglo-Norman

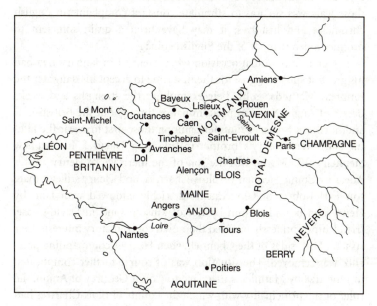

Map 7 Normandy and northern France to 1160

ruling family which broke out after 1066. But the two became inextricably linked as the Capetian kings Philip I and Louis VI and successive counts of Anjou and Flanders and other northern French powers gave enthusiastic support to first the Conqueror's son Robert Curthose against his father and then to Curthose's son William Clito against Henry I. Studies of the itineraries of all the Anglo-Norman rulers have shown just how much Normandy remained a priority for all of them. Since not all Norman families had participated fully in the conquest of England, and because the practice of dividing cross-Channel estates among sons caused some families to divide into Norman and English branches, there were 'Norman Normans' (if the expression can be forgiven) who tended to fan, in the words of the so-called 'Hyde Chronicler', the 'undying fire' of opposition to Henry I in Normandy. The duchy of Normandy was sustained by frequent military campaigns in France which required the transfer of taxation revenue from England. These wars were difficult affairs against enemies who were as technically adept as the Normans themselves. Even though Normandy's defences held, both the Conqueror and Henry I suffered notable defeats, in the former's case at Dol in 1076 and in the latter's at Alençon in 1118. The financial impact of these wars was such as to stimulate constant complaints in English chronicles and histories; it may have been a drain sufficient to produce a debasement of the English coinage.

The great ceremonial occasion when Henry I in January 1127 had his greatest subjects agree for the first time to accept his daughter the Empress Mathilda as his heir exemplifies the strengths and weaknesses of Anglo-Norman predominance throughout the British Isles and northern France. Prominent among those first to swear the fateful oath were Henry's brother-in-law King David I, his nephew Stephen of Blois who was the son of the marriage of Henry's sister Adela to Count Stephen of Blois-Chartres, and Henry's illegitimate son Earl Robert of Gloucester. All, richly endowed with land by Henry and bound to him by ties of kinship (and in David's case, friendship), ruthlessly pursued their own contradictory interests after 1135, on both sides of the Channel, when Henry's commanding presence was removed. The situation was of course further complicated in June 1128 by Mathilda's marriage to Count Geoffrey of Anjou, the ruler of the principality with which the counts of Blois-Chartres had long struggled for dominance on the River Loire: a long-standing enmity in France was thereby transferred into the politics of the British Isles after 1135.

Ireland, Scotland, and Wales all provided bases for the defeated of 1066 to launch futile attacks on their supplanter which very rapidly fizzled out. In seeking refuge and support in the western and northern parts of the British Isles, all were acting according to patterns established before the Conquest. In seeking assistance in Ireland, for example, Harold's sons were following a route which their father had followed in 1051 when Edward the Confessor had tried to banish Earl Godwine's family. The Welsh princes who assisted Earls Edwin and Morcar against William the Conqueror had helped earls of Mercia before 1066. In terms of the course of the Norman Conquest, only Edgar the Atheling's flight to Scotland had long-term consequences, through the marriage of Edgar's sister St Margaret to Malcolm III and their daughter Edith/Mathilda's subsequent marriage to Henry I in 1100. As the formidable nature of Norman military power became more evident, the pre-1066 English overlordship was rapidly resumed, as both Scottish king and Welsh princes formally acknowledged William the Conqueror's general supremacy. The irrepressibility later attributed to the Welsh by Gerald of Wales nonetheless applies to all the British and Irish during this period. Thus, in spite of the Peace of Abernethy of 1072 between Malcolm and William the Conqueror, which was renewed in 1080, King Malcolm remained an occasional irritant until he was killed in 1093, on his fifth invasion of northern England, by the Norman earl of Northumberland.

Zones of indeterminate influence between the core lands of every kingdom or principality provided an endless supply of combustible material for warrior elites whose fundamental ethos was war. The sustained, if usually unequal, rivalry of the English and Scottish kings for control over Cumbria and Northumbria is the best recorded of these areas of dispersed influence. However, the same problems were replicated countless times throughout Ireland, Wales, and Scotland, with power and control tending to be more liable to rapid change in Wales and Ireland where territorial rulership was less well established. The highly militarized frontier zone between England and Wales meant that warfare between Welsh and newcomers and Norman/French interventions in the wars of Welsh princes were almost endemic throughout the period, with territorial control fluctuating dramatically. The much larger area of northern England

and southern Scotland was never militarized in the same way as the Anglo-Welsh frontier. Politics were as a result much less fraught, and an event such as the Battle of the Standard in 1138 in which northern barons fought on both sides seems to have left no legacy of tension. David I's extensive use of warriors whose families had originated in northern France and his grants of land to them were mostly a means to confront the contested region of Northumbria. Late eleventh-century Wales was on occasion harassed by attacks from Ireland and the long-reigned king of Gwynedd, Gruffudd ap Cynan (1095–1137), Rhys ap Tewdwr of Deheubarth (d. 1093), and in 1102, more exotically, the Norman Arnulf de Montgomery, earl of Pembroke, were among many who used troops from Ireland to help fight their wars. Throughout Wales, Scotland, and Ireland, kings began to build earthwork fortifications on the model of many early Anglo-Norman castles. Although Henry II largely re-created the dominance of his Norman predecessors after 1154, the new assertiveness of England's neighbours achieved some success as the Irish and Scottish churches (but not the Welsh) freed themselves from the primatial claims of Canterbury and York.

It is highly unlikely that English kings, hard-pressed by wars in France and aiming to establish the legitimacy of their rule in England, ever sought to make conquests which were probably beyond their resources and which precedent did not justify. They undoubtedly believed that their overlordship was a continuation of what their English predecessors had exercised even if, in practice, the power they built up resembled more the imperial pretensions of the tenth-century kings than the pale imitation of Edward the Confessor's time. In this period, a less legalistic age than the century which followed, overlordship was never defined in writing and was probably thought of in personal terms. Much stricter and more onerous when applied to Welsh princes than to Scottish kings, by Henry I's time, as far as the Welsh were concerned, it meant regular attendance at the English king's court and his, or at least his agents', frequent intervention in the succession to Welsh kingdoms. David I's friendship with Henry I was clearly exceptional and gave a unique tinge to Anglo-Scottish relations. As the holder of the earldom of Huntingdon and king of Scots, David played out a dual role which put Anglo-Scottish political hostility into abeyance until after Henry's death in 1135. His rapid occupation of the northernmost counties of England after December

1135 does, however, suggest an opportunist who kept the traditional territorial and political aspirations of a Scottish king in the forefront of his mind. The practice of visiting the English court was resumed by his son Malcolm IV who most remarkably took part in Henry II's 1159 expedition to Toulouse. Warfare with a fully effective English king was not resumed until the time of William the Lion, who joined the 1173–4 revolt against Henry II, with catastrophic consequences for William.

For all the overwhelming military power of the Norman kings in England, their capacity to enforce their will was always in practice limited. Thus, although their methods of war were technically superior to those of their British neighbours, effective large-scale military intervention was always problematic. For rulers based principally in Normandy and the old kingdom of Wessex, Scotland was a distant and difficult land against which only demonstrations of power were possible. As early as 1072 Malcolm III retreated in the face of William the Conqueror's invading army until an agreement suitable to both sides was made. The same piece of theatre was repeated in 1080, except that the Conqueror decided that the task of leading the campaign could be left to his eldest son. The only invasions of Scotland from England to produce a decisive battle were those organized by William Rufus in 1094 and 1097 in support of Duncan II and Edgar, the sons of Malcolm III, in order to overthrow their uncle Donald Bàn; these interventions were arguably a matter of Scottish rather than British politics, since the issue was the Scottish kingship. Although Wales was closer to hand, under both William Rufus and Henry I large royal armies had a habit of losing momentum in the mountainous countryside, while the princes of Gwynedd in particular learnt quickly the tactical advantages of retreat into Snowdonia against opponents whose commitment to a decisive victory was in any case always in doubt. Contemporary chroniclers based in England had a habit of bemoaning the cost and absence of results of such campaigns. Yet as sharp reminders of the mailed fist which lurked within the kid glove of normal diplomatic relations, they surely served their purpose. Ireland remained beyond the Norman kings' reach, although both William the Conqueror and William Rufus are said to have contemplated intervention, perhaps because of the disruptive impact of military intervention from Ireland in the politics of the west of Britain. The meagre evidence suggests that after *c.*1072 the

English kings and the Irish high kings worked out a means to reinforce economic and ecclesiastical contacts and to control wilder elements. The dramatic impact after 1135 of the Scottish conquests in northern England and the Welsh revival shows only too clearly how different the balance of forces became once the intrusive might of the English monarchy was compromised.

The civil war between Stephen and the Empress Mathilda was an Anglo-Norman crisis with implications for most of the British Isles. It splintered the Anglo-Norman ruling elite and it suddenly removed the inexorable pressure which the Norman kings had exerted on their neighbours in Britain and northern France. Although the struggle did not begin in earnest in southern England until after Mathilda's landing at Arundel in 1139, it is a telling comment on the suddenness of the crisis that, with Henry I dying on 1 December 1135, the pregnant Mathilda and her husband occupied the strategically crucial fortress of Argentan in southern Normandy and David I much of Northumbria in December, and that a Welsh revolt was in full swing by March 1136. While these actions were certainly not coordinated, it is hard to believe that they were not pre-meditated on the part of the individuals or groups concerned. Collectively they are a comment on the relative fragility of Anglo-Norman domination of Britain. Subsequent events, however, reveal the limits of each of the participants' ambitions. Geoffrey refused to accompany his wife to England, King David restricted most of his activities to Northumbria and Cumbria and to retaining the earldom of Huntingdon, and the Welsh formed alliances with the great lords of the Anglo-Welsh frontier and supplied troops for the armies of the earls of Gloucester and Chester. In the longer term, and in spite of the disorder prevailing in England, it is striking how all rulers throughout Britain and Ireland remained active only within their own spheres of influence and how the potentially overwhelming strength of the English kingdom was rapidly restored as the central focus of politics. With Mathilda's son Henry (the future Henry II) emerging as the likely victor, it was David I who knighted him at Carlisle in 1149, while extracting a promise that Cumbria and Northumbria would remain under the rule of the Scottish kings. The Irish, much less directly involved in the conflict, in 1152 secured an agreement with the papacy whereby the Church in Ireland was freed from the claims of Canterbury.

Within England, the civil war was for a long time a stalemate.

Although Stephen's abilities have not been rated highly by historians, a fairer verdict should emphasize his persistence in the face of opposition far more widespread and formidable than any of his predecessors had faced. The closest parallel with the strategic problems he confronted is the circumstances with which Harold II had to contend in 1066, yet even this comparison is inadequate because Stephen's enemies were based on both sides of the Channel and because he was fighting a different kind of war whose chief objective was the control of castles. Several of Stephen's decisions in the first four years of his reign—most of them entirely logical—turned out badly, and once Mathilda had a secure base in the West of England and a group of strongly committed supporters, she was extremely difficult to dislodge. The lesson of Mathilda's brief period of dominance in 1141–2 after Stephen's capture at the Battle of Lincoln is, however, that she lacked the support to achieve conclusive victory and the desultory warfare concentrated in the Thames Valley during the mid-1140s came nowhere near producing a resolution. Studies of government during this period have shown the English kingdom divided roughly into four zones, two, the South-East and South-West, controlled, respectively, by Stephen and Mathilda, a third, much of the Midlands and the North, where neither was dominant, in which great magnates exercised local power, and a fourth controlled by David I, which stretched as far south as Preston in 1141–5. The prerogatives and responsibilities of taxation and justice continued to be exercised, but on a reduced scale. Aristocratic behaviour is difficult to categorize, but it would seem that, in general, efforts to exploit the situation for individual gain faded out as the years went by. Even the most powerful, such as Earl Ranulf of Chester, never cut themselves truly adrift from the raft of kingship; the actions of many might be violent, but the thinking of most was conservative and circumscribed by convention. The Angevin conquest of Normandy, the English Church's refusal to crown Stephen's son Eustace, and the advance to adulthood of the future Henry II made the latter an increasingly attractive prospect. Another stalemate, created this time by yet another decision by the Anglo-Norman aristocracy not to fight a battle at Wallingford in July–August 1153 in spite of the bellicose intentions of Stephen and Henry, led to peace negotiations and a settlement. The flexible formula of hereditary right was used to justify Henry II's succession. The overall framework of settlement, the so-called Treaty of Winchester, was constructed around the tried-and-tested mechanisms of an amnesty for all participants, a guarantee of title to all lands held in 1135, and the abandonment of acquisitions.

The construction of Henry II's rule around the agenda that he was Henry I's legitimate heir and that conditions should revert to their state before 1135, while representing a credible basis for settlement, was also a recipe for difficulties. What, for example, should happen to the likes of the king of Scots and the earls of Gloucester and Leicester, all of whom had made significant acquisitions fighting for Henry and his mother? The first two were bullied into submission, with Malcolm abandoning Cumbria and Northumbria in 1157, while the last named, a very capable man, became one of Henry's closest associates. In 1157 Henry led a large army into Wales and in 1155, for the first time, the conquest of Ireland was seriously discussed. As the ruler of territories much larger than those of his Anglo-Norman predecessors, Henry II must have looked formidable indeed. Within England most of the aristocracy rallied to his cause, and he gradually rebuilt his seriously reduced financial resources. The legacy was, however, in some respects a poisoned one. English royal revenue rarely returned to the level of Henry I's reign. Danegeld was abandoned, and Henry's zeal for judicial reform led by devious paths to the murder of the archbishop of Canterbury in his own cathedral. There was a great Welsh rising in 1163 and in 1173—leaving aside the exceptional conditions of Stephen's reign—a Scottish king fought against an English one for the first time for almost eighty years. Henry's achievements were ultimately great ones, but he operated within a framework not much changed from the time of his Norman predecessors. The nineteen years of Stephen's reign, if nothing else, had accentuated yet again the sense of difference between the major kingdoms of eleventh- and twelfth-century Britain and Ireland.

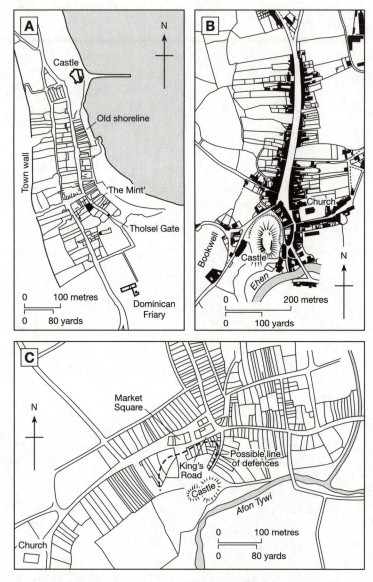

Map 8 Town and castle: Carlingford, Egremont, and Llandovery. Three boroughs that developed alongside twelfth-century castles, Carlingford, Louth (A), Egremont, Cumbria (B), and Llandovery, Carmarthenshire (C), illustrating a pattern repeated many times in different parts of Britain and Ireland.

Social bonds and economic change

Richard Britnell

Lordship in 1100

A comparison between the importance of lordship in the middle ages and the irrelevance of that concept in modern industrial societies must raise some of the most profound issues of social change over the last thousand years. In this chapter, we are concerned with the change occurring during the twelfth and thirteenth centuries, and insofar as this affected the lower levels of society. As a shortcut to understanding the power structure affecting society at these levels, it has often been assumed that particular forms of lordship which happen to be well represented in our sources were in fact dominant and represent the form and development of power as it affected society as a whole. The territorially compact manor, corresponding to a single rural settlement, with hall, home farm (demesne), and attached tenements occupied by unfree tenants (serfs) owing labour services on the demesne, has been adopted for this purpose as a model of lordship over peasants, for no better reason than that such administratively complex properties have left exceptionally detailed administrative records. A survey of British and Irish societies in the middle ages must rapidly expose the limitations of such models, for it is easy to show that manors of this kind did not cover most of the land even in southern and eastern England, and that elsewhere they were rare or absent.

Although lordship cannot be simplified in this way, its importance is not in doubt. In the case of England, Domesday Book conveys a very clear sense of its pervasive character and complex forms. William the Conqueror's surveyors of 1086 portrayed very effectively the patchwork of rights in the counties of England, distinguishing each unit of lordship as a manor. In Aldborough, for example, Uluric the sokeman was recorded as having held 80 acres as a manor in 1066. However, Domesday Book shows that manors varied considerably both in size and in their relationship to named territories. Some, like Leominster (Herefordshire), or Taunton (Somerset), contained a number of differently named settlements. Others, like the royal manors of Comberton and Haslingfield (Cambridgeshire) in 1066, occupied only a fraction of a named territory and had lordship over only a part of its population. Besides these differences, the internal structure of manors also varied. Many were divided between demesne land, whose produce was directly available for use by its lord, and land occupied by tenants, but there were no regular principles by which such a division was made. The land of some manors was wholly in the hands of hereditary tenants, and there were manors of this sort that had no halls of their own; the tenants paid their services elsewhere. At the other extreme were halls with no tenant land attached. This was characteristic chiefly of small manors, such as Eadmund's five-carucate manor at Thornton le Moor, and Asketill's six-carucate manor at Murton in the North Riding wapentake of Allerton.

In the wider perspective of Britain, the multiple estate was of particular importance. This was often of royal origin, with hall, with lands under the lord's direct control—demesne, bartons, wicks, berewicks—and with extensive rights of lordship over men living in settlements all around. Such an estate may be thought of as a peculiarly large and complex manor, though in many parts of Britain it was not described as such. Seignorial rights of this kind were commonly less dependent on lordship over ploughland, and less concerned with labour services, than the classic model of the manor would imply. Seignorial authority over such estates derived more from lordship over men than from lordship over land. This characteristic was expressed in eastern England by the use of the word 'soke' to signify the right to exercise jurisdiction over particular men or groups. In the more pastoral regions of Wales, Scotland, and Ireland, lordship over pasture land and livestock was at least as important for the lord's authority as rights over arable. In the north of England, the

Lowlands of Scotland, and the Scottish east-coast region, these extensive lordships took the form of a territorially defined 'shire': a central hall, usually with attached demesne lands and pasture rights, exercised jurisdiction over the men of a number of settlements and drew from them rents in kind and minor services. An English example is Hallamshire (see Map 9), whose sokemoot at Sheffield was attended by the freemen of the shire. These freemen were also responsible for helping the lord of the shire when he went hunting, and for various other services. In Scotland such shires were administered by a class of ministerial tenants known as thanes. This same system existed in native Wales, where it was still essentially a royal structure. Each royal hall, with associated outbuildings, was situated amid a complex of inland worked by the king's bond tenants, living in a distinctive type of settlement called a *maerdref*. The best-known example of this institution was the royal estate of Aberffraw on Anglesey, which had tenants of various sorts in several surrounding hamlets (see Map 10). A royal estate served, in turn, as an administrative centre for a *cantref* ('hundred farmsteads'), a territory including numerous townships, analogous to the English soke or primitive 'shire'. Some *cantrefi* became subdivided for administrative convenience into two *cymydau*, or commotes, each with its own royal centre, and in these circumstances the larger unity did not always survive. The royal hall at the centre of each *cantref* or *cymyd* was a centre from which the laws were administered. In Ireland, lordship over a dependent peasantry, exercised from clearly defined central points, was already well-established by 1100, but very little can be said about its organization in detail because it was so heavily modified after the English conquests of the later twelfth century and the earlier thirteenth.

Some generalizations about the nature of the bonds of rural lordship around 1100 are worth making, despite their wide variety, because they help us to understand how societies changed during the next two centuries. In the first place, lordship over rural populations was not as definite a relationship as simplified models suggest; there were many degrees of freedom. The freer a man, the more control he had over his time and other resources, and the more servile he was, the more he was obliged to work for someone else. The least free were slaves, who were commonly full-time farm servants with special responsibility for livestock. Secondly, lordship was not narrowly 'landlordship', since countrymen often owed attendance at a lord's

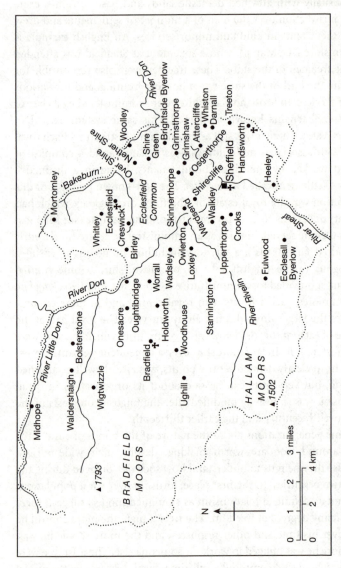

Map 9 Hallamshire. A reconstruction (by G. W. S. Barrow) of Hallamshire in the twelfth and thirteenth centuries and the places that belonged to it. Hallamshire was also known as the soke of Sheffield (the estate centre) or the soke of Ecclesfield (where the mother-church was placed).

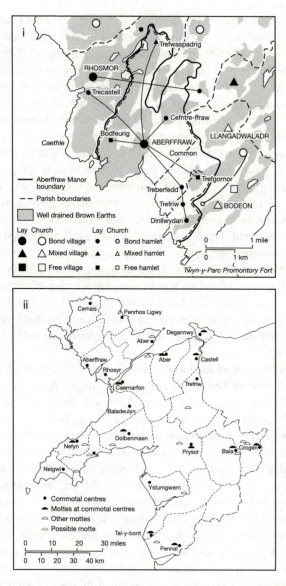

Map 10 i. The royal estate of Aberffraw. ii. The commotes of North Wales. In the thirteenth century Gwynedd was divided between commotes, each administered from a central royal hall (*llys*). The hall was supported by customary payments from the townships of the commote and by bondmen attached to the hall.

court, or paid tribute of some kind rather than a rent for land. Such personal dependence was intrinsic even to the most tightly manorial-ized regions of southern England, where customary obligations might be due from the family and its members (and so varied accord-ing to the size and composition of the family) rather than from the land as such. Thirdly, relations of lordship and dependence were characteristically defined, not by the legal structures known to royal administrations, but by local custom. There was nowhere a general framework of law that laid down what any particular tenant owed his lord, except in a narrow range of free tenures governed by documentary titles. The early Welsh laws relevant to peasant custom hardly contradict this conclusion, since they do not go back as far as 1100, are chiefly concerned with royal tenants, and vary considerably in regional detail. Finally, relations between lords and tenants were rarely controlled by written documents and depended rather on the memory of those involved. The only way to establish the truth about disputed obligations was to summon a group of responsible men to swear to what they knew. Even Domesday Book contains little information about the rights and duties of tenants; it records nothing about what all the 109,230 'villains' it enumerates really had in common.

The extent to which lords received money payments varied in different parts of Britain and Ireland. Domesday Book records 112 English boroughs and 41 other markets, and there were probably more. Beyond a line roughly from the Severn to the Humber estuar-ies, towns were mostly either non-existent or so small that their urban status is questionable (see Map C). The very fact that the geld assessments recorded in the survey relate to a royal tax on land implies a widespread circulation of money. Yet this complex of monetary and trading institutions was characteristic only of that part of Britain that Domesday Book surveys. Neither Scotland nor Wales had native currencies, English coins were not extensively available there, and though silver bullion was used for some important trans-actions, it was not appropriate for everyday local trade. Commercial development had encouraged the localized minting of silver in the Irish Sea region from the late tenth century, but the circulation of Hiberno-Norse coinage was restricted to eastern Ireland and other coastal parts. Irish coins minted before 1100 are rarely found, even in Dublin. This monetary tradition was faltering, in any case, and coins were becoming poorer in quality and fewer in number, to the point that minting ceased altogether about 1150. The Scottish economy, too, managed with little coinage before the 1140s.

With few markets and little money, the dues owed to even the most powerful lords had to be paid in service or in goods. The king of Scotland received income from his estates chiefly in the form of *conveth* and *cáin*, traditional rents in kind. The tribute due to the Gaelic lords of Ireland from dependent clients were similar; the ordinary commoner of Irish Gaelic society, the betagh (*bíatach*), owed few labour services and little or no cash, and took his title from the food rent (*bíad*) that he owed to a lord. In the 'shires' of Scotland and northern England, peasants owed light labour services but more substantial renders of grain, malt, poultry, and cattle. In Wales the commotes were divided into districts, from each of which free landowners owed food tributes (*gwestfa*) comprising bread, meat or cheese, and mead. Native rulers toured round the countryside, collecting dues owed to them in food and imposing the right to be billeted by their subjects. Welsh bond tenants owed a similar render of food and drink called a *dawnbwyd* ('gift of food'), which they delivered to their lord's hall.

Lordship 1100–1280

Between 1100 and 1280 one of the main stimuli for changes in lordship all over Britain and Ireland was an expanding market for goods and services, which benefited lords by allowing them to manage their property more profitably. The growth of demand by a growing number of artisans, tradesmen, and hired workers was met by increasing sales of produce, both from manorial demesnes and from hundreds of smaller producers who were able to produce surpluses above their household requirements. To some extent the improvement of estates implied squeezing more cash out of existing demesnes, often by taking them out of the hands of lessees and managing them directly in the lord's interest, a characteristic development of the late twelfth and early thirteenth centuries. It meant, too, taking advantage of rising land values to raise traditional rents. However, landlords also engaged in the competitive business of attracting settlement on their estates by creating small freeholdings, many of them in new towns and planned villages. Such entrepreneurship is the clearest indication that lordship was a mainspring of economic development. Many boroughs, both in England and Scotland, were royal foundations, but more were the result of baronial enterprise, particularly in regions of Anglo-Norman colonization. Examples of the combination of Anglo-Norman castle and new borough are numerous in southern England (as at Pleshey in Essex, or Devizes in Wiltshire), but the formula is more evident in areas of Anglo-Norman expansion. Many of the new towns of northern England, Wales, and Ireland were closely associated with new baronial castles (see Map 8), and some with royal castles, as at Newcastle upon Tyne and Carlisle. New markets and boroughs were often more related to the geography of baronial estates than to the current interests of traders. In southern Ireland, Theobald Walter, the founder of the Butler family (d. 1205), chose to divide his enormous lordship into seven administrative regions, each with a castle and demesne estate at its centre, and he planned an urban settlement at most of these centres.

There were several reasons for placing new trading communities by castles, particularly in a colonial context. It was convenient to have markets at a castle gate, where estate officers could supervise them and ensure that market tolls due to the lord were collected. Where money was scarce, estate officers liked to be able to intercept tenants at the point where they sold their produce, in order to ensure that rent payments had the first claim on available cash. In addition, castles were collecting points for produce from their lord's estate, and any surplus might conveniently be sold to an adjacent market community. In areas of Anglo-Norman colonization, the new nobility was particularly inclined to develop monetized trade because its members were less disposed to be resident than their predecessors, and had little chance of benefiting from traditional renders in kind unless these could be converted into cash. The close association of boroughs with castles in a colonial context is also attributable to the need to defend immigrant townsmen from hostile neighbours.

The growth of internal and external trade in England was accompanied by a sharp increase in coinage in circulation from an estimated £25,000 on average in the eleventh century, to £125,000 in 1180, £300,000 or more in 1218, and about £674,000 in 1278, an increase that far outstripped the concurrent growth of population. This increase is mirrored in the changing form of landlord–tenant relations. Throughout England, the settlement of rents by money payments was gaining ground relative to other forms, partly because of the multiplication of new money rents, such as those payable from the large number of new burgage tenements, and partly because lords preferred to take money from older tenures in place of produce or labour—by so doing they enjoyed greater flexibility in managing their incomes. By 1280, as the Hundred Rolls demonstrate, money was the predominant means of settling rent in midland England not only on free but also on villein holdings, and probably accounted for over two-thirds of the total value of rents.

The increasing use of money was meanwhile accompanied by expansion of the monetized zone. This was achieved partly by the increasing use of sterling outside England; even in Scotland, most payments were made in imported coin all through the period. Meanwhile, more coin was coming to be made outside English mints, particularly in Scotland. David I of Scotland started to mint coins about 1136, following his annexation of Cumberland at the height of the first great northern boom in silver-mining. The volume of Scottish currency in circulation perhaps reached £60,000 or more in 1250, and £180,000 or more in 1280, and since the Scottish currency at this period was minted to the sterling standard, this implies a Scottish currency about 27 per cent of that in contemporary England by the reign of Alexander III. Meanwhile, a new Irish monetary tradition was inaugurated after the English conquest, with the establishment of royal mints at Dublin about 1185, and at Waterford and Limerick after 1195, though at that time none of these mints struck anything larger than a halfpenny. King John reinforced this development of Irish coinage in about 1207, with pennies minted to sterling standard, though with a distinctive design. Thereafter, though Irish minting was discontinuous (the principal mintings being c.1207–11, 1247–54, 1276–9, and again, with a new issue, 1279–84), the volume struck rose to significant levels. By 1285, after several years of recoinage, the Dublin mint had put an estimated £40,000 into circulation, about 6 per cent of the English total. Though this undoubtedly reflected an increasing use of money in parts of Ireland, the monetization of the internal economy there in the later thirteenth century was inhibited by heavy exports of cash to the English royal wardrobe and exchequer. Little coinage was struck in Wales before 1200, though

English coins were first minted at Cardiff, St Davids, and Rhuddlan during the reign of William II. The imitation of English coins at Rhuddlan, on the authority of the lords of Gwynedd, illustrates the growing need for cash from the late twelfth century in this part of Wales.

Increases in the volume of currency accompanied a growing importance of monetary relations between lords and tenants at every level. At the very top, monetization offered new possibilities for the expansive monarchies of England and Scotland. By 1178 King William the Lion claimed the right to levy geld on land throughout Scotland, and the expansion of royal cash income justified the institution of an annual exchequer audit soon after this. There was an Irish exchequer in 1200, and King John was able to draw money revenues from the boroughs, from his demesne lands, and from feudal dues. The smaller administration of Gwynedd seems not to have established an exchequer with a permanent staff, though by 1274 it was compiling written accounts that were formally audited by officials of the prince's court. Similar developments were evident in the incomes of the lesser princes and lords, both lay and clerical. From 1140 money rents started to replace rents in labour and kind in southern Scotland, and by the end of the twelfth century money was used there for a wide range of rural transactions, including the renting of mills, fisheries and saltings, and the leasing of ecclesiastical tithes. In much of Wales, cattle and the products of pasture farming were still characteristically used instead of coin in the twelfth century, but in some regions the monetization of rents is in evidence. Rents formerly paid in flour and cheese on the estates of the bishopric of St Davids in south-eastern Wales had been converted to cash by the early thirteenth century. The earlier Welsh law books compiled in the late twelfth and early thirteenth centuries already specified a fixed commutation of the food renders of the king's freemen into money, but the commutation of rents was stepped up considerably by thirteenth-century Welsh princes in order to finance their military operations, and was further accelerated by the influx of English lords after the Edwardian conquest of 1282. Monetization of the economy was also expressed through much of Britain in an increasing level of receipts from judicial revenues, from licences and fees for services and liberties of various kinds, and from tolls on trade.

The widespread monetization of relations between lords and

tenants had consequences for the character of these bonds. It corresponded to the growth of a more bureaucratic approach to seignorial dues, since money obligations invited a higher level of precision in their levying and recording than other sorts of render. Money dues lent themselves more easily to negotiation in detail, and so encouraged a more legalistic attitude towards relations between lords and tenants. In addition, the availability of money in circulation widened the range of opportunities for lords to benefit at the expense of their subordinates, and so facilitated the imposition of heavier burdens. Such transformations epitomized the intensification of Anglo-Norman or English lordship over much of Wales, Scotland, and Ireland. In English Ireland they were associated with the reorganization of the land into manors with demesne land and dependent tenants, based to some extent on English models. However, many Irish capital manors of the thirteenth century, like those of the Butler estates in 1205, some of which exceeded 100,000 acres in size, would have corresponded in size and complexity to baronies in England, and contained sub-manors granted to knights and other free tenants. The betaghs who lived in small hamlets on such estates increasingly paid money rent, as they did on the lands of Sir Thomas de Clare in Youghal in 1288. Rising property values, the development of estates, and the growing use of money in relations between lords and tenants, often meant that lordship over land matured at the expense of lordship over men, especially in the multiplication of free rents. However, money payments also increased in many relationships of personal dependence where no tenure of land was in question. This is illustrated, for example, by the so-called common fine owed by all adult men to the lords of some English manors, and the chevage payments lords exacted from landless labourers on others.

In the absence of nationwide royal bureaucracies, kings depended on their magnates to maintain stability in the provinces. In its idealized forms strong lordship could supplement royal law in promoting social harmony between local interests. It might have patriarchal quality, especially when—as in Wales, Scotland, and Ireland—it overlapped with kin relationships. In other circumstances, however, lordship could be exploited to advance the local interests of the strong at the expense of the weak, whether within the law or outside it. Some of the worst abuses on record in England were committed during the civil war of Stephen's reign by magnates responding to the breakdown of royal authority; some imposed new labour services and money exactions, both on their own tenants and on others, for constructing castles and waging warfare. Even at other times, however, royal law courts rarely offered much protection to minor landlords or ordinary peasants against systematic bullying. The abuses of aristocratic power that historians of the fifteenth century used to think of as 'bastard feudalism' were already all too common in the twelfth and thirteenth centuries.

Community in 1100

In 1100 town life was localized and exceptional. Even middle-ranking towns, like Leicester and Nottingham, had fewer than 3,000 inhabitants, and the smallest had only a few hundred. England north of York, Ireland away from the east coast, Scotland, and Wales, were thoroughly rural. At the same time, country dwellers were more thinly scattered than their modern equivalents. The 268,984 people recorded in Domesday Book outside the boroughs occupied 13,306 recorded settlements, implying only 20 households in each, on average. Some under-enumeration of households has to be suspected in this calculation, but archaeological evidence abundantly supports the conclusion that small settlements and isolated farms were an important feature of the landscape in 1100. Documentary evidence for this would be even more marked if it could be extended outside the region of Domesday Book's coverage, since settlement sizes were smaller away from southern and midland England.

The small size of settlements has implications for the nature of communities in Britain around 1100. Early Irish and Welsh laws assume that families normally lived in clusters rather than scattered over the land, but such evidence cannot be read directly to imply close intimacy between neighbours, since we have no means of knowing the force of the status divisions that often split even small rural groups. Bonds between families in different settlements may often have been strong, especially in regions like Norfolk where settlements were close together. Small farmers were of necessity dependent on each other at key points in the agricultural year—sharing beasts to make up plough teams, or committing their beasts to a common herd—and this, together with the small size of settlements, implies that people normally knew something about their neighbours' personal affairs. This made viable the frankpledge system that was imposed shortly before 1100 over those parts of England firmly under Norman control, but foreshadowed in a law of Cnut of the early 1020s. Under this arrangement, the men of each vill were organized into 'tithings' and expected to answer for each other's good behaviour.

Everywhere there was some provision for administering the sacraments of the Church, often by groups of secular priests operating from mother-churches that played an important role in the regional dissemination of Christian teaching and pastoral care. Their scope for bonding communities was probably limited to comparatively few settlements. In the bigger rural settlements of south and central England, however, churches of this kind were being supplemented by thousands of parish churches, often with their own priests. Domesday Book's recording of churches is unhelpful for parts of the realm, but in Suffolk and Huntingdonshire, where an attempt was made to notice them, there were about 398 churches to serve about 722 named places. Churches were often founded by landlords, and in one sense represented an extension of seignorial rights. They nevertheless provided a focus for social interaction in a variety of ways, both liturgical and secular.

The institutions of lordship also imposed the need for communal organization, especially on those families that made a substantial contribution to the cultivation of demesne farms. It was expected in 1086 that each English vill should have a reeve or head-man (*prepositus*): the information collected for the Domesday Survey was to be attested both by the sheriff and barons of the shire concerned and also by the priest, reeve, and six men from each administrative vill. Although reeves served as estate officers, answerable to manorial lords, this did not preclude their also being recognized intermediaries who acted on behalf of rural communities. There was neither need nor occasion for precise constitutional definitions.

Rural settlements also developed more cooperative systems of land use. It is no longer supposed that the open, or common, fields of southern and midland England and Yorkshire date back in their mature form to the Germanic invaders of the fifth and sixth centuries. They developed subsequently, from less communally organized beginnings, chiefly to achieve a better integration of arable and pasture farming as more land was taken into cultivation. The chronology of development is obscure, but by 1100 at least some townships had field systems dependent on communal organization. Their formation was probably associated in many cases with the planning that occurred when the territory of a township was divided between different settlements, a procedure attested by the large number of modern parishes that share a name with a neighbour; the extreme example is that of the eight adjacent Roding parishes in Essex. The exceptional density of settlement in East Anglia in 1086 suggests that managed field systems were already widespread there, and probably more developed than in other parts of England.

The ownership of arable land was usually assigned to individual families, so that any common rights over it were limited to the periods when there were no growing crops. Nevertheless, many families throughout Britain, both in common-field areas and elsewhere, were free to common heathlands and woodlands all the year round, and such rights were accordingly, in some sense, attached to the community, though usually within the framework of royal or seignorial control. On either side of Epping Forest in Essex, for example, settlements had common wastes that included sections of the woodland, and their cattle and other livestock were pastured in the custody of a common herdsman, though the wastes in question were part of the royal forest and so subject to forest law. Local populations differed greatly in the extent of their pastoral resources, which were greatest away from southern England and often constituted a very prominent feature of local landscapes until abolished by the enclosure movements of later centuries (see Map 11). A characteristic feature of northern England, Scotland, and the upland parts of Ireland was transhumance between low-lying winter pastures and grazing on the hills, often several miles away, where herdsmen would live with their cattle during the summer months. A similar pattern of transhumance is suggested by some surviving buildings in the Welsh Black Mountain. In some instances nearby settlements shared the same common land. In 1086, for example, it was said that there was a common pasture for all the men of the Hundred of Colneis in Suffolk. It is rare to catch a documentary reference as early as this, but some system of intercommoning by men of a hundred or a northern 'shire' seems to have been widespread in the more pastoral areas of

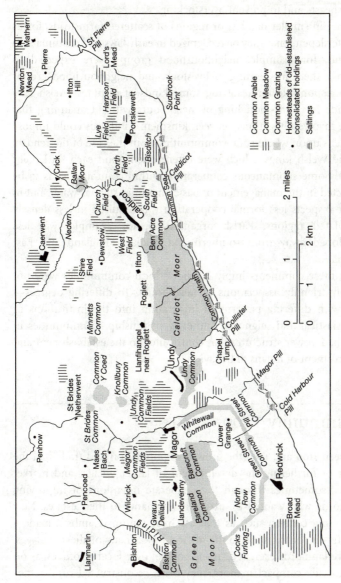

Map 11 Settlement and common land in Wales. Land held in common in south-east Monmouthshire, 1750–1850. Features of ancient land use here survived into a period for which we have adequate maps. Cultivated lands were separated by extensive areas of meadow and grazing characteristically subject to common rights.

Britain, such as the Lake District. The care of livestock required those who shared common rights to act together to provide supervision for their beasts and to prevent overstocking.

Even in smaller hamlets or regions of scattered farmsteads, forms of interdependence may be recognized in early laws and custumals. In Ireland, for example, neighbourhood groups were expected to arrange the joint-herding of livestock, and neighbourhood groups were responsible for resolving some kinds of disputes. Welsh laws provide for joint-ploughing by neighbours without assuming that these involve obligations between kinsmen. Landlords could impose burdens upon whole rural communities, as in the case of the renders to the Welsh kings, which were often levied upon each settlement (*tref*). Some spontaneous cooperation within communities is to be expected in the management of basic amenities such as water. But in other respects less formal cooperation was required in less densely populated regions. Parish organization, for example, was less developed away from southern and midland England and East Anglia.

As these comments imply, medieval local communities were not simply friendly associations of neighbours. To differing degrees— and with differing patterns of integration into the institutions of ecclesiastical and seignorial authority or kinship—communities in 1100 had power structures that contributed to the establishment and enforcement of norms of behaviour.

Community 1100–1280

Between 1100 and 1280 the growth of population and trade had the effect of furthering the development of larger villages and market towns, sometimes through the deliberate intentions of improving landlords who wanted to attract new tenants to their estates. New marketing centres, such as that at Great Linton (Cambs.), made a significant contribution to the nucleation of many medieval villages. Where landlords exercised strong control over local resources, as on territorially compact manors, they often reconstructed rural settlement patterns, as at Toft, Great Eversden, and Comberton (all in Cambs.), presumably to achieve agricultural improvements made desirable by the growth of population. Population growth not only brought about the physical expansion of settlements but also encouraged a widening of the range of occupations within them, so that families became more dependent upon neighbours for their particular needs. Little is known about how such exchanges were conducted, but it is doubtful whether they were characteristically negotiated with financial profit in mind. At the beginning of the period a silver penny, the lowest minted denomination of coinage, was too valuable for small household purchases, and it is unlikely that exchanges of eggs or fuel were normally for cash even in 1280, though by that time the monetary system was appreciably more accommodating. Such patterns of economic interdependence must have contributed to defining bonds of community, even though they mostly evade the written record.

Between 1100 and 1280 several institutional developments of outstanding importance for the life of rural communities were consolidated, extended, and in some cases innovated. Estate owners continued to build new parish churches, especially in the twelfth century, though their rights over them were often later granted to monastic houses. With more churches came the drawing of parish boundaries and the fixing of tithe obligations. The multiplication of churches, and development of the parochial system, was not confined to England. In Wales, where there were few parish churches before 1100, the framework of a parochial system was defined during the twelfth and thirteenth centuries, often based on pre-existing subdivisions of the commote. In Scotland the twelfth century was a turning point, in this as in so much else, as the time when the payment of tithes to local churches became more general and more effectively enforceable even in the most outlying parts of the country (see Map 12). The growth of the parochial system in south and east Ireland seems to have been accelerated in the late twelfth century by the English invasion. Though imposed upon local communities from above, these developments had many positive implications for the shaping of medieval communities. Parish organization may be less relevant to lightly populated parts of Britain, where church building and parish formation were inhibited by the poverty of local resources, but in much of Britain and Ireland it implied more cooperation between neighbours in church matters and facilitated secular activities such as the dissemination of news, the witnessing of deeds, and

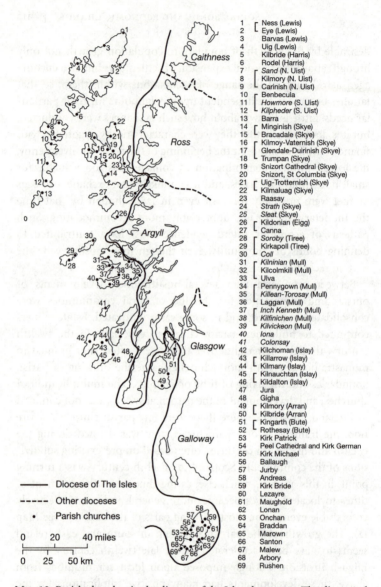

1 Ness (Lewis)
2 Eye (Lewis)
3 Barvas (Lewis)
4 Uig (Lewis)
5 Kilbride (Harris)
6 Rodel (Harris)
7 *Sand* (N. Uist)
8 Kilmory (N. Uist)
9 Carinish (N. Uist)
10 Benbecula
11 *Howmore* (S. Uist)
12 *Kilpheder* (S. Uist)
13 Barra
14 Minginish (Skye)
15 Bracadale (Skye)
16 Kilmoy-Vaternish (Skye)
17 Glendale-Duirinish (Skye)
18 Trumpan (Skye)
19 Snizort Cathedral (Skye)
20 Snizort, St Columba (Skye)
21 Uig-Trotternish (Skye)
22 Kilmaluag (Skye)
23 Raasay
24 *Strath* (Skye)
25 *Sleat* (Skye)
26 Kildonian (Eigg)
27 Canna
28 *Soroby* (Tiree)
29 Kirkapoll (Tiree)
30 *Coll*
31 *Kilninian* (Mull)
32 Kilcolmkill (Mull)
33 Ulva
34 Pennygown (Mull)
35 *Killean-Torosay* (Mull)
36 Laggan (Mull)
37 *Inch Kenneth* (Mull)
38 *Kilfinichen* (Mull)
39 *Kilvickeon* (Mull)
40 *Iona*
41 *Colonsay*
42 Kilchoman (Islay)
43 Killarrow (Islay)
44 Kilmany (Islay)
45 Kilnauchtan (Islay)
46 Kildalton (Islay)
47 Jura
48 Gigha
49 Kilmory (Arran)
50 Kilbride (Arran)
51 Kingarth (Bute)
52 Rothesay (Bute)
53 Kirk Patrick
54 Peel Cathedral and Kirk German
55 Kirk Michael
56 Ballaugh
57 Jurby
58 Andreas
59 Kirk Bride
60 Lezayre
61 Maughold
62 Lonan
63 Onchan
64 Braddan
65 Marown
66 Santon
67 Malew
68 Arbory
69 Rushen

Map 12 Parish churches in the diocese of the Isles about 1300. The diocese of the Isles, or Sodor, was founded in 1130. This map, showing parish formation there by 1300, impressively demonstrates the development of ecclesiastical organization in Britain, The italicized names are those of churches appropriated by religious corporations (monasteries or cathedral chapters). Such bodies received the tithe income and appointed a stipendiary vicar or chaplain to serve as parish priest.

the organization of local trade. In addition, the secular authorities made use of parochial divisions for defining fiscal and military burdens.

In no area of rural affairs was cooperation between lords and tenants likely to be more important than in the development of common fields. Under the stimulus of demographic pressure on the resources for growing food, these attained their most systematic forms in England in the twelfth and thirteenth centuries. In each common-field community most of the available arable land was distributed between two or three large heavily subdivided blocks, of which one was uncultivated and subject to common grazing each year. Not only were common rights over such fields systematized in many parts of England, but similar developments were occurring in parts of Wales and Ireland. The importance of Anglo-Norman or English direction should not be assumed, since the same tendency was evident in many parts of native Wales. Even in regions without common fields, the management of common rights often required more regulation than in the past, and to that extent required more cooperation between neighbours. Throughout the period 1100–1280 the need to secure agreement concerning the management of agricultural resources must be considered one of the most universal requirements of communal organization, since any change depended upon the active consent of those whose interests were affected. The multiplication of by-laws relating to the use of land, often registered in the court rolls of English manors, is one of the most apparent signs of this necessity.

The parallel developments of lordship and rural community were complementary, since agricultural regulation, the enforcement of by-laws, and the imposition of sanctions against misbehaviour all depended on cooperation between representatives of community and manor. Greater interaction between individuals, and between individuals and manorial lords, as indicated by the growth in the market for land after 1200, the growth of trade, and the growing importance of credit in everyday commercial relations, generated increased private litigation, and this was something that could be addressed by institutional innovation at a local level. In England the development of manor courts was a response to these various pressures. Even if, as some have supposed, the manor court, or hall moot, had Anglo-Saxon forebears, it was an institution that must have changed out of all recognition after 1100. Many features of manorial jurisdiction as practised in 1280 cannot have gone back more than a hundred years, because they so plainly echoed recent developments in superior courts. The recording of court business became common only from the later thirteenth century.

The development of local jurisdictions is difficult to parallel outside southern England for want of documentation, though it is likely to have been a widespread feature of the development of lordship. On the large English 'manor' of Knocktopher (Kilkenny), a court was held at Knocktopher itself, and subordinate manorial lords created their own manorial jurisdictions at least from the late thirteenth century—the evidence does not stretch back further. However, away from southern England the existence of large multiple estates meant that it was less common for a manor court to relate to a particular settlement. The halmotes of the bishop of Durham, to judge from later evidence, though they served only the bishop's own tenants, were more akin in their territorial scope to the hundred courts of southern England. Since they were attended by men from many separate settlements, such courts could not have had the same significance for the development of communities as the southern English manor court.

Though the institutions of lordship and community were complementary, tenants were in a position to organize resistance to lords they considered to be unjust, and from the late twelfth century onwards some such campaigns involved a high degree of collective commitment. Sometimes conflict took the form of local resistance to landlords, as when in 1276 men of Stoughton (Leics.) prosecuted the abbot of Leicester in the king's courts (unsuccessfully) for demanding villein services from them. Another recurrent cause of conflict between lords and communities was uncertainty over the extent of common rights, which became increasingly valuable as land values increased and control over pastures, marshes, and woodlands became more highly prized. Kings and magnates claimed considerable portions of pasture and forest, and there were many disputes concerning their use. An early and well-documented case of conflict concerns a marsh lying between Crowland and Spalding (Lincs.), over which men of several rural settlements in the wapentake of Holland tried to establish common rights in 1189 in opposition to the seignorial claims of Crowland Abbey; but they too were unsuccessful.

The growth of town life during the twelfth and thirteenth centuries was of particular significance for the formation of more complex communities. Occupational specialization, and inter-family economic dependence, was more advanced here than in the countryside. Town life also presented new challenges of economic and social organization to urban elites. Their reference group was a restricted one, including free burgesses but excluding labourers, servants, and other unenfranchised persons, whose lower legal status allowed them to be more easily controlled. The lords of boroughs often relinquished the task of managing their revenues by leasing them out, sometimes to the freemen as a body. This last practice, especially common in the larger royal boroughs of England and Scotland from the late twelfth century, required formal cooperation between burgesses that is well indicated by the creation of seals to authenticate the acts of borough communities. Lincoln had such a seal by 1200, York by 1206, Barnstaple by 1210, Berwick by 1212, Perth by 1219, Dublin by 1229. The administration of such chartered communities was headed by an elected mayor or by two elected bailiffs (*ballivi*) in England, and by provosts (*prepositi*) in Scotland. The Dubliners were authorized by the English crown to appoint their own mayor and provosts from 1229. In England towards the end of the period it was becoming more common for these officers to be advised by small elected councils of twelve to twenty-four members; such councils are recorded in Ipswich, Lincoln, Leicester, London, Northampton, Oxford, Cambridge, Great Yarmouth, Winchester, and perhaps Exeter by 1280. Few boroughs had as much self-government as these royal ones, but even in those still firmly subject to seignorial control the more influential townsmen often developed the ecclesiastical and legal institutions of the town to exercise some control over its affairs.

Communities became more diverse in size and power structure in the course of the twelfth and thirteenth centuries, but the contrasts can be drawn only with difficulty. Smaller settlements were perhaps more effective in organizing agricultural innovation, such as the stinting of commons or the draining of fens, whereas larger groups were better at organizing forms of self-government and shared ceremonial. One important difference between settlements of different kinds, and between different parts of Britain and Ireland, is strikingly apparent from the geographical distribution of extant documentary sources, which come preponderantly from southern England. Though most of the social bonds of daily life remain hidden from us even there, in such contexts mutual interdependence was becoming more apparent, more monetized, and more subject to negotiation, while forms of organization were becoming more explicit, more subject to formal procedures of decision-making, and more governed by written documents. The resulting surge of written evidence, especially during the thirteenth century, leaves the world of small hamlets and dispersed farmsteads—the world of the English Pennines and the Lake District, or of most of Scotland, Wales, and Ireland—underrepresented, by comparison, in the historical record. Most detailed observation of life in medieval communities relates, inevitably, to better documented, larger settlements that were a sign of the times but (like housing estates at the present day) socially and spatially distinctive.

Historians evaluate what they know of medieval communities very differently, and for a balanced view it is necessary to hold conflicting impressions in conjunction. There is a venerable historical tradition that contrasts the community values of medieval society with the capitalist individualism of the present day. Because of the nature of rural institutions, and especially parochial ones, countrymen were indeed expected to cooperate regularly, and not only in supplying the material necessities of life. For example, there were annual celebrations at Christian festivals, or at harvest time and other key points of the agricultural year. Other historians have a more sceptical attitude to the virtues of medieval communities. Quite apart from the systematically depressed status of women, families were divided by irreducible differences of status and of wealth, and these divisions had significant implications for family welfare. In the various settlements that made up Halesowen (Worcs.), richer families employed the poor on harsh terms, made loans to them at extortionate rates of interest, and used their distress to acquire land that would otherwise have been unavailable. Though the word 'community' may often accurately reflect medieval legal usage, or be appropriate for describing some forms of active and regular cooperation between families, idealistic egalitarianism was very foreign to the values of the dominant groups.

Kinship in 1100

A distinction between community and kinship has to be made in analysing the bonds of society because even the inhabitants of hamlets were rarely members of a single family group. Irish laws of the seventh and eighth centuries suppose at times that neighbours were kinsmen, but at other times this assumption was already relaxed. Though many English place names suggest a remote pre-Conquest period when hamlets were occupied by the members of a single kin, this was no longer so by 1100. Nevertheless, rural families often had kinsmen at hand, and people felt strongly that some transactions were better conducted with kinsmen than with neighbours. Where there was little money and no provision for public assistance, the boundaries between commercial and non-commercial transactions—between a gift, an exchange, a loan, and a sale—were often barely perceptible, and nowhere more so than in dealings between kinsmen. It is difficult to document this side of family life, which largely falls outside the bounds of both legal prescription and narrative record.

The individual household unit seems to have been characteristically small throughout Britain and Ireland, even when property was shared between a wider kindred. Apart from the economic interdependence between husband, wife, children, and resident servants that was vital at a time when a large amount of agricultural labour was on family farms, and most manufacturing was domestic, it was the responsibility of the head of each household to discipline its members. This usually implied that men exercised authority over their wives, children, and servants.

One important determinant of how different groups of people conceptualized the family was custom relating to the inheritance or transfer of land. Amongst the most servile groups of the population such rights were still non-existent or tenuous. In the villein townships of eleventh-century Gwynedd, land was allocated by royal officers, who equalized the share each villein received regardless of his descent, and there are traces of a similar form of tenure amongst neifs on the *maerdrefydd* of the Honour of Denbigh. It is impossible to say how far similar insecurity characterized the more dependent and servile ranks of the rural population elsewhere in Britain or Ireland in this period, but it seems likely that the kinship ties of people whose lords could move them about at will were exceptionally fragile. However, outside such dependence, among ordinary English peasant families rights of inheritance were widespread, even if often weakly formalized. It would be difficult otherwise to explain the entrenched local variations in practice that are to be found in later records.

Primogeniture (inheritance by the eldest son) was widespread in midland and southern England. The new titles to land created after the Norman Conquest, when granted by hereditary tenure, were similarly regarded as heritable by primogeniture, and this subsequently became established as the norm for freehold properties under English common law. In lands of predominantly Celtic tradition, meanwhile, though royal office was usually regarded as indivisible, land was not. The custom of dividing land between heirs remained general even for the most free and noble estates. After the death of the great Somerled, king of Argyll and of the Hebrides, in 1164, his lands and following were divided (not without prolonged conflict) between his sons Dugald, Angus, and Ranald. As this example illustrates, lordship was intrinsically more problematic where there was no undisputed heir. Among lower social ranks inheritance customs do not so clearly distinguish the area of Anglo-Norman domination, chiefly because of the considerable variety of local customs in England. Partible inheritance was, for example, a distinct feature of Kentish gavelkind tenures, which were classified as free, and also survived amongst customary tenants in parts of northern and eastern England.

Because of such differences in laws relating to the transmission of property, more distant kinship links were variously perceived in different parts of Britain and Ireland. They were less important in England, and in areas of intensive Anglo-Norman penetration, and most important where Celtic traditions were strong. There is no clear statement of the inheritance rights of kinsmen over English free tenures at this time; the legal treatise known as *Glanvill* (c.1187–9) assumes that the most remote heir that would need to be considered would be the descendant of an aunt or uncle of the deceased, but other writers propose various wider limits to inheritance claims. In Wales, inheritance customs among freemen made it necessary to keep track of family relations in the male line back three generations (that is, as far back as the great-grandfather of the deceased), beyond which all rights were extinguished. This meant not only that agnatic third cousins had a right to inherit land for which there was no closer heir, but also that, even if there was an heir, they had a right to demand a resharing of the inheritance to preserve their status. Kinsmen within this degree also had a right to veto the alienation of land. The early Irish laws show similar customs, and Scottish tradition may also have been like this, though the absence of written laws leaves the question doubtful. In England land was often regarded as belonging to a particular 'blood', but the rights of a family in regulating the disposal of property were significantly weaker than where Celtic customs prevailed.

In detail there were differences between the rules of different legal traditions relating to marriage and the legal status of women. The Welsh and Irish remained aloof from the crystallizing of canon law relating to marriage that was taking place through most of Latin Christendom during the twelfth century, and this meant that their customs became increasingly exposed to criticism by outsiders. They treated marriage much more as a social contract than as a sacrament of the Church, and customs relating to sexual union, marriage, and the legitimacy of children allowed men significantly more discretion than those favoured by canon law. Social acceptance of concubinage amongst those who could afford it, and the relative ease of divorce, meant that legitimacy was a complex issue. In Wales, too, the practice of *cynnwys* allowed a man to legitimize the offspring of extramarital partnerships by formal adoption. These customs explain why reformist English archbishops of Canterbury from Lanfranc to Pecham occasionally upbraided the Welsh and Irish for loose living. Differences in marriage custom were paralleled by differences in the extent to which women could exercise or transmit property rights. In the Anglo-Saxon legal tradition women were unambiguously bearers of such rights, whether as heiresses—in the absence of male heirs—or by right of marriage or as the beneficiaries of gifts. The Norman Conquest did not imply any break with this tradition, even in military tenures: Domesday Book records a number of women landowners, including the Conqueror's own niece, Judith, countess of Huntingdon, the widow of the recently executed Earl Waltheof, from whom the title to the earldom of Huntingdon passed through the successive marriages of Judith's daughter and heiress to Simon de Senlis (*c.*1090) and to David of Scotland (1113). In 1100 Henry I's coronation charter promised that, with the assent of his barons, heiresses should be allowed to succeed to the lands of deceased tenants-in-chief. Women did not have such clear rights to succeed, or to transmit legal rights, in lands of Celtic tradition, which systematically privileged agnatically related male relatives. This meant that however important women were as social intermediaries and conveyors of status in these societies, they were landowners only in exceptional circumstances.

Besides being of fundamental significance for the transmission of property, family membership was also one of the most powerful determinants of social status. At the lowest end of the social scale this was self-evidently true of slaves, but it was also true of many other categories of tenant—the English villein, the Scottish neif, the Welsh *taeog*, and the Irish betagh. In the upper ranks of society, though nobility was weakly and variously defined, there was no question that ancestry was of decisive relevance to rank. This was as true of Celtic traditions as of the Anglo-Normans. The propensity of the Celtic nobility to delight in genealogies owed more to status criteria than to legal or economic interest. In the early eleventh century one branch of the powerful Ó Néill family drew up a pedigree that traced its descent for twenty generations. Gerald of Wales says that the Welsh set such a high value on pedigree that they would prefer to marry into noble families than into rich ones.

Amongst the Welsh, Irish, and Scots alike, kinship groups among free men constituted more extended and substantial political groupings than they did in England. The *ceann cineil* or *toiseach cloinne* in Scotland, the *cenn fine* in Ireland, and the *pencenedl* in Wales were all alike 'head of the kindred', with recognized powers over the households within their branch of the family. They offered some form of protection and a guarantee of justice in exchange for tribute. However, despite these similarities, the political significance of the extended family was not uniform throughout Wales, Scotland, and Ireland. Some families were conspicuously more powerful than others. In much of Scotland and Ireland the heads of some lineages wielded considerable territorial power as kings. Such authority became the basis for forms of extensive clientage, in which relationships of economic and political subordination paralleled real or blood relationships, so that very large kindreds embraced a wide range of status differentials. In this context ties of kindred were tightened by lordship rather than loosened. The Irish *fine* and the Scottish *clann* were sometimes political forces powerful enough to contest the occupation of lands at the expense of both rival families and less free occupants. Pride of family among such kindreds had a lasting influence on the form of family names. The characteristic O' of Irish surnames derives from the Middle Irish *úa*, meaning 'descendant of' (from the Old Irish *aue* meaning 'grandson of'), and the Mac of many Irish and Scottish surnames is from *mac*, meaning 'son of', which in earlier formulations is often *mac meic*, 'grandson of'. Because they emerged from notable concentrations of power in the hands of heads of families, Scottish and Irish names in O' and Mac relate to particular powerful and distinguished ancestors. The Níall remembered by the powerful Ó Néill family was supposedly a head of family as far back as the fifth century.

Kinship 1100–1280

Although it is tempting to suppose that the growth of monetized relationships during the twelfth and thirteenth centuries undermined the cohesiveness of families, it is far from obvious that this should be so. Insofar as patterns of kinship were changing during these centuries as a result of economic change, the causes were much more ambiguous and more indirect than a straight commercialization of intra-familial bonds, which have proved exceptionally resistant to such pressures even to our own day.

Within individual households, the growing independence between households attested by the growth of local trading probably increased the tendency for women and children to engage in distinctive work. In rural areas they were often employed for dairy work, and for weeding and mowing, though not for ploughing and reaping. This aspect of family life is nowhere well documented before 1280; and most of the evidence is from England, but the same changes are likely to have ensued wherever the range of occupational specialization widened. The selling of produce in local markets and fairs was often, it seems, the responsibility of wives and daughters, and the wives of householders had increasing opportunities for commercial brewing, which was at this time a part-time domestic industry. Domesday

Book's account of Hereford already implies that brewing was an activity for wives, and in the early twelfth century the prescribed punishments for baking and brewing offences at Newcastle upon Tyne were specifically for women. Brewing was an expanding trade in the twelfth and thirteenth centuries, and women were chiefly responsible for its development. The growth of cloth-making mostly for the home market, but in places such as York, Beverley, and Lincoln for overseas sales as well, also created increasing employment for women in the spinning and preparing of yarn. These tendencies were most marked where towns were most developed, notably in southern and eastern England, but they must to some extent have been experienced more widely. There is nevertheless no reason to suppose that a variety of roles within the family, and particularly the urban family, undermined its integrity as an economic unit or reduced the authority of its head. The precariousness of a life in trade ensured that family members would have to pool their resources, and the characteristically small size of cottages, peasant farms, or the artisans' houses, ensured that there was a high degree of reciprocity within the home. In many craft activities it is likely that, as in later centuries, husbands, wives, and older children worked together. There were laws, too, to ensure that married women could achieve little by way of financial independence even if they wished, since their husbands were liable for their debts.

Relationships between parents and children, and in more extended kin groups, remained significant for the welfare of individuals in a variety of different ways. In some contexts economic and social change probably strengthened their importance, since rising land values, and the growth of dependence upon commercial transactions, meant that hereditary claims became more valuable. Litigation over individual tenements, as recorded in the court rolls beginning to be numerous towards the end of the period, sometimes shows the value of remembering family links. In Wales the rights of hitherto servile families over property characteristically increased with the sharp decline in the number of bond manors worked by servile labour and the associated transformation of precarious tenures into heritable ones. Amongst wealthier families kinship ties were important even for those without inheritances, since fathers would often acquire land specially for the purpose of setting up their children. In some places such transactions dominated the land market, systematically enhancing the position of wealthier families, and often strengthening their family ties, at the expense of those poorer families who were driven to dispose of land in order to pay debts.

The responsibility of a family for the welfare of its members remained, too, a recognized principle of the more extended kinship relations that continued to distinguish free landowners in Wales, Scotland, and Ireland through the twelfth and thirteenth centuries. It was still often the case in 1188, according to the *Description of Wales* by Gerald of Wales, that ordinary Welsh families could recite their family tree back for six or seven generations, and the fact that he was so impressed implies that this was a point of contrast with the English. Providing for less fortunate family members was in these contexts a duty of family chiefs, whose political status increasingly varied in different political contexts. Away from the lands controlled by the English and Scottish monarchies, heads of politically important kindreds exercised royal authority, like the O'Neill kings of Tyrone, the O'Connor kings of Connacht, the MacCarthy kings of Desmond, and the MacSorley kings of Argyll. Where their royal status came into dispute during the course of the period, as notably in Scotland, heads of distinguished families might be redefined as noblemen under the crown. The head of the MacDuff family in Fife, descended from King Dubh in the late tenth century, was recognized as earl of Fife by the early twelfth century. Elsewhere, in native Wales, the office of *pencenedl* would appear to have survived only where it was absorbed in some way into royal administration. Yet in all these instances family custom ensured some distribution of property to members of a property-owning kindred, and required the head of the family to make some provision for unfortunate kinsmen.

Not everyone was able to benefit from family ties. Among the poor, with their very restricted expectations from family connections, growing pressure on resources in the English countryside meant that families became more fragmented, imposing a greater demand for self-reliance on individuals. The centripetal force that held families together where there was enough family property to sustain a growing number of conjugal families contrasted, in places such as Halesowen, with the centrifugal force that drove non-inheriting offspring away from families deficient in land. Poverty and over-crowding on family tenements inhibited marriage and reproduction and, especially when compounded by misfortune, constituted 'push factors' that contributed to family dispersal. Family members for whom no adequate provision could be made might find a new livelihood away from the family home, on new land, as self-employed artisans, or in some form of dependent employment. Many became servants outside their parents' home, even if their parents employed servants from other families, presumably because the parents in question found it more difficult to exploit their own offspring than to exploit those of other people. Other unsupported family members became 'the naked poor', far from any effective support from their own kindred. Some drifted townwards, drawn by the prospects of institutional almsgiving, casual employment, or crime. As this implies, the poor were more likely than the better off to be without an effective kinship network, even in rural society. Evidence from Halesowen shows that smallholders and cottagers were less likely to have kinsmen on the manor than large or middling tenants.

Even where more extended family responsibilities prevailed, and where land was divided between heirs, the system worked better for some than for others. Rivalry between family chiefs encouraged conflict between families, and between branches of the same family, either in the form of cattle raiding or in more determined competition for land and power, so that the extended family was more often like a war-band than a friendly society. Such destructive conflicts directly benefited those powerful enough to offer leadership or protection. New lineages battled their way to power throughout the period. The Scottish MacDonalds, Macdonnells, and MacConnels, for example, are all named from Somerled's grandson, Donald, who died sometime in the mid-thirteenth century, after having made a reputation for piracy on the western seaboard of Scotland. Such aggressive families created innumerable victims. In other instances, families gained relative to others more peacefully, as a result of political favour. The prosperity of the Tudor family was founded on wealth accumulated in the service of the thirteenth-century princes of Gwynedd by Ednyfed Fychan and his sons. Families that lost out in the competition for land, for whatever reason, were in no position to protect the welfare of their less fortunate members, so that poverty and destitution were far from unknown in Wales, Scotland, and Ireland amongst those whose kindreds could not help them. Amongst unfree families, family connections were even more doubtful as a source of security. One of the reasons for the declining number of unfree tenants in Wales was that their land was being taken over by men of free lineage.

The economic opportunities of the twelfth and thirteenth centuries sometimes enabled men to improve their lot by migration. This is most apparent in the development of urban employment, which depended upon the continuing migration of families away from their previous bases in search of the superior opportunities that a town could provide. A survey of Stratford-upon-Avon made in 1251–2 exhibits the contrast between the names of the bishop of Worcester's manorial tenants, who were often identified by patronymic or metronymic surnames (such as Alfred son of Eynulf and Thomas son of Cicely), and the tenants of the small borough there, who were often identified by their place of origin or by their occupation (such as Richard of Bagendon and Richard the Tanner). These names may

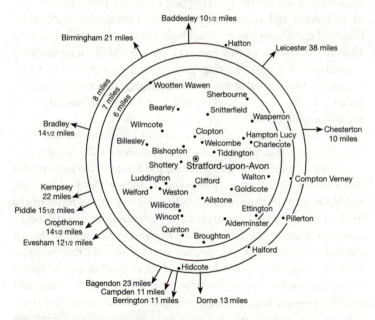

Map 13 Origins of the inhabitants of Stratford-upon-Avon in 1251–2. The map uses the evidence of 57 names of the form 'Richard of Bagendon' to show that many derived from places within eight miles of Stratford.

therefore be used to chart the territory from which migrants were attracted (see Map 13). Contrasts were even stronger in Wales and Ireland, where the English and Anglo-Norman names common in the borough contrasted with the Welsh and Irish names of the rural settlements nearby. Some migrant families retained a connection with their place of origin, especially if they were sufficiently wealthy to have business connections. Migration into most towns, too, was predominantly over short distances—less than twenty miles—so that supplanting of kin relationships was likely to be partial and gradual. However, the much longer distances over which many men migrated to the larger towns, and especially to London and its surburbs, makes it unlikely that they were all able to maintain contact with their families in any regular fashion. Moreover, even very small towns in areas of new development—especially in Wales, Scotland, and Ireland—were able to draw new inhabitants over long distances. Many migrants into Dublin in the twelfth century were drawn from Wales, south-west England, and the Midlands (see Map D). In the migration of new settlers from England to Carmarthen and Cardigan, or to Dublin and Dundalk, or from the Lothians to St Andrews, bonds of community were strengthened at the expense of bonds of kindred. Migration of this sort was not necessarily followed by a re-creation of the old kinship pattern in a new environment; as migration became intrinsic to the changing structure of society, urban families experienced complex patterns of migration in successive generations.

As in the case of the medieval community, there are grounds both for supposing that kinship ties were stronger in the twelfth and thirteenth centuries than they are now, and for doubting whether this was a wholly enviable feature of medieval society. On the one hand, kinship ties could be protective and supportive as the result of the hold of family members over scarce economic and institutional resources. Care of the elderly was everywhere the responsibility of children able to help. As English court roll evidence becomes available, members of well-established local families can be found supporting each other in conflicts both within courts of law and outside. This has been strikingly observed, too, in the earliest court rolls of the lordship of Dyffryn Clwyd in the earlier fourteenth century. Yet kinship ties often implied some families triumphing over others in various ways. They could offer little support to the many members of families lacking strong legal or customary property rights. As in more recent times, too, the authority of heads of households, likely to be enforced by blows and beatings when challenged, was also a dubious blessing, buttressed as it was by all the royal, seignorial, and communal institutions of law and order.

Figure 5 The south doorway of Kilpeck church. Kilpeck, built in the early twelfth century, is one of the finest minor churches in the Romanesque style surviving in England, and it is as noteworthy for its sculpture as for its structure. The richly decorated south doorway shows that the Romanesque of the West Midlands was receptive to decorative forms that were in origin Anglo-Saxon. But note also, on the main shaft of the left jamb, two warriors, each in trousers, who are placed one above the other—the one carrying a cross, and the other, a sword. The motif of superimposed figures has parallels at Maillezais (Vendée, France), a church on the pilgrimage route to Santiago de Compostella.

The Church and Christian life

Brian Golding

Shortly after his appointment as papal legate in Ireland, Gilbert, first bishop of Limerick, wrote a tract, *De statu ecclesiae* (*Concerning church order*). This may have been intended as a statement of intent for the reforming council of Rathbreasail (1111), at which he presided as legate, or alternatively as a digest of its conclusions. It laid out, clearly and schematically, the organizational structure of the Church. From the perspective of Rome the Irish Church was regrettably archaic; there were too many bishops but no territorial dioceses, the jurisdictional authority of the bishops was circumscribed, while abbots and their monasteries enjoyed considerable autonomy and spent as much time in ministering to the laity as in prayer within the cloister. In every respect this ran counter to contemporary orthodoxy. Gilbert showed, quite literally diagrammatically in the earliest manuscripts of this text, how matters should be ordered. The Church was an elaborate pyramid, which itself contained other interlocking and smaller triangles. At the base were the laity, divided, according to a tripartite scheme commonplace for several centuries, into those who worked (or ploughed) at bottom left, those who fought, next on the right, and above them those who prayed, presumably, though this is unclear, the pious laity. Above these on the left side stood the parish, the basic building-block of the secular (i.e. non-monastic) Church, with its priest and attendants, the deacon, subdeacon, acolyte, exorcist, reader, and doorkeeper. On the right side of the pyramid was the monastery, with its abbot and his subordinate monks. Over both parish and monastery were set the diocesan bishops, who were themselves subject to archbishops, archbishops to primates, and primates to the pope who stood at the apex. The whole of this ecclesiastical pyramid was, Gilbert explained, the mirror image of another temporal structure where the emperor corresponded to the pope and so on down the scale, with the knight as the priest's equivalent.

Gilbert's elegant model would have been inconceivable two or three generations earlier. It offers a well-articulated normative structure under the papacy. Yet papal supremacy was a recent development: our period coincides with the emergence of a new-style, centralized papacy under Leo IX and Gregory VII and their immediate successors, and the consolidation of the 'papal monarchy', through the efforts of such great legislators and administrators as Alexander III and Innocent III. Traditional rights and privileges enjoyed by bishops and laity alike were eroded as the papacy extended its prerogative in all areas of church life, from the appointment of bishops to the canonization of saints, from the proclamation of holy war to the overarching authority of papal legislation. The whole is underpinned by new orthodoxies disseminated through the new centres of learning, especially Paris for theology and Bologna for law. This centralized orthodoxy was mirrored by a corresponding hardening of attitudes towards outsiders: heretics, Jews, and homosexuals.

Dioceses

In England Gilbert's ideal diocesan structure largely accorded with reality. By the mid-eleventh century the arrangement was much as it would be till the Reformation (see Map F). Only two new dioceses, Ely (1109) and Carlisle (1133) were established: Ely carved out of the huge diocese of Lincoln, and Carlisle established for the region of southern Strathclyde recently brought under English control. Some sees were relocated, particularly in the 1070s, including Lincoln from Dorchester-on-Thames and Chichester from Selsey. In 1072 bishop Herfast moved from Elmham to Thetford: in 1094 or 1095 the see moved again, this time permanently, to Norwich. In 1078 Sherborne moved to Salisbury (Old Sarum), but in 1219 the bishop moved again from the cramped and unsatisfactory hilltop to the riverside site of

[New] Salisbury. In the north-west Midlands arrangements were more complicated. Lichfield transferred to Chester in 1075, papal confirmation for the next bishop's move of headquarters, to Coventry, was granted in 1102, and from 1228, following increasing tension between the rival claims of Lichfield and Coventry, the bishop became known as bishop of Coventry and Lichfield.

Diocesan organization elsewhere was significantly influenced by Anglo-Norman conquest. In Wales territorial bishoprics, with their accompanying administrative structure, were only really established in the first half of the twelfth century, the chief catalyst being the vigorous campaigns of the two rival bishops of south Wales, Urban of Llandaff (1107–34) and Bernard of St Davids (1115–48), to consolidate the areas of their jurisdiction. In both instances claims centred on rights to the territories of old mother churches (the *clasau*) as well as on the rightful coincidence of their boundaries with those of regional principalities. In north Wales, the diocese of St Asaph was created in 1143, carved out of the earlier, larger diocese of Bangor (see Map F). Yet these developments cannot be seen solely in terms of alien conquest. Both Urban and Bernard were Anglo-Normans, the former a priest from Worcester diocese who fiercely condemned Norman spoliations when it was his own church's interests that were threatened. Bernard had been the chancellor of Edith (Mathilda), wife of Henry I, and likewise defended the rights of St Davids against the claims of Canterbury to metropolitan status. Just as their counterparts were doing in England, both Urban and Bernard went to great lengths to appropriate the relics of the conquered in order to increase the renown and prestige of their churches, Urban bringing the bones of Dyfrig back from Bardsey island, while Bernard launched several expeditions to find the bones of St David.

North of the border we find similar complexities and interplays, this time between English and Scots, against a background of increasing homogeneity within the Western Church as a whole (see Map G). Here Irish influence remained strong until the twelfth century, though the move to territorial bishoprics began earlier in Scotland than in Ireland. The greater number of Scottish bishoprics existed before the reign of David I, although several may have been without a bishop for a long time before his accession in 1124. By the end of the twelfth century, thirteen dioceses had been established, and ten of these on the mainland were recognized by Rome as constituting the

Ecclesia Scoticana: they were effectively a province. By an anomaly, however, none of the ten bishops had the status of archbishop or metropolitan. As in Wales, episcopal boundaries sometimes marched with those of secular lordships, and many bishoprics owed their origin to the existence of earlier mother-churches whose lands they had taken over. As the twelfth-century Scottish kings expanded their jurisdiction northwards, new bishoprics were established in Caithness and Argyll, using the boundaries of secular lordships. Orkney and the Isles remained anomalies. Both belonged to Norway and were subject to the ecclesiastical jurisdiction of Nidaros (Trondheim). The Isles were ceded to Scotland in 1266, but Orkney remained a Norwegian dependency until 1469. Similarly, Galloway did not become subject to Scottish ecclesiastical jurisdiction until the fourteenth century, having previously recognized the authority of the archbishop of York.

The case of Ireland was rather different. Long-standing differences in social and ecclesiastical structures meant that the concept of the territorial bishopric was largely unknown. Traditionally the authority of abbots overrode that of bishops, and the lack of a coherent organizational structure brought a corresponding laxity of practice, though this was perhaps exaggerated by outsiders eager to portray the native Irish as barbarians to further their political agenda. The first territorial bishopric was that of Dublin, probably established sometime in the middle of the eleventh century and closely connected with the see of Canterbury, which had some claim to primacy over Ireland. The Anglo-Norman archbishops of Dublin were correspondents of both Irish kings and clerics. Outside the dioceses associated with the Danish settlement, Dublin, Waterford, and Limerick, things were rather different, and it was only in 1111 at Rathbreasail that territorial bishoprics were established across the country. These were divided into two provinces, Armagh and Cashel. This 'ecclesiastical engineering', as it has been described, was completed in 1152 when the council of Kells-Mellifont created two further archbishoprics, Dublin and Tuam, under the primacy of Armagh (see Map E).

English dioceses varied considerably in size and wealth. Some, such as Lincoln or York, extended over several shires, while others included only one or two shires, as did Chichester and Hereford. Kent was divided between Canterbury and Rochester. The bulk of episcopal revenues was derived from landed endowments, mostly of pre-Conquest origin, though additional income came from the possession of some parish churches and other sources such as markets and fairs. By far the wealthiest see was Winchester, with an income of nearly £3,000 per annum in 1291, when an assessment was made for the purposes of papal taxation, followed by Durham (£2,700), Canterbury (£2,140), and Ely (£2,000), while the poorest, Rochester, enjoyed less than £200. These were substantial differentials: the richest bishops ranked with the most prosperous earls, the poorest with relatively minor barons. Yet no English see was as badly off as those in Wales: even St Davids, whose possessions had recently been boosted by Edward I, had an income of only £105, while St Asaph, with £22, was poor indeed.

Parishes, parish churches, and chapels

But it was not only the diocesan structure that was being strengthened. At the grass-roots the holy landscape that had been created over centuries was transformed. This trend towards a tighter organization was Europe-wide, as apparent in Scandinavia as in Spain, and was nowhere more obvious than in the creation of the parish. At the beginning of this period, the parish as it is understood today scarcely existed outside a few areas of England; by its end there were over 8,000 such basic units of ecclesiastical organization, whose boundaries and number were to remain virtually unchanged till well into the nineteenth century. In England the 'parish system' was essentially complete by the last quarter of the thirteenth century. But this administrative grid was superimposed upon a much more complex and older structure. It was usually centred on a mother-church, or minster, sometimes with subordinate chapels, serving an extensive *parrochia*, an arrangement that gradually gave way to the new framework of independent churches responsible for much smaller units, the parishes. The initiative for this radical reform probably came from the bishops, such as Wulfstan of Worcester or Archbishop Lanfranc of Canterbury, who was responsible for a substantial programme of parish creation in Kent. This administrative reform, combined with the desire or need of Anglo-Norman lords to establish churches on their own estates, acted as a powerful catalyst to parochial church building. So too did the increase in population which was such a marked feature of this period. Consequently, new churches were created and old ones expanded, and the registers of thirteenth-century bishops are full of references to the consecration of new churches. In Scotland a similar transformation is found, though it began perhaps a generation or more later than in England and went further in the south, which was more subject to English influence, than the north. Here also there was an ambitious programme of church building in the twelfth century, as favoured churches and chapels were transformed into parish kirks. The initiative for this change seems to have come, at least indirectly, from David I (1124–53), whose insistence on the payment of teind (tithe) gave the new parishes unprecedented economic resources, though, as in England, there were considerable discrepancies in income between churches.

In many instances old-style minsters were transformed into communities of Augustinian canons, as happened, for example, at Aldgate in London, where, in 1107–8, the Priory of Holy Trinity, an Augustinian foundation, took over the rights and endowments of an earlier minster dedicated to St Mary Magdalen. North of the border, the same phenomenon can be observed, as at Whithorn, where c.1175 the old community, probably consisting of secular canons, became a Premonstratensian abbey. In Wales, too, the *clasau*, which bore strong resemblances to the English minsters, went into decline: many passed into Augustinian hands; others, as at St Davids, formed the nucleus of cathedral chapters, and some became parish churches in the modern sense. While some of these changes can be attributed to the new Anglo-Norman order, keen to impose its own notions of ecclesiastical structure on an alien and 'barbaric' people, and at the same time to appropriate church lands for themselves and their monastic foundations, native princes were also responsible. It is no surprise to find the early twelfth-century prince of Gwynedd, Gruffudd ap Cynan, being praised by his biographer for his extensive church-building activity, nor the *Book of Llan Dâv* recording the consecration by Bishop Herewald of some twenty churches in his diocese. The great Lord Rhys of Deheubarth was influential in the endowment of his new Premonstratensian abbey of Talley with lands taken from one of the most ancient *clasau* in Wales, Llandeilo, centre of the cult of St Teilo.

Ireland, however, had its own distinctive pattern of development. Here, parishes were unknown before the beginning of the English penetration c.1170, and development subsequently in the Gaelic west and north was along very different lines from those which became normal in English Ireland. Vast rectories, covering areas which can often be related to ancient sub-kingdoms, existed in the west and north, and many chapels, but no parishes in the English sense. Even in English Ireland, development was often slow. In County Louth, for example, the parish of Beaulieu was in process of formation as late as the fourteenth century.

But to limit discussion in any part of the British Isles to the parish churches is to miss half the picture, for there were also perhaps the same number of chapels, often maintained by the laity. Some were of very ancient foundation, dating back to the early Christian period, particularly in Celtic regions, such as Cornwall, which possessed the densest concentration; others testify to the filling-up of the country-side and the need for local chapels for new and often marginal communities far from the parochial centre, and perhaps inaccessible through poor communications. They might be oratories built in sub-urban areas to cater for a growing urban population or to serve as market chapels; many were found in areas of dispersed settlement or remained *in situ* following the shifting of settlement to a new centre; some were originally private chapels or built for the tenants of one lord; others might be founded on newly reclaimed land, later developing into fully fledged parish churches or, conversely, enjoying only an ephemeral existence. Their subordination to the parish church was carefully monitored. Their congregations were normally required to attend the parish church on greater feast days, while attempts, not always successful, were made to ensure both the dependence of the chapel's clergy on the mother-church and that rights of baptism, marriage, and burial were retained in the mother-church's hands. Not surprisingly, disputes between parish churches and chapels were frequent, as the former sought to maintain a monopoly of baptism and burial.

Private chapels certainly seem to have been on the increase, though it is hard to be sure in the absence of episcopal registers prior to the thirteenth century. Chapels had long been found in castles, where their staff frequently provided secretarial and other administrative support within the household, and seignorial churches were often found in close association with thegnly residences in late Anglo-Saxon England. Certainly in the thirteenth century possession of a private chapel was a status symbol, though lesser gentry families might well receive this privilege. Licences could be temporary or permanent and granted for many reasons, including distance from the parish church and a patron's physical incapacity. In 1292, Bishop Oliver Sutton of Lincoln licensed a chapel for Walter of Molesworth whose mother was old and whose wife was extremely fat, so that they could not attend their parish church. A year later, he gave a similar licence to Hugh of Bibbeworth and his wife, since the road to the parish church was so difficult during winter and his wife could not attend church during pregnancy. It is clear that private chapels were already being built in the twelfth century. That of Stoke Orchard (Glos.), which, after many vicissitudes, remained in private hands until 1946, was probably built by a member of the Archer family in the second half of the century. Shortly afterwards, its walls were elaborately decorated with a narrative cycle of scenes from the life of St James of Compostella which constitute the only known example in England, and perhaps in western Europe. The iconography is sophisticated and for the most part follows literary sources familiar from the twelfth century. A similar version of events is found in the contemporary *Gemma ecclesiastica* of Gerald of Wales, a didactic work prepared for the clergy of his archdeaconry of Brecon, where the story is introduced with an explicit apology that it is intended for the edification of the less learned. That such a narrative is found on the walls of the private chapel of a lesser lord witnesses to the wealth of instructional decoration that would have been found on the walls of all churches at this period.

Pilgrimages, shrines, and holy wells

It is probable that Stoke Orchard's patron had himself been on pilgrimage to Compostella, which was among the most popular destinations for pilgrims of all classes. Wealthy pilgrims might grant property in England to monasteries which had provided them with hospitality along the way, as did Oliver de Merlimond, steward to Hugh de Mortimer, who gave lands in Herefordshire to St Victor at Paris, and whose church at Shobdon (Herefs.) appears to have close artistic affinities with churches along the pilgrimage route, particularly in Poitou. The pilgrimage, undertaken for spiritual and/or temporal healing, as penance, or as holiday, was central to the religious life of the laity. Some might combine a pilgrimage to Jerusalem with crusading activity and, though most of the documented crusaders are of knightly origin or above, a unique surviving list of those who took the cross in southern Lincolnshire at the end of the twelfth century indicates that many artisans and poor labourers were also anxious to go. Pilgrimage to such a distant site was inevitably expensive, and often laymen are found mortgaging their estates to religious houses in order to raise the necessary finance. If pilgrimages to Jerusalem, Compostella, and Rome were normally restricted to the wealthy, there were other, national shrines closer to hand. Amongst them, that of Thomas Becket, murdered at Canterbury in 1170, was pre-eminent. Offerings at his shrine peaked in 1220, when his bones were translated from the crypt to a new shrine. Another major shrine, that at Walsingham, did not achieve prominence until the very end of this period, and is predominantly a cult-centre of the late middle ages, but it had its origins in the construction by a local gentry woman, Richelde de Fervaques, c.1120, of a replica of the Holy House at Nazareth, a rare indication of lay piety of this sort.

The usual focus of pilgrimage was the corporeal relics of the saint. They conveyed power and authority, which might be both spiritual and temporal. No wonder their seizure was a frequent event. The removal of the relics of Gwenfrewi (Winifred) from Holywell to Shrewsbury Abbey in 1138 was at least as much an indication of a new Norman hegemony in Wales as it was of the monks' devotion and desire to promote pilgrimage. Similarly, John de Courcy identified himself with native Irish devotion when he discovered the bodies of St Patrick, St Brigid, and St Columba in a cave and had them translated to Down Cathedral. Relics might also carry dangerous political charges, as Edward I recognized when he seized the prize Welsh relic of the Holy Cross. Though relics might most often be publicly honoured and visited at a shrine, they themselves might also travel and be carried around in a reliquary. In the Celtic regions, where relics were more usually associative than corporeal, these often took the form of a bell once owned by the saint, a crozier, or a book. Frequently in the guardianship of hereditary keepers, who were descendants of monastic stewards and whose office occasionally survives to the present day, they would be brought out for ritual use, not only for cures, but also in oath-swearing and cursing ceremonies. They might even function as talismans in battle, as did the Monymusk reliquary carried at Bannockburn (1314) and the book-shrine of the Cathach, containing a manuscript allegedly written by Colum Cille (Columba), the battle standard of the O'Donnells. Peripatetic relics might be used in fund-raising campaigns. In the late eleventh century, Walter of Cérisy, the first abbot of Evesham, sent the bones of its Anglo-Saxon founder, Ecgwin, on a successful tour of southern England to raise money for the abbey's rebuilding, a course of action followed a few years later by several French and Flemish houses, most notably in 1113. In this year, the canons of Laon cathedral brought their relics to southern England, where they enjoyed mixed success, generosity being sometimes tempered by hostility from those who feared that 'charity-fatigue' might deprive local churches of offerings.

Though by this period the heyday of the local saints had passed, to be superseded by the growing appeal of national or supranational figures like St James or St Thomas Becket, many local cult-centres continued to flourish, such as those at Pennant Melangell (Merioneth.), with its remarkable, if restored, twelfth-century shrine, Bampton (Oxon.), which honoured an otherwise unknown Saint Beornwald, or Whitchurch (Dorset), with its shrine to St Whyte. More recently canonized or locally revered figures included bishops such as Thomas Cantilupe of Hereford, hermits like Robert of Knaresborough, monks such as Gilbert of Sempringham, or examples of lay piety such as Margaret of Scotland. Some were unfortunate victims of homicide, as was William of Norwich, whose alleged 'martyrdom' was attributed to the local Jewish community, or William of Rochester, a Perth fisherman of some piety who was attacked and killed at Rochester by his travelling companion while on pilgrimage to Jerusalem. Yet another was Simon de Montfort, baronial rebel or political martyr, according to one's point of view: all provided a focus for piety and role models for their supporters.

Below these shrines in the hierarchy of cult were other focal points of devotion, some long-lasting, others ephemeral. Many of these were centred on miraculous images and holy wells. The history of these sites is by definition obscure, and often revealed only in place-name evidence in the writings of later antiquarians, but it is clear from synodal legislation and episcopal registers that the Church's attitude to them was ambiguous. Though some wells, like that of Tottenham (Middx.), were accepted or at least tolerated, many came under suspicion. In the parochial undergrowth official supervision and control were most difficult: here abuses and pagan practices were most suspected and heterodox opinions might flourish. How far veneration of medieval holy wells indicates a continuation of pre-Christian activity remains hotly contested, and certainly some represented late medieval cults. It is certainly true that many wells whose veneration was popular in origin were taken over by local churches and monastic communities, while others were condemned. In 1102, the council of Westminster forbade the veneration of wells, along with 'the bodies of the dead', presumably a reference to unauthenticated relics, without episcopal licence. Hostility appears to have intensified during the thirteenth century, but the crucial issue remained one of ecclesiastical authorization.

In 1240 synodal statutes for the diocese of Worcester ordered local clergy to forbid gathering for the veneration of wells at Cerney (Glos.) and outside Gloucester. That this prohibition is found along with others forbidding consultations of sorcerers and sorceresses, and especially condemns those who consult Jewish fortune-tellers, suggests that wells were being similarly used for divination. The statutes for the diocese of Wells (1258?) echoed the Fourth Lateran Council (1215) in prohibiting the veneration of newly found relics, unless with papal sanction, and also of 'stones, wood, trees, or fountains on account of anyone's dream or deception'. The Exeter statutes of 1287 explicitly condemned such acts as heretical. That these canons were taken seriously is indicated in contemporary episcopal registers. In 1290 Bishop Sutton of Lincoln ordered the archdeacon of Oxford to forbid the veneration of St Edmund's Well, where miracles were being alleged in St Clement's parish outside Oxford. He was also concerned to stamp out unauthorized miracle cults. In 1296 the archdeacon of Buckingham was ordered to close Edmund earl of Cornwall's private chapel on his manor of Hambledon. Not only was the oratory unlicensed but reports of healing miracles had encouraged people to make unauthorized pilgrimages. Four months later, the fuss had died down and the chapel, now licensed, was allowed to reopen.

Dissent

Yet by contrast with much of western Europe, particularly southern France and northern Italy, formalized, organized heresy was almost unknown in Britain and Ireland, though in the 1160s a small group of Cathars from Flanders or Germany arrived in England. Henry II summoned a council at Oxford in 1166 to deal with them, and they were mercilessly expelled from the town. Any contact with them was prohibited, and the group died of exposure in the harsh winter. As attitudes in the west hardened against heretics, so they hardened against Jews. This intolerance is chillingly illustrated at the Council of Oxford in 1222, when an Oxford deacon who had converted to Judaism and married a Jewish woman was burnt for heresy, the first such example of the death penalty being imposed for heresy in medieval England. In Banbury during the same year, a lay couple were walled up alive. The man styled himself Christ, refused to enter the church, and mutilated himself in imitation of Christ's wounds. The woman, who in one source is said to have led the man astray through her magical arts, called herself the Virgin Mary and had allegedly made a chalice and patten of wax, claiming to be able to administer the sacraments.

The parish clergy: preaching and teaching

The generality of parish clergy remained ill-educated. Many were poor vicars. These priests acted in the place of rectors, who enjoyed most of the Church's revenues. By the end of this period, many rectories were in the hands of monasteries, which either served the church themselves or appointed a secular priest. In spite of episcopal efforts to ensure that vicars received due remuneration, their economic standard of living was often no better than that of the peasantry they served. Moreover, their own morality was sometimes questionable. Though papal reformers had condemned clerical marriage since the mid-eleventh century, the frequent reiteration of prohibition by bishops testifies to its survival. In Wales it remained common even in the thirteenth century, and as late as the mid-twelfth was apparently no bar to advancement through the ranks of the higher clergy. Thus, David fitz Gerald, bishop of St Davids (1148–76), was married and had at least two sons. Nor was condemnation of clerical marriage universal. The Cistercian abbot of Ford, writing of Brihtric, priest of Haselbury Plucknett in the mid-twelfth century, speaks with no obvious rebuke of Brihtric's wife, while Brihtric's son succeeded him in his priestly office. More reprehensible were the temporary liaisons formed by priests, while others, though not formally married, lived permanently with one woman.

Amongst the parish priest's duties spelt out by Gilbert of Limerick was the obligation to preach, though how far this was generally carried out during the twelfth century is a moot point. Indeed, how far any of the clergy preached to the people in this century is uncertain. Some bishops certainly *wrote* sermons, and perhaps delivered them at synods and the like, and the surviving sermon collection of Herbert Losinga seems to indicate that some of his sermons were intended for a lay audience. Abbot Samson of Bury St Edmunds is said to have preached in the vernacular to his English audience, going so far as to erect a pulpit in the abbey church so that he might be heard clearly. Bishops might preach at church consecrations or at the translation of relics, or go on occasional preaching tours, particularly to promote crusading fervour. Most famous of these expeditions was archbishop Baldwin's circumnavigation of Wales in 1188 which inspired his companion, Gerald of Wales, to write his great *Itinerary*. In this instance we know that Baldwin usually preached in Latin and relied on local interpreters to translate into Welsh. Other preaching might be yet more charismatic. In 1200, Eustace, abbot of Flaye in northern France, visited south-eastern England. Roger of Howden's contemporary account of his mission sheds a different light from that of episcopal prescriptions on what was expected of the laity and on their beliefs. Eustace's first act was to bless a holy well at Wye (Kent), where many healing miracles were reported and a woman was cured of demoniac possession. Moving on to Romsey (Kent), he struck the wall of the church—healing waters immediately flowed forth. He also persuaded many to give up the sin of usury and to take the Cross. He encouraged devotion to the Host as well as daily almsgiving. It was opposition to the latter that appears to have inspired his disillusioned return to Normandy, but he soon returned to England. This time his campaign was particularly focused on Sunday observance. He had already preached against the common practice of holding markets on Sundays and, armed with a letter he claimed had been sent down from heaven demanding the keeping of Sunday, he preached with great initial success in York, urging both Sunday observance and due respect for other feast-days. All trade and the hearing of court cases were prohibited in churches and churchyards. His converts pledged that they would give one farthing from every five shillings' worth of goods sold to provide lights in the church and for the burial of paupers, and Eustace set up collecting boxes for this purpose in every parish church.

The emergence of the friars in the thirteenth century unquestionably stimulated the preaching of sermons on a regular basis at parochial level: so, too, did synodal legislation that followed norms established at the Fourth Lateran Council (1215). Bishops closely associated with the friars, such as Grosseteste of Lincoln (1235–53) and Thomas Wallensis of St Davids (1248–55), or friars themselves like Pecham of Canterbury (1279–92), were perhaps particularly ardent promoters of preaching, but an increased emphasis on the sermon is everywhere apparent. This was accompanied by growing efforts to transmit orthodoxy and 'high' theology to the parishes.

The Fourth Lateran Council's emphasis on teaching was reflected too in the growth of a new literature intended for the edification and sometimes the readership of the laity. As well as stipulating annual confession, penance, and communion, it also ordered the provision of teaching in the vernacular by the local clergy. Spurred by such injunctions, reforming bishops urged their clergy to preach in English, and Latin texts were increasingly translated into the vernacular, often through the friars' initiative. By the end of the century, books of hours had appeared, books of private devotion that were owned by individual clerics as well as by the laity. They testify to the dynamic of lay spirituality, and perhaps also to growing lay literacy. There was a remarkable flowering of vernacular Welsh religious literature during the thirteenth century, including miracles of the Virgin, commentaries on key texts, such as the Creed and Paternoster, while court bards produced elaborate religious poetry; and the Black Book of Carmarthen, one of the most important collections of medieval Welsh verse, probably compiled in the early thirteenth century, contains a great deal more. Nor was this literature intended only for a male audience. Even before the Lateran Council we find saints' lives written for women, sometimes in Latin, as was the life of St Margaret of Scotland for her daughter, Edith/Mathilda wife of Henry I of England. Occasionally, women wrote Anglo-Norman hagiographies themselves. Clemence, nun of Barking, produced a life of St Catherine, and though Barking was perhaps exceptional for the range of its learning during the twelfth century, nuns from other communities are known to have written lives of St Edward the Confessor and St Etheldreda of Ely. More often, women commissioned, or were given, translated lives. Matthew Paris translated his Latin life of St Edmund of Abingdon into French verse for Isabella de Forz, countess of Aumale, who is also known to have borrowed other translated hagiographic texts from Matthew, while towards the end of the century a Welsh aristocratic lady, Efa ferch Maredudd, commissioned a translation of that most intractable of Christian texts, the Athanasian Creed, from the friar, Gruffudd Bola.

But of the spirituality of lower social levels we know little, apart from exemplary stories of the extraordinarily pious or impious found in hagiographies and other didactic works. Thirteenth-century bishops enjoined regular churchgoing, but how far such injunctions were obeyed is debatable. That they were needed may indicate some indifference on the part of the laity to what now appeared to their pastors and teachers to be basic religious obligations. Most parishioners encountered their Church at the sacraments of baptism and marriage, and at burial, and their spiritual understanding was transmitted orally and visually, through wall-paintings, stained glass, and the like. But in a conflict between the moral teaching of the Church and deeply entrenched custom, the Church might teach in vain. To the scandal of Archbishop Pecham and many others, the teaching of the Church on marriage as a sacrament did little to undermine the Welsh view of it as a contract that might be terminated by divorce.

Monasticism old and new, hermits, and anchoresses

To renounce the world was the ultimate expression of lay piety. Those who did not go this far might nevertheless insure their souls and those of their family by founding or patronizing a religious community. Here they might find, beside the prayers of the religious, a refuge for themselves, and a family burial place. Such patronage spanned the social spectrum, from kings who richly favoured such abbeys as Westminster, Dunfermline, Cashel, or Strata Florida, to peasants who might collectively make a small donation to a local house. In 1066 the choice was, however, limited. In England there were only some thirty-five communities for men, fewer than ten for women. All were Benedictine, and many had been founded by the kings of Wessex or the higher aristocracy during the preceding two centuries. Consequently, some were extremely wealthy and their distribution was largely dictated by the political geography of late Anglo-Saxon England, most being found in the Wessex heartland, the West Midlands, and East Anglia. Moreover, not only did these communities have aristocratic founders: their own recruitment was exclusively aristocratic, particularly in the case of the nunneries. Further north there were none: such great communities as Jarrow-Monkwearmouth having disappeared in the political convolutions of the Danish invasions.

In Celtic and Gaelic regions the monastic tradition was very different. Here Benedictine monasticism was unknown, and the religious communal life, regarded as archaic and corrupt by many contemporary commentators, was based on houses of secular canons, who might hold property in common, and who were often responsible for providing for the spiritual needs of a large local area. In Ireland, though not in Wales and Scotland, the hereditary abbots of large communities like Armagh enjoyed greater jurisdictional authority than the attenuated episcopate. These customary practices proved resilient in Ireland. Nevertheless, the twin tides of English colonialism and the influence of a reformed papacy swept much away; and in Ireland as well as Wales and Scotland, the new monasticism proved attractive to native as well as Anglo-Norman and English leaders.

In the closing years of the eleventh century, and during the twelfth, the range of monastic options broadened dramatically. New-style communities based on a rule, first provided by St Augustine of Hippo, but refined and made more austere at the end of the eleventh century, emerged. A significant factor in their success was the wide range of services they provided. At one end of the spectrum some communities, often developed from groups of hermits, scarcely differed, if at all, in their asceticism from new orders of reformed monks, such as the Cistercians. At the other end, some played an important social role, undertaking educational and charitable work and serving in parish churches. Augustinian foundations were by far the most common in twelfth-century Britain and Ireland, considerably exceeding their more high-profile contemporaries, the Cistercians. They proved especially popular with rulers such as Henry I of England and David I of Scotland, as well as with members of the royal court, eager to demonstrate their new-found prestige, but lacking the considerable resources needed to establish a 'traditional' Benedictine abbey. In any case, the opportunities for Benedictine foundations were drying up, as the rapid colonization of the countryside meant that there were far fewer extensive estates available, other than on the agricultural or political frontier.

And it was here that were founded many of the new orders. Chief amongst these were the Cistercians, first established in England, at Waverley, in 1128 and in Wales, at Tintern, in 1131. Five years later, they had reached Scotland where Melrose, founded by David I, was colonized from English Rievaulx, which was soon to become the largest and most prestigious Cistercian abbey in Britain, under its charismatic leader, Ailred. Before entering Rievaulx as a monk, Ailred had spent much of his early life at David's court. It may well have been his influence that led to Melrose's foundation. We can assume that David I sanctioned the foundation of Dundrennan Abbey, the first to be made by any of the new orders in Galloway, in 1142. Nevertheless, at Dundrennan and elsewhere the native rulers were also patrons of the new movement. The first Cistercians in Ireland were established at Mellifont in 1142, through the support of Malachy, and Malachy, though at various times bishop of Bangor and Down, and archbishop of Armagh, was above all a monk. He was deeply attracted to the Cistercian life, and Bernard of Clairvaux wrote his biography. He was also responsible for the promotion of the Augustinians in Ireland, particularly (though not exclusively) those following the customs of Arrouaise, near Arras. By the end of our period there were about thirty-five Cistercian abbeys in Ireland, eleven in both Wales and Scotland, and about sixty in England, including Savigniac houses, which the larger order absorbed in 1148. Most of these had been founded before 1152, when the order notionally banned any new foundations.

These new orders were all influenced by the eremitical tradition: many indeed emerged from communities of hermits. They brought a new emphasis on asceticism, manual labour, and withdrawal from lay society, demanding a return to the original austerity and purity of the Benedictine Rule. Not all religious necessarily joined a monastic community. Hermits were familiar figures throughout medieval England. They might be found in woods or marshes, upon or underneath bridges—which they frequently bore responsibility for maintaining—in churchyards, or in cells attached to a church, where they remained till death. Of their popularity there can be little doubt: it is significant that in the Arthurian romances, for example, it is most often to hermits rather than the 'established' clergy that the knights turn for spiritual consolation or advice. They were often consulted by the clergy. Gerald of Wales visited a hermit at Newgale, who gratified him by assuring him that his opponents in his struggle for the bishopric of St Davids would be duly punished. The Somerset hermit, Wulfric of Haselbury, was a confidant of his near-neighbour and later biographer, the learned Cistercian John of Ford, and it has been suggested that Wulfric acted as an interviewer of prospective Cistercian recruits. Geoffrey, abbot of St Albans, supported a number of hermits in the vicinity of his abbey and was a close friend of Christina of Markyate. Indeed, most twelfth-century bishops, as well as kings, maintained hermits on their payroll. Hermits came from a wide social range. Caradog of Rhos was a member of the household of Rhys ap Tewdwr of Deheubarth. A knight named William founded a hermitage which was later endowed by Hugh de Lacy and became the Augustinian priory of Llanthony Prima. A Derby baker became a hermit in Depedale, later the Premonstratensian house of Dale. Several emerged from an urban or trading environment: Christina of Markyate came from the Anglo-Danish patriciate of Huntingdon, Robert of Knaresborough from the very same milieu in York. Godric of Finchale was a huckster made good. He became a successful international merchant, was both a pirate in the eastern Mediterranean and a pilgrim, until he finally settled down as a recluse a few miles outside Durham. All of these, it has frequently been observed, were of native, non-Norman stock and often functioned as intermediaries between the colonizers and the colonized.

Anchoresses, though they might be formally dedicated to poverty and the strict enclosure and seclusion that was a metaphor for death itself, sometimes, like their male counterparts, acted as counsellors. The instructional texts of Ailred of Rievaulx and the early thirteenth-century *Ancrene Wisse* condemn anchoresses who teach, act as scribes, keep livestock, and set themselves up in business. They often employed servants, as did the three anchoresses at Kilburn (Middx.) in the early twelfth century, who were attended by two servant girls and a kitchen boy. During this period they were always more numerous than male hermits or anchorites, and this predominance increased during the thirteenth century, when there was seemingly a very significant growth in their numbers. Their social status varied considerably: they were recruited from both urban and rural environments, some were widows, a few were aristocrats. Two daughters of William de Braose were both anchoresses: Annora, the widow of Hugh de Mortimer, and Loretta, widow of Robert fitz Pernel, earl of Leicester (d. 1204), who was an anchoress at Hackington, outside Canterbury, for nearly fifty years. During this time, Loretta acted as a sponsor of the Franciscans and intervened in a number of legal cases on behalf of friends, both lay and ecclesiastical.

The life of an anchoress was one route whereby a woman desirous of leading the religious life could find fulfilment. At the time of the Conquest there were fewer than ten nunneries: most were in Wessex, some were extremely wealthy, all were the preserve of the higher aristocracy. A few new nunneries were founded after the Conquest, but the real expansion only came with the new orders in the twelfth century. In their attitude to women, monastic reformers ranged from those who regarded them as intrinsically tempting and hence to be totally avoided, through those who found a place for them so long as their life was carefully regulated, to those who like Robert of Arbrissel, the founder of Fontevraud, actively encouraged women in his ministry and order. Fontevraudine nunneries were few in Britain, the most important being Amesbury, but other orders flourished. In Ireland the way was led by the

Arrouaisian canonesses; in Scotland the majority of women religious followed a Cistercian observance, though here as elsewhere the scope of their incorporation within the order, which was always suspicious of women, remains controversial. The most interesting experiment in women's religious life was the Gilbertine Order, founded by Gilbert of Sempringham (Lincs.) from a nucleus of an anchoretic community, which was given its rule c.1148. This was an order of some thirty houses, of which the majority were for canons only. About a third, however, were double houses, dual communities of nuns and canons. Though increasing suspicion of their proximity meant that no new foundations were made after c.1200, and though their geographical range was confined to eastern England, they remained popular with benefactors, particularly from the knightly class.

However, choice of monastic affiliation was not only influenced by spiritual factors: local and national politics also played a major role. This was particularly the case in early Anglo-Norman England and during the conquest and colonization of the Celtic territories. Though post-Conquest magnates might choose to patronize existing abbeys, those which antedated the arrival of the new monasticism were more often despoiled, sometimes to provide endowments for new foundations, sometimes to increase the lord's own demesne. Choice depended in part on whether the new family was already well-established in Normandy, in which case they would normally continue to favour communities they had founded in the duchy with grants of English estates and churches. Such properties might develop as 'alien priories' and acquire some autonomy from their mother house, from which they were normally staffed, while smaller cells might consist of only one or two monks whose role was essentially administrative and economic rather than spiritual. Some larger Norman abbeys, such as Bec, might possess several priories across the Channel, and these priories continued to present accounts to, receive visitations from, and have their priors appointed by, the mother house, until the outbreak of war with France in 1294 led to the temporary seizure of their estates by the crown. This policy was frequently repeated in the following century, until the final suppression in 1414 of all priories that had not gained their autonomy.

Robert of Mortain, William I's half-brother, is typical of these patrons in making most of his donations to his family monasteries at

Mortain and Grestain, which developed an alien priory at Wilmington (Sussex). But it was not only the very powerful who made such foundations. In Somerset William de Falaise founded Stogursey as a cell of Lonlay, endowing it with lands locally and also with property in Wales. The Falaise inheritance passed to the de Courcys, and when John de Courcy occupied Ulster at the end of the twelfth century, Stogursey in its turn was given lands there, and these formed the nucleus of its daughter community of St Andrew-in-Ards. Similarly, after the establishment of the de Lacy lordship in County Meath, Llanthony Prima, a Lacy foundation, acquired substantial interests there. Some other great lords might even establish new monasteries in England which were independent though staffed by Norman monks, as did Roger de Montgomery at Shrewsbury. Yet others founded Cluniac priories, the first English community being established at Lewes (Sussex) by William de Warenne. But increasingly, Norman lords directed their giving to existing English houses and demonstrated their new loyalty and cultural assimilation by choosing burial in them rather than, as had Robert of Mortain, burial in their Norman foundations. Colonization might be peaceful and by invitation. The first abbot of David I's great abbey of Holyrood came from Merton (Surrey) and was of English not Norman stock. The first abbot of Dunfermline was Geoffrey, prior of Canterbury, while David I's Cistercian foundation at Melrose was established by monks from Rievaulx. This influence was also reflected in architecture. Durham cathedral inspired the building of Dumfermline abbey church; both Durham and Dunfermline influenced the building of Kirkwall cathedral, though in this instance the choice of design seems to reflect, not colonization, but a desire by the Orkney earls both to enhance their status through imitation of a great dynastic mausoleum, as was Dunfermline, and to promote their dynastic saint, St Magnus, to the kind of reverence given to St Cuthbert at Durham.

Friars

Early in the thirteenth century, the monastic map of western Europe was transformed by the emergence of the mendicant friars. Their milieu was very different from that of traditional monasticism with its emphasis, most marked amongst the twelfth-century orders, on withdrawal from the world. The friars represented a new kind of spirituality which stressed corporate as well as individual poverty, was at home in the towns, and saw its mission essentially as one of conversion rather than contemplation, in which preaching was as central as prayer. Like the Augustinians before them, but to an even greater extent, the friars were 'to teach by word and example', and it was this teaching function, initially particularly directed against heretical movements prevalent in southern France and northern Italy, that gained them the support of the papacy. Though at first the Franciscans placed rather greater emphasis on apostolic poverty and the Dominicans (or Friars Preachers) on preaching and the study of theology, within a few years there was a convergence of practice, and for the most part they were scarcely distinguishable from each other. The mendicants enjoyed rapid and phenomenal success, attracting support not only from the crown and aristocracy, who frequently employed them as confessors and advisers, but also from urban patrons.

The Dominicans were first established at Oxford in 1221 and came to London by 1224, the year in which the Franciscans came to England. Within a few weeks, the latter had set up in Canterbury, London, and Oxford. Their rapid growth continued, though not quite as dramatically, and by 1284 there were about fifty communities in England, and about forty Dominican houses. A generation later than the Franciscans and Dominicans, two smaller mendicant orders arrived in Britain, the Carmelites and Austin friars, as well as more transient, less organized groups, such as the Friars of the Sack, who enjoyed an ephemeral existence until all their houses were closed early in the fourteenth century. In Scotland there were eleven Dominican friaries by 1300, the first being settled in 1230 at Edinburgh. Of these, eight were founded by Alexander II, whose significance for the Scottish Church was as great as that of David I a century earlier, and whose royal patronage of mendicants parallels that of Henry III and Edward I in England. There were also six Franciscan houses, of which the earliest, Berwick (1231) and Roxburgh (1232), were also founded by Alexander.

That there were relatively few friaries in Wales occasions little surprise. The mendicants were almost exclusively an urban initiative, and twelfth- and thirteenth-century Wales was notoriously under-urbanized. By the middle of the thirteenth century there were five Dominican friaries in Wales, of which the first appeared in Cardiff sometime before 1242, but only three Franciscan houses, the first being founded by Llywelyn ab Iowerth (d. 1240) at Llanfaes (Anglesey), the town whose growth he did so much to foster. Nevertheless, by the end of the thirteenth century, there may have been more friars in Wales than Cistercians, and Archbishop Pecham of Canterbury (himself a Franciscan) compared their spirituality favourably to that of the Welsh secular clergy. Individual houses generally flourished in spite of political vicissitudes, as when the Dominican friary at Bangor was destroyed in the troubles of the 1280s. As elsewhere, friars were soon appointed as bishops. Anselm le Gras, a Franciscan, became bishop of St Davids in 1231, the Dominican Hugh went to St Asaph in 1235, and a Welsh Dominican, Anian II, was to have a long and politically active career in the same see. Though not himself a Franciscan, Thomas Wallensis, who became bishop of St Davids in 1248, had been a distinguished master of the Franciscan school at Oxford during the course of a notable academic career in both Oxford and Paris, as well as serving as archdeacon of Lincoln during his mentor Grosseteste's episcopate. Men like Thomas and his near-contemporary John Wallensis, who became lector of the Franciscans at Oxford and then a regent-master at Paris, stood in the front rank of thirteenth-century academic and pastoral theologians. It is also likely that the Welsh mendicants were behind the substantial translation of didactic texts, as well as poems and biblical paraphrases for both clergy and laity, that marks the late thirteenth and early fourteenth centuries, such as *Penityas*, a translation of the Dominican Raymond of Pennafort's *Summa* on penance.

Across the Irish Sea, we find a similar pattern, though here the texts appear to be in Latin rather than the Gaelic, even when the authors, such as Malachy, a Franciscan of Limerick, whose *Venenum Malachie* enjoyed a widespread popularity, were native Irish. The mendicants had certainly enjoyed substantial success in Ireland. The Dominicans first settled in Dublin and Drogheda in 1224, the Franciscans in Cork and Youghal a few years later. By the end of the century, there were twenty-four Dominican and thirty Franciscan as well as eight Carmelite and three Augustinian friaries. Though first established in Anglo-Irish towns, they were soon found in Gaelic regions also.

Poor relief and hospitals

Charitable obligations had long been incumbent upon monasteries and greater churches. Often that obligation was incorporated into monastic ritual, and expressed in the feeding of the local poor, at certain times in the church year, but monasteries might also provide famine relief in times of emergencies. Evesham Abbey looked after many of the refugees who flooded south following William I's harrying of the north in 1069, and Margam imported corn from across the Bristol Channel to feed the poor at its gates. Bishops, too, like Robert de Bethune of Hereford, who provided for a stated number of paupers on a daily basis at each of his manor houses, might provide for the local poor. By the twelfth century, however, poor relief and care for the sick were becoming more institutionalized with the foundation of hospitals, normally organized on quasi-monastic lines. Many of these were the result of episcopal initiative. Bishop Henry of Blois of Winchester founded the hospital of St Cross just outside his city. Both St Cross and the almost contemporary foundation of St Mary at Chichester, whose care was vested in the dean and chapter, continue to the present day. In 1232 Bishop Hugh Foliot of Hereford founded St Katharine's Hospital by the marketplace of Ledbury. It was intended to cater both for the spiritual and material needs of the sick and aged poor, as well as those of travellers. Typically, this holistic approach was expressed spatially, in that the hall and chapel were indivisible, with the latter at the east end of the complex served by chaplains celebrating Mass for the souls of the founder and benefactor. Other founders included prosperous merchants such as Gervase 'the Rich' of Southampton, who founded God's House Hospital c.1197, and royal servants like Rahere, a member of Henry I's court, who, consequent upon a vision whilst on pilgrimage to Rome at the church of San Bartholomeo, founded a great priory and hospital at Smithfield, just outside London: the hospital—and part of the priory church—survive as 'Barts'. Rahere's king was also a hospital-founder, establishing St John's at Cirencester before 1135.

Bishops

Though the majority of the bishops of twelfth- and thirteenth-century England came from aristocratic or gentry backgrounds, there were notable exceptions, such as Thomas Becket, of Anglo-Norman mercantile origins, and Robert Grosseteste, of obscure rural parentage in Suffolk. To some extent at least, the Church always remained a career open to talents, in which men of lowly rank could rise to great distinction. There were three chief routes to preferment: royal service, a monastic career, or service in an episcopal or other large ecclesiastical household. It is hard to find general trends in appointments. Thus, for example, while the balance may have gradually swung away from those with a theological to those with a legal background, many thirteenth-century appointments were of distinguished theologians who were personally learned and who had a deep commitment to clerical education and reform, and sometimes to political reform as well. Pecham, the Franciscan archbishop of Canterbury, is an outstanding example of this group. Though Henry I was conspicuous in his promotion of royal servants, all English kings used such promotions as a means of rewarding loyal service, at relatively little cost to themselves. These appointments were often successful, sometimes mediocre, rarely scandalous. Monastic appointments, though attacked by polemicists such as Gerald of Wales, were relatively few. Only about 17 per cent of the English episcopate were recruited via this route between 1066 and 1215, and a similar proportion thereafter, when friars also figured occasionally. These monastic bishops include some of the most notable figures of the medieval Church, including Lanfranc, Henry of Blois, and Hugh of Avalon.

Bishops were also used as instruments of colonization. Though Edward the Confessor's episcopal bench had been far from exclusively Anglo-Saxon in make-up, William the Conqueror ensured that his appointments to replace retired, dead, or deposed bishops were of continental origin, and by the end of his reign there was only one native survivor of the 'old guard', Wulfstan of Worcester (1062–95). In Wales, William Rufus appointed Hervé, a Breton, as bishop of Bangor in 1092. Hervé was, however, expelled by the Welsh c.1109, when he was transferred to the quieter environment of Ely.

Thereafter, the intrusion of Anglo-Norman bishops beyond Offa's Dyke accelerated, though it was far from comprehensive, even after the Edwardian conquest at the end of the thirteenth century. About 70 per cent of all bishops appointed during this period could be defined as Welsh, and the percentage is higher for the dioceses of south Wales. Of course, their loyalty to the English crown had to be assured, but when they did act against royal interests they were conditioned by political and/or religious rather than by ethnic concerns.

Though some Irish sees had formal links with Canterbury before 1170, it was only following Henry II's intervention in Ireland that Anglo-Norman or English clerks were appointed to Irish sees, and the picture here is very nuanced. Anglicization fluctuated: some dioceses, unaffected by foreign settlement, continuing to appoint Irish bishops throughout the period, even though the choice of bishop was predominantly influenced by the English crown. Only occasionally were ethnic considerations explicitly articulated, as they were at Armagh in 1201, while in 1217 a royal writ ordained that no Irishman was to be elected bishop 'since by this our land is disturbed'. Such blatant intervention brought papal condemnation (not wholly effective), and during the thirteenth century appointments continued to reflect in varying measure interests of the crown, local lords, both native and settler, and the cathedral chapters themselves.

Academic standards in the episcopate varied hugely. Some, like Anselm and Grosseteste, rank among the greatest minds of the European middle ages, some were of notorious stupidity, though we should beware of taking the strictures of contemporary commentators such as Gerald of Wales or Matthew Paris at face value. But most were at least competent, some outstanding. Many were concerned to raise pastoral standards within their diocese: in Scotland, Bishop David de Bernham of St Andrews, a contemporary of Grosseteste, did much to promote good practice among his clergy, and another contemporary, Thomas Wallensis of St Davids, was similarly noted for his concern for his flock. Moreoever, a number of secular cathedrals were also flourishing centres of learning. Though they did not rival the nascent schools of Paris, Bologna, or even Oxford or Cambridge, Hereford, Salisbury, and Lincoln were able to attract individual scholars of great intellectual power. At the end of the twelfth century, Hereford contained a vibrant community, especially in science, which included a woman *geometra*, Dina, who used an astrolabe to calculate the height of the cathedral tower. These schools did not necessarily coalesce into organized centres, but in 1262 Giles of Bridport, bishop of Salisbury, founded de Vaux College for the study of the liberal arts and theology. Though it never developed into a full-blown university, de Vaux continued to function for many generations, perhaps especially to train priests for the south-western dioceses.

The nature of their job meant that medieval bishops were always on the move, conducting visitations of parishes and monasteries, holding diocesan synods, visiting their estates, consecrating churches, confirming children, though this might, as the author of the *Magna Vita* of St Hugh of Lincoln disapprovingly remarks, entail no more than the perfunctory sprinkling of children without the bishop dismounting from his horse. Even conscientious bishops, and there were none more so than Hugh himself, found it difficult, if not impossible, to do more than cover in a very cursory manner the vast areas of such dioceses as Lincoln or York. On the way, bishops would stay at their own manors, and at episcopal castles or palaces, some of which were of considerable grandeur. Those of Bishop Roger of Salisbury at Devizes and Sherborne rivalled those of the king himself, the bishops of Lincoln controlled a considerable network of palaces, while even in remote St Davids, Bishop Bek (1280–93) rebuilt Llawhaden castle in splendid style. He also maintained castles at St Davids itself and Lamphey, as well as having minor residences scattered throughout the diocese. By the thirteenth century, too, most bishops of England and Wales, including those of St Davids, maintained residences in London. Some bishops were constrained by their other responsibilities, both ecclesiastical and secular. The mighty Henry of Blois, bishop of Winchester, probably spent more time in Rome, Cluny, or on royal business, than he did in his own diocese, while other bishops, particularly curial appointments, were more wilfully negligent.

Following the Norman Conquest of England, new bishops embarked on lavish rebuilding programmes that were sometimes intended to reveal the authority and prestige of the new regime. Two curialist archbishops, John Cumin (1181–1212) and Henry le Blund of London (1213–28), are associated with different stages in the building of, respectively, St Patrick's cathedral and Holy Trinity cathedral in Dublin. In many instances, however, the new churches reflected architectural developments elsewhere in western Europe, such as the Rhineland; and not all rebuilding was consequent on changes in the political landscape. Bishop Urban's twelfth-century rebuilding—which was supported by indulgences granted by the pope and archbishop of Canterbury—of his tiny cathedral at Llandaff was doubtless motivated partly by convenience, but especially by a desire to promote his church and its saints, particularly Teilo and Dyfrig, against the rival claims of St Davids and Hereford. In England, the twelfth-century rebuildings of both Norwich and Canterbury cathedrals followed the success of the cults of St William and St Thomas Becket.

Papal authority and national and local churches

At the apex of Gilbert of Limerick's pyramid stood the pope. The degree of papal intervention—or interference, as kings like William I or Henry II would see it—in the country's ecclesiastical affairs was modulated by the relative strengths of the papacy and secular government. At times of relative papal weakness, as during much of the late eleventh and twelfth centuries, when there was a succession of anti-popes, lay authorities clearly enjoyed more autonomy. Conversely, during times of political turmoil at home, the papacy sometimes had more opportunity for action. Relations were also determined by the policy of individual bishops. Lanfranc stubbornly refused to attend Gregory VII's synods at which papal policy was articulated. Grosseteste saw the Roman curia as the source of all evil within the Church: Archbishops Anselm and Theobald, on the other hand, were prepared to suffer exile for their loyalty to the papal reform programme. Yet Anselm's views were not as clear-cut as this summary implies. He did indeed go into exile rather than abandon his observance of the papal decree of 1099 condemning the lay investiture of clergy with churches and ecclesiastical offices, and forbidding the homage of clergy to laymen. But for him the central issue was that of obedience to the pope, not the intrinsic merits or demerits of papal reform.

Whatever the individual case, the room for papal manoeuvre was especially limited by two factors: first, as Stalin noted centuries later, the papacy had no divisions; secondly, Rome was a long and arduous journey from the British Isles. The roads to Rome were well-trodden, but they were not easy. Even in the best travelling conditions, when local weather and politics alike were favourable, letters and legates took weeks to arrive. Papal involvement in national ecclesiastical affairs, therefore, was always conducted at one remove, either through the employment of papal legates, whose authority in theory—and sometimes in practice—trumped that of the metropolitans, or by the use at local level of papal judges-delegate appointed to hear and determine ecclesiastical lawsuits. The native legate, Bishop Christian (Gilla Crist) of Lismore, is associated with Henry II's council at Cashel in 1171–2. But these solutions were not perfect: papal legates might be foreign appointments and hence occasion resentment; and if they were local, their own agenda sometimes overrode papal policy, as happened, for example, during the legateship of Henry of Blois. Papal policy might also be conveyed via bishops who visited Rome to attend synods or, in the case of metropolitans, to collect their *pallium*, the stole that signified their authority. A third channel, and one that was perhaps ultimately the most effective means of transmitting policy to the localities, was the general papal council. This period saw six, four at the Lateran palace, and two at Lyons, of which the Fourth Lateran Council (1215) was the most significant. Nine English bishops, two Welsh, and about twenty Irish attended, besides abbots of some of the most considerable monasteries in the British Isles. But it was not just their presence at Rome in 1215 which brought the papal programme home: it was the continuing incorporation of this policy into diocesan synods, which became a major feature of thirteenth-century episcopal legislation.

In other less beneficial ways, the papacy became increasingly involved in the local Church. Papal taxation, often collected on the pretext of funding a crusade, could be onerous and was resented. Even more insidious was the practice of papal provision, whereby the pope appointed his nominees, a number of them Italian, to clerical positions, particularly to prebends in cathedrals. This has often been seen by both contemporary and modern commentators as the most harmful impact of papal interference, which sometimes occasioned physical violence. Certainly, most of these appointments were absentees, many were foreigners, but pluralism and absenteeism were rife everywhere, and it can be argued that the practice of appropriating parish churches to monasteries, as happened to over one-third of English and a staggering 86 per cent of Scottish parishes, was at least as conducive as papal provision to poor arrangements for the cure of souls. Episcopal insistence that adequate provision should be made for the parishioners where the rectory was appropriated in this way may have lagged behind the actual growth of appropriation.

Yet even as the papacy extended its universal authority, it might also contribute to the creation of national, secular identities. In 1192 Celestine III declared that the *Ecclesia Scoticana* was subject to the papacy alone and was free from the primatial claims of York. Though thereafter the papacy might seek to achieve accord between the two kingdoms, or support English claims to sovereignty, the acknowledgement of the theoretical existence of an autonomous Scottish Church may have contributed to the development of ideas of Scottish national sovereignty.

The Church in medieval Britain and Ireland was marked, as everywhere in western Christendom, by a quickening trend from localization to centralization. It had always had a theoretical claim to a supranational universality, but it was only following the emergence of a revitalized papacy that this could become fully operative. This process can be seen over a wide spectrum. Church or canon law was increasingly codified and given universal validity, a process that culminated in Gratian's great 'concord of discordant canons', or *Decretum* (*c.*1140), and its expansion by Gregory IX in the *Decretals* of 1234. Churches were increasingly dedicated to, and children named after, universal saints. Homogeneity was also encouraged by the growth of international monastic orders, most notably the Cistercian, with its carefully articulated rule, and elaborate system of visitations that ultimately led back to Cîteaux itself. Individuals and communities crossed permeable national boundaries. A number of Anglo-Norman monasteries received Norman monks, not least in order to further the Conquest. Anglo-Norman monks from Canterbury were brought to Dunfermline, and other individual monks from English houses were appointed bishops of newly subjugated Celtic lands. After an adventurous career which included service with the Norwegian king, Turgot, who was English, became a monk at Durham, and then bishop of St Andrews. Bishop David of Bangor had been a clerk of the emperor Henry V. Monks from Clairvaux settled at Rievaulx. Cistercians from Yorkshire established abbeys in Norway in the 1140s. At least one Irish monastery was colonized by Welsh monks. Early in the twelfth century, Irish monks founded St James's Abbey, Regensburg, and its daughter houses in southern Germany. Regensburg monks, who may have been Irish or German, returned to colonize Cashel, while monks from Würzburg founded another abbey at Ross Carberry. Such ethnic heterogeneity could lead to trouble, as it did in some English monasteries after the Conquest, and in the Cistercian houses of Ireland. Here, long-standing tensions between Irish monks and abbots, on the one hand, and Anglo-French, on the other, culminated in a full-scale rebellion by Mellifont and its daughter houses against Cistercian authority. At his subsequent visitation (1228), Stephen of Lexington brought in new French and English monks, insisted that all monks, whatever their nationality, confess in French or Latin, and ordered that the rule should be expounded in French and Irish monks encouraged to study abroad. Stephen was a member of an extraordinary family of apparatchiks: one brother was a curialist of Henry III, another was a royal justice. The political ascendancy now belonged to England, ecclesiastical ascendancy to Rome, cultural ascendancy to France. Stephen's visitation illustrates in microcosm the new order of the thirteenth century.

Figure 6 The Lismore crozier was made (so the inscription on it tells us) for Mac Meic Áeducáin, bishop of Lismore from 1090 to 1113. The wooden core was covered with sheets of bronze, decorated with gold filigree and coloured glass. The monsters that make up the crest have parallels in other Irish metalwork of the period. The crozier was designed as a reliquary: a cavity in the crest contained a tiny piece of wood and in the crook were found a scrap of cloth and a further reliquary in the shape of a small bronze box.

5

Cultural affinities

Henrietta Leyser

'So William became King', wrote Eadmer, monk of Canterbury, of the events of 1066; 'what treatment he meted out to those leaders of the English who managed to survive the great slaughter, as it could do no good, I forbear to tell.'[1] Eadmer's pursed lips need no special explanation. Within a year of the Conquest the Anglo-Saxon cathedral at Canterbury had been gutted by fire (possibly by arsonists). Within three years of this event, Eadmer had to submit to the leadership of an archbishop, Lanfranc, whose initial plans made few concessions either to the architectural or to the liturgical traditions of the Anglo-Saxons. Having accepted perhaps with some reluctance, the English oddity of a cathedral staffed by monks, Lanfranc had begun to erect a building of the same dimensions as his church at Caen, with stone from Caen, to provide it with a calendar that would as far as possible match that of his former monastery at Bec, and to introduce new constitutions modelled on those of Cluny, the great Burgundian abbey which became the pattern of reform for Norman monasteries in the eleventh century.

Not so long ago historians took the speed and resolution displayed by Lanfranc in his early years as archbishop as evidence of the decadent and stagnant character of the Anglo-Saxon Church in particular, and in general of the efficiency of the new regime. Despite the emphasis of revisionist historians on the vitality of the institutions of pre-Conquest England, the suspicion still lingers that culturally England was something of a backwater in the eleventh century and that despite the benefits this 'first entry into Europe' would bring, it

---

[1] *Eadmer's History of Recent Events in England*, trans. G. Bosanquet (Philadelphia, 1964), 9.

would never catch up, could never hope to match the achievements of France. Furthermore, even if early eleventh-century Britain and Ireland had been bound together by the trade routes of the Anglo-Scandinavian empire, in the new Anglo-Norman era the Celtic and Gaelic kingdoms were destined to sink back into their particular corner of what was already a remote part of the world. Yet whatever currency such views have gained, it is doubtful if Lanfranc himself would have recognized them.

Texts and languages, old and new

In the years 1066–70, when still abbot of Caen, Lanfranc would already have come to know something of the splendours of the church over which he was to rule: Caen in particular was the recipient of much of the ecclesiastical booty William I distributed throughout Europe. It received gifts 'so precious in both material and workmanship that they deserve to be remembered to the end of time'.[2] As archbishop, Lanfranc defended with vehemence the dignity and privileges of his new position, insisting on an authority that extended not simply over York, but over the whole of the British Isles. This claim he could buttress only with reference to the Anglo-Saxon past, to a very particular reading of Bede's *Ecclesiastical History*, laced with a generous helping of fantasy and forgery—it is in the Anglo-Norman hagiography of Goscelin, a monk of Saint-Bertin who spent his later years at Canterbury, that Canterbury's first archbishop, St Augustine, becomes a preacher in both Ireland and Northumbria 'embracing the other world of the British ocean with his apostolate'. For this was the paradox of conquest. Throughout the country, newly built cathedrals and castles gave evidence of Norman power and military might exercised by foreigners who yet insisted the inheritance of Edward the Confessor was legitimately theirs: how else indeed to defend an act of acquisition that to many contemporaries smacked so clearly of barefaced robbery?

The alleged lawfulness of the Conquest and of the rights it was

---

[2] *The Gesta Guillelmi of William of Poitiers*, ed. and trans. R. H. C. Davis and M. Chibnall (Oxford Medieval Texts; 1998), ii. 42.

thought to bestow were easier to proclaim than to prove. In the end, the legitimacy of William's claim was demonstrated by obliterating the reign of Harold from the official record. Rights in land were to be proved or disproved with reference to the state of affairs on the day of Edward the Confessor's death (5 January 1066). Not the least of the Normans' problems in this rewriting of history and of the English in coming to terms with it was the lack of the necessary documentation. Eadmer in the 1090s noted how 'men of the present day under stress of difficulties of one kind or another search laboriously into the doings of their predecessors, anxious to find there a source of comfort and strength and yet, because of the scarcity of written documents which has resulted in the events being all too quickly buried in oblivion, they cannot for all their pains succeed in doing so as they would wish'.[3] For despite the sophistication of the Anglo-Saxon state, it still belonged, in Michael Clanchy's terminology, to an age of memory rather than of written record. The distinction is vital, not only because it makes intelligible many of the disputes of the Anglo-Norman period, but above all because it throws light on how it could ever have been possible to see eleventh-century England as intellectually isolated, rescued from barbarity only by Norman longships.

The transition from memory to written record has to be set, not in an English or Norman, but in a European context. Europe in the eleventh century has been described by Karl Leyser as being on the eve of its 'first revolution'. This was a revolution that depended on the circulation of new texts, on the reinterpretation of old sources, on the making of new histories. It is here that the foundations of the twelfth-century renaissance were laid. At stake were shifts from ritual to law, from custom to codification, from self-government to centralization. The pope played a key role in these events. Rome inspired a vision of a Europe united by faith, by a uniform liturgy, and by the precepts of canon law; significantly, William fought at Hastings under a papal banner. And when some few years later his appointees as abbots began to import patristic texts into their new libraries, they did so not because of their horror at not finding them in England—for in many cases they were not available in Normandy either—but simply because of the renewed interest in such texts across Europe. Nor were England's intellectual links at this time only

---

[3] *Eadmer's History of Recent Events in England*, trans. G. Bosanquet, 1.

with Normandy. Abbot Baldwin of Bury St Edmunds (1065–97/8), who was very active in acquiring such texts for Bury, made full use in doing so of his links with the monastery of St Denis in Paris, where he had been a monk before coming to England in the 1050s.

The flurry of scribal activity in late eleventh- and twelfth-century England was, then, fuelled by the dovetailing of a European movement with the particular needs of a new ruling class. The new legal texts translating Anglo-Saxon legislation into French and Latin belonged to the same movement and likewise served the needs of England's new rulers. They demonstrated the intention of the Anglo-Norman kings to uphold the law which they inherited from their Anglo-Saxon predecessors. The tract known as *Leges Edwardi Confessoris* (*Laws of Edward the Confessor*) has attracted attention not least because there was, in Edward the Confessor's reign, no such text. The title, however, was added very late, and the text itself can probably be accepted as a genuine work of the early twelfth century. A mere glance at these compilations alerts the reader to a consequence of the Conquest it is high time to address: the introduction into the language of the new ruling class and of government of a new vernacular, French, and of a new role for Latin.

Pre-Conquest Britain, for all its many links, cultural and political, with continental Europe, was in the use it made of its vernaculars odd. Anglo-Saxon, the language of government in England, coexisted with Welsh, Cornish, Norse, Cumbric, and Gaelic—none Romance languages. For such speakers, Latin had always been a strange, alien, and bookish tongue. It was his despair at the Latin learning of his subjects that had made King Alfred (871–99) so vigorously promote translations into Anglo-Saxon of those texts he considered it 'the most necessary for all men to know'. This led also to his sponsoring the compilation of that work of 'national' history, the Anglo-Saxon Chronicle. An offshoot of this Alfredian Renaissance is the collecting together sometime around 1000 of vernacular works of poetry and prose, most notably of *Beowulf*. The French-speaking conquerors of 1066 found none of this intelligible: to their ears Anglo-Saxon was barbaric and uncouth. Despite the ways in which this linguistic divide could be bridged—by, for example, the use of professional interpreters—and the existence, quite soon, of mixed marriages whose offspring were exposed to both languages, the gulf that now opened on this account between newcomers and natives was deep and much resented. It threatened to split religious communities and to create an underclass: witness the traumatic scene at Christ Church, Canterbury in 1076 when a monk went mad and the bewildered bystanders could not understand each other. And witness, too, the bitterness of Brihtric, priest of Haselbury Plucknett, in Somerset, when the local hermit, Wulfric, enabled a dumb man to speak both French and English, for Brihtric himself spoke only English, and, as he said, could never speak in the presence of the higher clergy.

The miracle giving speech to the dumb man occurred in the first half of the twelfth century; by the end of the century bilingualism would not have been so unusual; nor perhaps would Haselbury Plucknett's priest have felt so isolated. For English was now not only, in Ian Short's phrase, the 'class-inclusive vernacular' of the native English, but also of the French-speaking minority, who now learnt French because it was the genteel language. Among the minority, some of the higher clergy were now, to our knowledge, trilingual, and unlike those known to Brihtric, willing to speak in each language as appropriate. Abbot Samson of Bury St Edmunds (1182–1211), as we are told by Jocelin of Brakelond, spoke well in French and Latin, and could read English 'most elegantly', but spoke in his native Norfolk dialect when preaching to the people. However, as this reference to Abbot Samson implies, to speak English was one thing, to read it quite another. To write it was different again, and soon after the Conquest, English lost, together with its status as the language of government, its status as the language of historical record, the Anglo-Saxon Chronicle withering in sure and steady stages—1066, 1079, 1130, 1154, each marking the death of local versions that formerly had comprised the corpus.

By 1154 the traditions the Anglo-Saxon Chronicle had represented long seemed outmoded, both in style and in stance. Within a decade of the Conquest, those Norman 'spin-doctors' William of Poitiers and William of Jumièges had completed tendentious, highly wrought Latin histories of the Normans and their deeds, designed to blacken King Harold and to legitimize William's invasion and conquest of England. No less learned but different in tone were the works of historians of the next generation, notably William of Malmesbury and Henry, archdeacon of Huntingdon, for whom it no longer seemed so clear that Saxons were bad and Normans good. The conflicts, suspicions, and animosities so characteristic of the immediate post-Conquest years were now giving way to various attempts at integration. The marriage of Henry I to Edith/Mathilda, great-great niece of Edward the Confessor, was a union which could be interpreted as fulfilling Edward's prophecy as he lay dying that peace would come again to England when the truncated green tree he had seen in his dreams, was reassembled and began again to 'bear fruit from the old love of its uniting sap'.[4] Moreover, as if to promote the example of his own marriage, Henry is said to have arranged other such matches 'and by all other means he could contrive, federated the two peoples in firm amity'.[5] William of Malmesbury himself was the child of just such a mixed marriage; so too was Henry of Huntingdon. For both men what mattered was not the immediate aftermath of conquest but how now to appropriate and claim the Anglo-Saxon past. William's sense of himself as the heir of England's first national historian, Bede, sent him both into the archives of his monastery and on travels all over England. Unusually, England already had in the Old English *Secgnan* a gazetteer of saints' names, their cult centres, and notable topographical features. William, in his *History of the English Bishops*, takes this much further, giving histories of every diocese, descriptions of the situation and buildings of each see, evaluations of every saint. Henry of Huntingdon likewise relies heavily on Bede, as indeed his patron Bishop Alexander of Lincoln had requested he do. Henry is also an advocate of direct observation: readers should themselves be pilgrims and he is happy to suggest shrines to visit. In all of this it is possible to perceive something of the spirit that lay behind the Domesday Survey in 1086 and the commissioning of Domesday Book, the desire, that is, to know inch by inch just what the country that had fallen so precipitately into Norman hands held—how many pigs, how many oxen, how many saints, how many kings, how much history.

---

[4] *The Life of King Edward who Rests at Westminster*, ed. and trans. F. Barlow (Oxford Medieval Texts; 1992), 118–19.

[5] Walter Map, *De Nugis Curialium (Courtiers' Trifles)*, ed. and trans. M. R. James, rev. C. N. L. Brooke and R. A. B. Mynors (Oxford Medieval Texts; 1983), 436–7.

New perspectives

How much history: but whose history was it? Arguably, the greatest of all the Anglo-Norman historians was Orderic Vitalis (1075–c.1142), again a child of a mixed marriage and a disciple of Bede's, but who unlike either William of Malmesbury or Henry of Huntingdon, spent his working life in Normandy, having been sent at the age of 10 to become an oblate at the monastery of St Evroul. Orderic's *Ecclesiastical History*, despite its scope and the attention paid in it to England, was nonetheless written in the first instance for the monks of Orderic's house. It is possible—and has indeed been argued—that for Orderic England and Normandy were one, culturally and politically. Yet already in his lifetime it is possible to detect the emergence of a new Anglo-Norman identity that rests on a crucial distinction between Norman English and the Normans of the Continent; this identity, moreover, depended for its articulation on the creation of further distinctions between English and Britons.

The histories of both William of Malmesbury and Henry of Huntingdon were in content decisively Anglocentric. When Henry referred to 'our kingdom', the kingdom was England; when William wrote about 'our people', he meant the English. Henry refers many times to the island of Britain. Yet he also tells his readers that 'Britain' is the name formerly given to 'England'. In William's vocabulary, the name 'Britain' belongs to antiquity. He acknowledges, to be sure, the existence of peoples living beyond the confines of England; but those who lived there were perceived by him to inhabit a different and inferior cultural zone: in short, they were 'barbarians'. William uses this term explicitly to describe the Welsh and Scots and inferentially the Irish. 'What would Ireland be worth,' he asks, 'without the goods that come in by sea from England? The soil lacks all advantages, and so poor, or rather unskilful, are its cultivators that it can produce only a ragged mob of rustic Irishmen outside the towns; the English and the French, with their more civilized way of life, live in the towns and carry on trade and commerce.'[6] By the mid-twelfth century, such

[6] William of Malmesbury, *Gesta Regum Anglorum* (*History of the English Kings*), i, ed. and trans. R. A. B. Mynors, R. Thomson, and M. Winterbottom (Oxford Medieval Texts; 1998), 738–41.

views were commonplace. Thus to John of Salisbury, the Welsh were 'rude and untamed'; the Scots were to William of Newburgh 'an uncivilized race', and their 'uncontrolled savagery made them thirst for blood'; the Irish, according to Gerald of Wales, were 'so barbarous that they cannot be said to have any culture'.

Reasons for the rhetoric that equated Briton with barbarian are not hard to find: such views typically justify intervention and conquest. In the work both of Orderic Vitalis and of William of Malmesbury, it was the English themselves who, despite a promising start, had by 1066 sunk to such a state of decadence and ignorance that they were in need of reform at Norman hands. Some hundred years later, this newly invigorated English people would in turn 'civilize' their neighbours. Rhetoric of this kind invites and deserves scepticism. As ever, there is a more complicated picture to be drawn.

Let us begin with the 'barbarians' of Scotland. Of especial interest here is the way in which, already in the late eleventh century, the kings and aristocracy of lowland and especially eastern Scotland formed links of kinds that would make it possible eventually for them to be represented and to represent themselves as Francophile. Queen Margaret of Scotland, who was herself of English descent, the sister of Edgar Atheling, is portrayed by Turgot, her biographer, as bringing learning, culture, and church reform to the court and kingdom of her illiterate husband, Malcolm III, all for the greater glory of God and the dignity of the royal house, and all tending, as we can see, towards a new cosmopolitanism. Encouraged by her, merchants came by land and sea from diverse countries, bringing with them many precious kinds of merchandise unknown before in Scotland. At the instigation of the Queen, the natives bought garments of various colours and different kinds of personal ornaments. 'Arrayed at her instigation in different refinements of dress, they bore themselves so that they seemed to have been in some sense reformed by this elegance.'[7] Margaret's part in the early growth of Scotland's trading networks was perhaps less than Turgot believed. Nonetheless, in this period, courts and monasteries were important centres of demand for merchants, and Margaret was a queen and the patron of monasteries. In Turgot's words we glimpse a luxury, international trade, serving new cultural needs.

---

[7] *Early Sources of Scottish History, A.D. 500 to 1286*, ed. A. O. Anderson, repr., ed. M. O. Anderson (Stamford, 1990), ii. 68.

When Margaret died, she was buried at the Benedictine priory of Dunfermline, a house she herself had founded, and whose first monks had come, with Lanfranc's blessing, from Canterbury. In the event, the new orders arriving in the twelfth century, proved to be much more influential in the religious life of Scotland than the Benedictines. Yet a scene had been set which enabled lowland Scots to keep abreast of and even to rival the cultural and religious changes being introduced into England, and eventually to regard some of their compatriots, the men of Galloway and Argyll, with a degree of contempt on account of their lack of polish and indeed their 'barbarism'. Such men spoke 'Gaelic' or 'Erse' (Irish), whereas lowland Scots spoke—and in the fourteenth century wrote—'Inglis': this is the language of Barbour's epic, *The Bruce*. We have practically no earlier vernacular literature from Scotland, but in the stirring poem by Jordan Fantosme on the 1173/4 rebellion of the Young King Henry, aided and abetted by William of Scotland, particular condemnation is reserved for the men of Galloway and the north who disregarded William's command that the Church be spared. 'That miserable race, on whom be God's curse, the Gallovidians, who covet wealth, and the Scots who dwell north of the Forth have no faith in God, the son of Mary: destroy churches and indulge in wholesale robbery.'[8] Likewise in *The Romance of Fergus* (c.1209), an Arthurian story set wholly in Scotland, the eponymous hero, Fergus of Galloway, is depicted as something of a buffoon, a rustic simpleton whose upbringing has in no way prepared him for civilized society.

The Romance of Fergus was long assumed to be of French provenance, on no grounds other than that it was written in French. It is, however, possible, as proposed by D. D. R. Owen, that its author was William Malveisin, bishop of Glasgow and subsequently of St Andrews (d. 1238). This suggestion is of particular interest, since it may also have been William who was responsible for the completion of the St Andrew's *Music Book*, a work owing much to compositions from Notre Dame in Paris. Taken together, Fergus and the *Music Book* can be seen as giving colouring to the charge levelled some years earlier against King William (d. 1214) to the effect that he was more French than Scottish. Whatever the resentments such criticism may

[8] *Jordan Fantosme's Chronicle*, ed. and trans. R. C. Johnston (Oxford, 1981), lines 684–8.

suggest, there can be no doubt that it was in fact the skilful manoeuv-rings and alliances of Scottish rulers that enabled them to integrate Anglo-Norman settlers, to imitate their ways, and yet to keep a measure of independence: indeed, the Anglo-Normans in Scotland were in a real sense Scotticized. A striking sign of the rulers' success came in 1192, when Pope Celestine III finally declared the Church of Scotland to be the 'special daughter' of the papacy and as such free from the jurisdiction of the archbishops of either Canterbury or York. Some fifty years later, in 1249, we can observe the fusion of old and new in the inauguration rites of Alexander III at Scone. The bishop of St Andrews, together with the bishop of Dunkeld and the abbot of Scone, participated and, although it is unlikely that the king was crowned, the archbishop of St Andrews may have laid hands on him. Following ancient tradition, however, the royal pedigree was recited by the king's poet. In the succession crisis that followed Alexander's death in 1286, it was St Andrew himself who was depicted on the seal of the Guardians and declared to be the 'leader of the compatriot Scots'.

In Ireland, as in Scotland, the desire for independence from the English metropolitan, culminating in the recognition of the primacy of Armagh in the mid-twelfth century, had more than ecclesiastical support. Here, too, the issues were in part political, but above all they were cultural. Twelfth-century Ireland, *pace* Gerald of Wales, was not a land full of the strange marvels and outlandish happenings with which he filled his *History and Topography of Ireland*—as, for example, the cow which, not long before the coming of the English, had intercourse with a man and gave birth to a man-calf in the mountains around Glendalough. Nor were its inhabitants 'a wild and inhospitable people', of whom it could be said 'All their habits are the habits of barbarians'.[9] There is, nonetheless, a sense in which it can be claimed that the Irish were 'different': never having been conquered by Romans, they had taken to classical learning (via Christianity) with avidity while still preserving their vernacular culture. According to early Irish law, kings, clergy, and poets shared a privileged and sacred status; it is no accident that from nowhere else in early medieval Europe has so much vernacular literature survived. But to

---

[9] Gerald of Wales, *History and Topography of Ireland*, trans. J. J. O'Meara (Harmondsworth, 1982), 101–2.

acknowledge the richness of its native culture is not to suggest that the Irish were insular or 'primitive'. Thus, many of the seeming peculiarities of Irish law once attributed to archaic Irish practice have now been traced to Old Testament sources; similarly, sheelanagigs, those carved images of women with large vaginas that adorn a number of Irish churches are not, it now transpires, ancient Irish fertility symbols but imports from twelfth-century France. It is with such cautionary tales in mind that we need to approach the cultural survivals of medieval Ireland.

Twelfth-century Ireland did not need the Normans to become a player on the European scene. The coming of the Cistercians has been looked at elsewhere in this volume, but there were many other links with the Continent besides those furnished by the white monks. Irish kings were a cosmopolitan lot with interests in the exotic—trophies include a fragment of the True Cross and a camel—and a fondness for pilgrimages to Rome. Romanesque churches (most notably Cormac's chapel on the Rock of Cashel) bear witness to the eclectic tastes of travelled patrons (see Figure 11). Despite the undoubted damage caused earlier by Vikings, in the late eleventh century and the early twelfth, Irish centres of learning were again flourishing. School-books from Glendalough point to a study of traditional texts that was continuing alongside that of newer works, such as Chalcidius' trans-lation of Plato's *Timaeus*. The year 1174 saw the death of Flann Ua Gormáin, arch-lector of Armagh, a man who, so his obituary tells us, had spent 'twenty-one years learning among the Franks and Saxons and twenty years directing the schools of Ireland'.[10] Manuscript evi-dence, in the form of lecture notes, suggests that in the 1130s Flann Ua Gormáin had been in Paris at the feet of Peter Lombard. Against this background it is not surprising to find in Ireland, as elsewhere in Europe, scribes and scholars whose interest in the past was matched only by their excitement at the intellectual developments of the present and whose concern was to make of the two seamless cloth.

Three great manuscript collections extant from twelfth-century Ireland—the *Book of the Taking*, the *Book of the Dun Cow*, and the *Book of Leinster*—contain between them a wealth of vernacular legend and lore, notably tales of the heroes Finn and Cu Chulainn

---

[10] Quoted in M. Richter, 'The European dimension of Irish history in the eleventh and twelfth centuries', *Peritia*, 4 (1985), 328–45, at p. 338.

and of dwellers from the Otherworld. According to Áed, the abbot of Terryglass responsible for the *Book of Leinster*, 'some things in it are the delusions of devils, some things are poetic images, some things are like truth, some not, and some things are for the pleasure of fools'.[11] Modern scholars debate how far these collections represent ancient, faithfully transmitted oral sources, and how far they have been decisively reshaped to accord with the twelfth century's renewed interest in classical tales and methods of composition. Irish metal-work perhaps presents an appropriate parallel, for it was in the eleventh and twelfth centuries that much care, expense, and artistic skill was lavished on old treasures. Thus, the iron bell that was believed to be St Patrick's was given a costly new shrine, built of bronze plates decorated with gold and silver filigree; the Lismore crozier, the staff of St Carthach (d. 637), was likewise adorned in gold and silver with red, white, and blue millefiori on the crook, biting beasts on the crest.

How Irish culture and society would have developed but for the English campaigns of 1169–71 and the subsequent English settlement we cannot know. What is certain is that the invasion left deep scars and divisions and led to an intensified sense of what it meant to be Gaelic Irish as opposed to Anglo-Irish. The lack of Irish manuscript collections comparable to those which have been mentioned, and datable to the period *c.*1150 to *c.*1350, may be fortuitous in the present context; equally, it may indicate that writing in the vernacular slowed down in this period. As for the new conquerors and settlers, unlike the Normans in England, they did not succeed in appropriating the native past, and, as far as we know, made no attempt to do so. Gerald of Wales's summing up of the situation in his *Conquest of Ireland*, written just before the death of Henry II, captures the mood of imperial intransigence and sheer lack of comprehension that lay behind the system of cultural and political apartheid finally enshrined in the Statutes of Kilkenny (1366). In Gerald's view, the Irish 'deserved to suffer the confusion attendant on invasion and conquest by foreigners, since their misdemeanours and vile practices demanded this punishment'.[12] Much would happen in Ireland— including, regionally, much peaceful if uneasy coexistence of Irish

[11] Quoted in K. Hughes, *The Church in Early Irish Society* (London, 1966; repr. 1980), 273.

[12] Gerald of Wales, *Expugnatio Hibernica* (*Conquest of Ireland*), ed. and trans. A. B. Scott and F. X. Martin (Dublin, 1978), 23.

and English—before it was prescribed at Kilkenny that Englishmen, under pain of losing their status as such, were to avoid 'the manners, dress and language of the Irish enemies'. But Gerald's intemperate language shows that this fourteenth-century attitude had deep ideological roots in the past.

For a view now from the perspective, not of conquerors, but of those threatened by conquest, let us move to Wales. One of the most moving laments provoked by the Norman Conquest is the poem of Rhigyfarch the Wise, eldest of the four sons of Sulien, bishop of St Davids. Sulien is described in his obituary (1091) as 'the most learned and most pious of the bishops of the Britons, and the most praiseworthy for the instruction of his disciples and his parishes'. Rhigyfarch's brother, Ieuan, attributed their father's learning to his visits to both Scotland and Ireland whence he had returned 'storing the treasure in his shrewd mind'. Their own work testifies, in Ceri Davies's phrase, to the 'vibrancy of Latin learning' in Wales on the eve of the Norman Conquest. Thus, in Rhigyfarch's *planctus* clear echoes can be heard of the despair felt by Boethius at the end of Roman civilization:

Why have the blind fates not let us die? Why does the earth not consume us, nor the sea swallow us? Now an unheard-of rumour comes to our ears: it says that free necks are subjected to the yoke. Nothing is of any use to me now, but the power of giving: neither the law, nor learning, nor great fame, nor the deep-resounding glory of nobility, not honour formerly held, not riches, not wise teaching, nor deeds nor arts, not reverence of God, not old age; none of these things retains its station, nor any power. Now the labours of earlier days lie despised; the people and the priest are despised by the word, heart and work of the Normans.[13]

Over the next two hundred years, such strains were to be repeated, and there were to be frequent expressions of Welsh hatred of Anglo-Norman power. *The Chronicle of the Welsh Princes*, for example, speaks of how unbearable were 'the tyranny, injustice, violence and oppression of the French'.[14] Yet the Welsh were able to maintain and develop a cultural identity that both drew on and inspired scholars and poets across Europe.

---

[13] Quoted in C. Davies, *Welsh Literature and the Classical Tradition* (Cardiff, 1995), 26; see also ibid. 16, 18.
[14] Quoted in R. R. Davies, *Domination and Conquest: The Experience of Ireland, Scotland and Wales 1100–1300* (Cambridge, 1990), 27.

To address the controversies that surround the production of Welsh vernacular literature in this period is a gargantuan task; and it is necessary at the outset to distinguish between the prose works, notably *The Four Branches of the Mabinogi* and the poetry of the court bards, the Gogynfeirdd. Let us begin with the poetry. Traditionally, the first of the Gogynfeirdd, is Meilyr Brydydd (*fl.* 1100–37), chief poet to Gruffudd ap Cynan, prince of Gwynedd (1095–1137), a ruler whose career and fame as victim, captive, and ally of the Anglo-Normans bear witness both to the intricacies of Anglo-Welsh politics and to the vitality of the court culture of Gwynedd. Anglo-Norman historians, including Orderic Vitalis, barely mention Gruffudd, but in Wales, within decades of his death, a Latin biography, later translated into Welsh, depicted him as a renaissance prince, a ruler of Trojan ancestry, the protector of lesser kings, a stern fighter but also the patron of gardens and orchards and of so many churches that they shone throughout Gwynedd like stars in the firmament. And in the elegy composed for him by Meilyr, Gruffudd is 'the hope of lands', 'leader of the Welsh', and capable of sending packing a king of England.[15]

Gruffudd's descendants managed to hold power throughout the twelfth and much of the thirteenth centuries. Praises for his dynasty and for Wales continued to be sung by the Gogynfeirdd—of whom we have the names of thirty-four—until ultimately in 1282, when Llywelyn ap Gruffudd was killed in revolt against Edward I and the time came instead for lamentations:

> With Llywelyn's death, gone is my mind,
> Heart frozen in the breast with terror,
> Desire decays like dried-up branches.
> See you not the rush of wind and rain?
> See you not the oaks lash each other?
> See you not the ocean scouring the shore?
> See you not the sun hurtling the sky?
> See you not that the stars have fallen?
> Have you no belief in God, foolish men?
> See you not that the world is ending?[16]

[15] *Gruffudd ap Cynan: A Collaborative Biography*, ed. K. L. Maund (Woodbridge, 1996), 182–6; and see also *History of Gruffudd ap Cynan (1054–1137)*, ed. and trans. A. Jones (Manchester, 1910), 154–5.

[16] Gruffudd ap yr Ynad, trans. in *The Oxford Book of Welsh Verse in English*, ed. G. Jones (Oxford, 1977), 32.

The apocalypticism here is reminiscent of Rhigyfarch ap Sulien's *planctus*; yet even when all allowances have been made for poetic licence, there can be no need to dismiss as mere rhetoric the anguish of either writer. But nor should the poignancy of their verse be allowed to simplify the very complex relationship between England and Wales in the centuries between them, years of cooperation as well as of conflict. And here, ecclesiastical politics, as in Scotland and in Ireland, had their role to play. If we return for a moment to the first of the Gogynfeirdd, Meilyr Brydydd, and to Gruffudd and his court, we pick up a sense of jarring contradictions.

Meilyr died in about 1137. He had asked to be buried on the Island of Bardsey, a famed pilgrimage site off the coast of north Wales, reputedly the resting place of the bodies of twenty thousand saints that thus deserved the name 'the Rome of Britain'. In 1120, in a ceremony at which Meilyr was probably present and Gruffudd most certainly was, the relics of St Dyfrig (in Latin Dubricius), purportedly a sixth-century prelate of Llandaff, were translated from Bardsey to Llandaff. Urban, bishop of Llandaff at the time, was an empire-builder: three times he went to Rome in an effort to create and consolidate the rights and privileges of what was for Wales a new-style territorial diocese. His acquisition of Dyfrig's relics was a part of this policy—it gave Urban claims to lands considered to be part of the saint's patrimony. What it was not was any kind of celebration of the independence from England that a Welsh Church of the sixth century had claimed and that in the eleventh and twelfth centuries the bishops of St Davids badly wanted. Urban, in his rivalry with St Davids, did not hesitate to support Canterbury's primacy over Wales. In this he was not alone. In 1120, the year of the translation of Dyfrig's relics, David, Gruffudd's nominee for the see of Bangor, and as such the bishop who was to authorize the translation, was consecrated at Westminster and acknowledged the authority of Canterbury on this occasion. We do not know whether it would have occurred to him to do otherwise. David may have been Welsh by birth—as was Urban—but it would have been hard to find anyone with a more European background. David had been educated at Würzburg in Bavaria. He returned to England, to the court of Henry I, to find himself chosen to accompany the princess Mathilda on her journey to Germany to marry the emperor Henry V; and he was subsequently chosen by Henry V to be the official historian of his expedition to Rome in 1111.

It was with such that Gruffudd's Gogynfeirdd rubbed shoulders; there is good reason to suppose the circle surrounding the prose writers of medieval Wales was every bit as cosmopolitan.

The tales in the *Four Branches of the Mabinogi*, *Pwyll*, *Branwen*, *Manawydan and Math*, are, by contrast, likely to strike the reader as particularly archaic, deeply rooted in Celtic mythology or Indo-European traditions or both. Consider the tale of Rhiannon, heroine of *Pwyll*, in which Rhiannon is wrongfully accused of killing and eating her new-born baby and by way of punishment made for seven years to act as if she was a horse, ready to give rides on her back to visitors from the gate of the court into the great hall. In one interpretation this is explicable only if we know and understand that Rhiannon is descended from the Celtic horse-goddess Epona; the fact that Gerald of Wales in his *Topography of Ireland* claims that king-making rituals of Ulster still include the king-elect having intercourse with a mare, on which he and his people then feast, arguably adding semblance to the idea of lingering horse-worship among the backwoodsmen of Celtic lands. But trawl other, non-Celtic sources, as Jessica Hemming has recently done, and the picture changes. William of Malmesbury and William of Jumièges, it transpires, each describe incidents in which rebellious and contrite sons—in Normandy and Anjou, respectively—have to carry saddles on their backs. Rhiannon's punishment is not, then, or not only, explicable just as some throwback to the Celtic pagan past.

Rhiannon and her saddle point towards the larger question: what was the context in which the Welsh narrative prose of this period was written? We have in all eleven tales besides *The Four Branches*: these include the Arthurian adventure story *Culhwch and Olwen* and three Arthurian romances, particularly notable since each has its counterpart in the more celebrated poems in French by Chrétien de Troyes. Despite the impossibility of accurately dating these texts, literary scholars tend to agree that *Culhwch and Olwen* belongs to a considerably earlier period than the romances. Two further questions therefore must be asked: first, what is the relationship between Geoffrey of Monmouth's best-selling account of Arthur in his *History of the Kings of Britain*, written in Latin *c*.1136, and these vernacular tales; secondly, what is the explanation for the apparent French takeover of a British hero? But first let us consider the region which was such a hothouse of literary production.

Linguistic evidence favours the south-east of Wales as the home of Middle Welsh prose; this is a region that included Glamorgan and Gwent and disputed territory in what is now Herefordshire. In the twelfth century this and the surrounding area were a melting-pot of languages and cultures: Welsh, Norman, English, Breton, Lotharingian. To this brew must be added the various ingredients from Europe which scholars and pilgrims, particularly those who had travelled along the route to St James in Compostella or to St Jean d'Angely had brought with them. Hereford itself had as its bishop a Lotharingian, Robert Losinga (1079–95), described by William of Malmesbury as an abacist and astronomer, and around whom gathered a circle whose influence and interest in the new Arabic learning coming from Spain survived well into the twelfth century and beyond. His interest in mathematics he is likely to have shared not only with his fellow countryman Walcher, a keen astronomer, who was living in England by 1091 and was prior of Great Malvern at the time of his death in 1125, but also with his Welsh neighbours. The manuscript in which Rhygyfarch's *planctus* occurs contains also a correspondence between Raoul of Liège and Ragimbold of Cologne discussing a mathematical problem. The ways in which study of the new mathematics may have influenced local ecclesiastical architecture is not yet clear. But it is perhaps significant that the parish church at Kilpeck, famed as an example of the Herefordshire school of sculpture, and itself indebted both to indigenous traditions and to the newer fashions from western France, is said to have been one of the earliest churches in the region to have had the innovative rib-vault. It is also worth noting the close relationship that exists between the decoration of the new cathedral which Bishop Urban was building for himself at Llandaff in the 1120s and for which he had so recently required the relics of St Dyfrig, and the sculpture of both Kilpeck and Hereford Cathedral.

Geoffrey of Monmouth and Arthurian romance

Middle Welsh prose emanated, then, from an area full of intellectual and cultural excitement. Here, too, belonged Geoffrey of Monmouth, author of the best-selling *History of the Kings of Britain*, a work which traces the rise, apogee under Arthur, and subsequent fall of a British empire. Geoffrey spent much of his life in Oxford, but he was closely associated with south Wales. In all probability his family had come originally from Brittany before settling near Monmouth. Although the British book from which Geoffrey claimed to derive his knowledge is probably a literary fiction, there can be no doubt that Geoffrey would have been well acquainted with the Arthur of Welsh legend and had ready access to native traditions. In Geoffrey's narrative it is at Caerleon-on-Usk, some twenty miles from Monmouth, that Arthur holds court, and it is Dyfrig, now styled primate of Britain, who makes Arthur king. The insoluble problem lies not in spotting Geoffrey's local allegiances but in guessing his wider purpose.

In 1136, at about the time Geoffrey was writing his *History*, the Welsh were seizing the chance offered by the death of Henry I to shake off the rule he had imposed upon them. An invincible hero would have suited them well—and indeed in *Culhwch and Olwen* that is how Arthur, 'chief of the princes of this land', is portrayed. Not so in Geoffrey's *History*. Mighty conqueror though he is, Geoffrey's Arthur ends his life not in glory but in defeat, betrayed by his own nephew, deserted by his wife. The hope that he might come again to lead the Britons to further and final victories is not extinguished, but nor is it unambiguously promised—small wonder, then, that the Welsh, when they came to translate Geoffrey's *History*, added extra text guaranteeing his return. Small wonder, too, that Henry II felt it necessary to lay claim to Arthurian majesty and at the same time to prove once and for all that Arthur was indeed dead and buried and on English soil, by ordering the monks of Glastonbury to find his tomb.

Geoffrey's *History* was many things to many people. It furnished at one and the same time an origin legend for Britain, and an explanation for its demise, a model of kingship and an examination of the human frailty of those who held power. Its success was phenomenal, not least because it provided a backcloth against which the new aristocracies of Europe could elaborate and explore the codes of behaviour and value systems appropriate to their increasingly chivalric world. It has been a long held assumption that the trendsetter of this world was France—home of Capetians, Cistercians, tournaments and crusades, and the cradle of learning. Since the Normans were to be regarded as French, it was axiomatic that one way or another they would bring England up to date. It is time now, still with Arthur in the frame, to look at this picture through a different lens.

In the mid-1150s, a French version of Geoffrey's *History* appeared, the work of Wace, a clerk of Caen. Wace's *Roman de Brut* was not simply a translation: it included an elaborated Arthurian section and, unlike Geoffrey, mentioned the Round Table. Since a copy was presented to Eleanor of Aquitaine, it may soon have become known to Henry II, who had married Eleanor in 1152. But this is not likely to have been Henry's first encounter with Arthur. As a young boy, some 9 or 10 years old, Henry had spent time, perhaps more than a year, in the household of Robert, earl of Gloucester, lord of Glamorgan, the only person to appear three times as a dedicatee in copies of Geoffrey of Monmouth's *History*. There is little or no evidence that the romances of Chrétien de Troyes circulated at the Angevin court in this period. Nevertheless, a passage in *Erec et Enide*, is arresting in this context. The coronation of Erec and Enide takes place at Nantes, where Henry invested his son Geoffrey with the duchy of Brittany in 1169. Those who assembled at Nantes, in Chrétien's poem, came

> from many lands, from diverse places.
> Kings and counts of many races,
> Normans, Bretons, Scots, and all,
> and folk of England and Cornwall,
> great lords from Wales down to Anjou,
> from Germany and from Poitou.
> There was no noble chevalier,
> or lady, sage and debonair,
> none brave, rich, or magnificent,
> who did not gather there at Nantes,
> assembled by the king's decree.[17]

[17] Chrétien de Troyes, *Erec et Enide*, trans. Dorothy Gilbert (Berkeley, 1992), lines 6613–23.

All the best and fairest knights and ladies were at Nantes, summoned by the king. Not named, however, is anyone from the lands of Henry II's rival, the Capetian king of France. Chrétien, like Wace, cast his Arthurian stories in French, not out of any deference to the king of France, but because it was his mother tongue and that of genteel, chivalric society. It was also the tongue of Henry II, the king of England, duke of Normandy, and count of Anjou, who ruled a greater extent of France than the Capetian kings of this period, and that of Eleanor, his queen, whose inheritance also included Poitou.

Chrétien's *Erec et Enide* is one of the three poems already mentioned for which there is an analogue in Middle Welsh prose. It seems unlikely that there will ever be any conclusive way of determining which was written first, and it is arguable that in the last resort this is a question which matters less than the acknowledgement of a shared milieu. Easy interchange between the Welsh, French, and Breton communities of south Wales and the Marches was facilitated by the use of professional interpreters (*latimarii*) whose job it was precisely to act as intermediaries between the different language groups. The fact that ultimately it was with the work of Chrétien rather than anonymous Welshmen that Arthurian romance came to be associated should not blind us to the debt he and others of his circle owed to Celtic sources. The suggestion that Marie de France was a regular visitor to Cardiff Castle may be impossible to prove; yet it is beyond doubt that her *lais* are deeply rooted in the local traditions and geography of south-east Wales. Instantly recognizable too is the Celtic context of the great romance of *Tristan and Isolde*, whose first redactors were the Anglo-Norman Thomas and the Norman Beroul.

To insist on an insular background for these particular master-pieces of medieval European literature is not intended as an exercise in chauvinism but rather as a recognition of internationalism. As Elizabeth Salter has argued, as far as mainstream culture is concerned, what is 'peculiarly English' in the second half of the twelfth century 'is also peculiarly Angevin and to that extent therefore European'.[18] To see England in the twelfth century as an intellectual dependency

---

[18] E. Salter, *English and International: Studies in the Literature, Art and Patronage of Medieval England*, ed. D. Pearsall and N. Zeeman (Cambridge, 1988), 19.

of France is to give it an isolation, both within the British Isles and in relation to the rest of Europe, that it never had. Under the Angevins, England belonged to a closely integrated European setting. The courts of its rulers were cosmopolitan, their literary and their political ambitions far flung. When Diarmait Mac Murchadha left Ireland in 1166 to seek help from Henry II, it was not to England that he went to find the king but to Aquitaine. Royal marriages connected the kings of England to Germany, France, Castile, Sicily. Royal brides, seemingly, took Arthurian stories with them, but there were also new stories to be told, set within ever wider circles. In 1177 Henry and Eleanor's daughter, Joan, married William II of Sicily. At just about the same time the Herefordshire clerk, Hue de Rotelande, wrote for his lord of Monmouth the tale of *Ipomedon*, a romance set in Apulia, Calabria, and Sicily. It was also in the 1170s that Peter of Blois obtained a place in the household of the archbishop of Canterbury, to whom he was chancellor. Peter had first been a student at Bologna and Paris before going to Sicily to be tutor and clerk of the seal to William II. The close resemblance between the figures of St Paul in the chapel of St Anselm at Canterbury—a painting widely considered to be the finest medieval mural to have survived in England—and the Capella of Palatina in Palermo is almost certainly the result of Peter's influence.

New cathedrals and new eclecticism

Canterbury in the 1170s was an exciting place to be. The murder of Thomas Becket in 1170 and the great fire four years later provided a reason and an opportunity to rebuild the cathedral in ways which would glorify the martyr and provide a fitting setting for the many pilgrims who were already flocking to his tomb. This in turn initiated a great wave of cathedral rebuilding across the south of England, similar in scale to that which had followed the Conquest, as bishops strove to update their cathedrals in rivalry with the new Gothic style of Canterbury. How and to what extent the cathedrals of either period simply imported ideas (along with the stone) from across the Channel and how far they were innovative is the topic to which we should now turn.

In the decades after the Conquest, every cathedral in England was rebuilt, every one of them (except Worcester) under the aegis of a bishop newly arrived in the country. Particularly telling was the destruction of the Anglo-Saxon minster at Winchester, the heart of the old kingdom of Wessex, and its supercession by a building of extraordinary length for its time, outstripping even St Peter's in Rome. Like the massive Norman cathedral at Durham, side by side with the castle there, the New Minster, as it was called, at Winchester dominated the city, an overpowering reminder of the conquest which had just taken place. Yet many of these cathedrals looked grander than they were, and design faults, or perhaps jerry-building, caused a number of fiascos. At Winchester itself, in 1107, the new tower collapsed; so too, some four years later, did the tower at Ely. Yet more striking is the determination of the patrons of these new cathedrals to achieve variety and their readiness to make what have been aptly called, by Eric Fernie, 'wayward choices' in pursuit of this end. Winchester, for example, was designed to include all the latest features of both French and German Romanesque. As the eleventh century drew to a close, such choices brought about the return of Anglo-Saxon features. Thus, at the abbey church, later the cathedral, of Ely it is possible to identify two phases of building, the unmoulded arches of the first period (c.1082–93) giving way just decades later to the more decorative style characteristic of Anglo-Saxon taste. Likewise at Canterbury under Anselm (1093–1109), its second archbishop from Normandy, Anglo-Saxon motifs began to appear in, for example, the foliage capitals in the crypt, the inspiration here seemingly coming from Anglo-Saxon manuscripts in the cathedral's library.

It is the second rebuilding of Canterbury Cathedral in this period, beginning c.1175, that truly heralds the arrival of Gothic in England. The master mason chosen for this task was a Frenchman, William of Sens, who from the start seems to have wanted to produce a building as Gothic as he knew how to make it. William had, nonetheless, to work within the constraints imposed both by the surviving fabric of the old cathedral and by the wishes of the community; ironically, it was his successor, William the Englishman, who seems to have been able to work, unhampered, to French designs, and to him fell the building of Becket's shrine chapel. But despite the great prestige of the new building, those who strove to emulate it were not content to be simply imitative. As at St Denis, the great Gothic abbey in Paris, care had been taken at its rebuilding earlier in the century to honour and reclaim the Merovingian past, so too in this later rebuilding of English abbeys and cathedrals was this legitimation by appeal to the past of central importance. Particular rivalries might heighten this concern. In the west of England, for example, the competition between the churches of Wells and Glastonbury, each hoping to become the seat of a bishopric, led to both insisting on the glories of their past at the same time as each strove to create a distinctive architectural character for itself. The abundance of chevron ornament at Glastonbury and its total absence at Wells provide just one example of the contrast between these two buildings. Contrasts have also been drawn between the richness of Lincoln Cathedral and the comparative austerity of Salisbury, as if these two represented different streams of thought within the early thirteenth-century English Church. Perhaps so, but what is most striking is the agreement among architectural historians that English Gothic, after the building of Canterbury, was idiosyncratic, innovative, and barely indebted to France. The loss of Normandy in 1204, the interdict under King John, and the Battle of Bouvines in 1214 are reflected in the architectural record in a new mood of 'Englishness' and insularity—until, that is, the rebuilding of Westminster Abbey under the patronage of Henry III.

Henry III's church at Westminster (see Figure 9) shows the influence of three churches which were all closely associated with the kings of France: Reims Cathedral, the church of St Denis in Paris, and the Sainte-Chapelle there. Intended as a shrine for St Edward the Confessor, it was also to be Henry's own mausoleum, and the central crossing was to provide a worthier theatre for coronations than these ceremonies had enjoyed since they became indissolubly associated with the abbey in the late eleventh century. In short, the rebuilding of the abbey was an attempt to provide English monarchs with an auditorium they had since the Conquest lacked, where the sacrality of kingship, in which Henry III, like his brother-in-law Louis IX of France, fervently believed, could be proclaimed, celebrated, and enhanced. It was hugely expensive, and not all saw the point. Matthew Paris mocked the new church by placing over his drawing of it a stag's head with lolling tongue, to signify the contribution made by forest fines, as he believed, to the sums involved. And he leaves us a little uncertain whether he shares the doubts expressed by some about the authenticity of the relic of the Precious Blood of Christ procured by Henry for his new church, which he reports at length, or accepts Robert Grosseteste's demonstration of its authenticity, which he also reports. We do not know how many were inclined, with Matthew, to mock the king's enterprise in rebuilding the abbey, although we do know that Edward I, Henry's son, never bothered to complete the lantern tower planned by his father to illuminate the coronations of future kings. But Henry III's church at Westminster came much too late, was too expensive, and too closely associated with a questionable ideology of kingship to inspire imitation or topple English Gothic from the eminence it now enjoyed.

Manuscript illumination, like the design of great churches, was subject to many different influences which it is now hard to disentangle. It is, for example, now difficult to discover how far English artists were attracted to Romanesque forms of decoration in the late eleventh century; but we do know that some English scribes—Eadmer among them—learnt to write in Norman script subsequently. Nor did the full development of Romanesque decoration imply an absence of eclectic features. By the mid-twelfth century it had become unusual in England for a monastery to maintain a scriptorium from its own resources, and normal to entrust work to professional scribes and artists, though these might do some of their work in the monastery, and the monks of St Albans Abbey were early exponents of this practice. The St Albans Psalter (c.1120–30), a magnificent example of twelfth-century manuscript art, is famous for, among other splendid features, its cycle of miniatures in the Romanesque style which were the work of a professional artist known today as the Alexis Master. Yet in having full-page illuminated miniatures, it revived an Anglo-Saxon practice, albeit in a style which borrowed now from Flanders, Italy, and Lotharingia (see Figure 7).

The eclectic tastes of the Anglo-Norman elite in this period are illustrated in the artistic patronage of Henry of Blois, abbot of Glastonbury (1126–71), bishop of Winchester (1129–71), who was a grandson of the Conqueror. The Winchester Psalter (completed by 1161) belongs to the years of his episcopate and so do the beginnings, at the very least, of the Winchester Bible; and although neither can be securely attributed to his patronage, both have strong links with his circle. The Psalter, in its iconography—for example, its depiction of the mouth of Hell—and in its layout, owes much to Anglo-Saxon

Figure 7 The St Albans Psalter, p. 70: Christ breaking bread at the supper at Emmaus. The twelfth-century St Albans Psalter revived the Anglo-Saxon tradition of full-page miniatures, while the typically elongated figures are heavily indebted to Ottonian art. The scene of Christ breaking bread at the supper at Emmaus had special relevance to Christina Markyate, the holy woman for whom the Psalter seems to have been especially adapted.

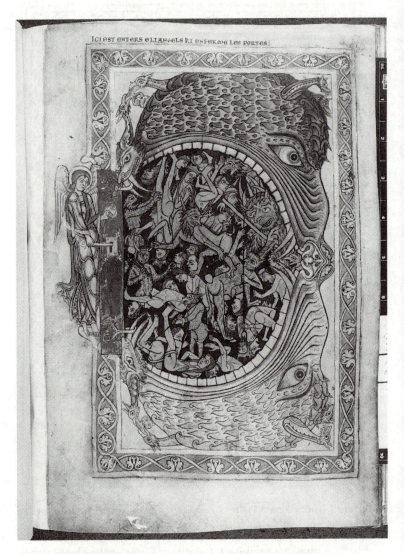

Figure 8 The Winchester Psalter: the vision of Hell. This image, from the twelfth-century Winchester Psalter, of an angel locking the damned into Hell, is a striking example of the continuation into the Anglo-Norman period of Anglo-Saxon iconography, for it is from pre-Conquest sources that the image of Hell as the mouth of an animal is taken. The caption in Old French reads ICI EST ENFERS E LI ANGELS KI ENFERME LES PORTES.

exemplars (see Figure 8). But the Byzantine-style illustrations of Christ and the Virgin may well have been copied from an Eastern diptych. Of the six artists who worked on the Bible, three are also thought to have had direct knowledge of Byzantine art. Although the Bible was never finished, it remains a work of astonishing lavishness and grandeur, a beneficiary, perhaps, of Henry's donation to the cathedral scriptorium in 1170. An enamel plaque made for Henry by a Mosan goldsmith appropriately depicts him prostrate under the inscription 'Henry alive in bronze, gives gifts to God'. Henry, it should not be forgotten, had been educated as a boy at Cluny; from an early age, then, he had become accustomed to the richness of Romanesque—not for him the puritanical tastes that shortly after he took office were being introduced into the north of England and into Scotland, Wales, and Ireland by the Cistercians.

Henry of Blois's interest in dramatic sculpture is attested both by his love for work in black Tournai stone—of which the font in Winchester Cathedral is a particularly fine example—and by the aplomb with which he bought up pagan statues from Rome to take home to adorn his episcopal palace at Wolvesey. Regrettably, neither this palace nor the new buildings Henry oversaw at Glastonbury, where there was a great fire in 1184, have survived. However, excavations have retrieved sufficient fragments to make it possible to get an idea of their character and indeed to suggest that for the inspiration behind their sculptural programme, Henry may have been indebted to St Denis, the great Gothic abbey whose façade was consecrated in 1140, a year when he was certainly in Paris.

New audiences for written English and new uses for Arthurian legends

From the time of the Conquest until the thirteenth century—and indeed beyond—there can be no doubt of the elite status held by the French language. Nonetheless, to suggest that Old English as a written language was ever quite dead and buried would be misleading. For reasons at which we can only guess there were in the twelfth and thirteenth centuries scholars for whom it mattered. In the twelfth century, these included the Canterbury scribes of the Eadwine Psalter, whose Old English gloss of the Psalms and Canticles suggests reasonable proficiency in Old English; and in the thirteenth, the work of the Tremulous Hand of Worcester (so called because the writing is indeed shaky) reveals the existence of a monk ready to spend a lifetime glossing some 50,000 words from at least twenty Old English MSS, mostly into Latin but sometimes into Middle English. Perhaps, like Henry of Huntingdon, though without his real familiarity with the language, such scholars were excited by the rhythms and the alliteration they found in Old English. In the early thirteenth century, and only ten miles from Worcester, the poet Layamon was translating Wace's *Roman de Brut* into Middle English, scrupulously eschewing insofar as he could all words of Romance origin in order to use Germanic vocabulary. Such labours may in part have been inspired by antiquarian interests, but we must also consider the ways in which, in the thirteenth century, both new pastoral concerns in the wake of the Lateran Council of 1215 and new political configurations worked together to provide an audience eager for literature in their own 'Inglis tong'. Culturally, an emphatically new sense of Englishness now kept abreast of—perhaps even anticipated—the political seachange of the thirteenth century in England. Thus it was that in c.1250 the tale of King Horn, of which there is a late twelfth-century Anglo-Norman version, appeared now in Middle English, the first of many romances in this new vernacular.

One of the most celebrated and—along with *King Horn*—one of the earliest pieces of Middle English literature is the *Ancrene Wisse*, written, or so it is supposed, in the early thirteenth century for a small community of anchoresses settled somewhere in the west of England—possibly indeed not far from Worcester. Of particular interest here is the fact that it was written for women, for it may well be that women in England had a key role to play in both the preservation and development of English as a vernacular. It is likely that in the immediate post-Conquest years many of the Anglo-Norman aristocracy will have learnt to speak at the knees of Anglo-Saxon wet nurses, and this may have been crucial in determining the speed with which English became a vernacular used by all classes. Subsequently, the fact that women were debarred from the priesthood and that, in consequence, few were taught Latin meant that there would be an ever-growing demand for works both of spiritual guidance and courtly entertainment in the language or languages they could read. Increasingly, the language of preference was English, and French gradually came to be regarded as the language of foreigners, of those foreigners, indeed, into whose hands England in 1066 had wrongfully fallen. The Middle English chronicle attributed to Robert of Gloucester is important in this context. This is a composite work, containing an account of the struggle between Henry III and Simon de Montfort that was indeed written by Robert, a monk of Gloucester, *c.*1270, but revised at the end of the century. The xenophobia that had flared up in England in the reign of Henry III is well expressed here. In Robert of Gloucester's eyes, through the influence of Henry's queen and his Poitevin advisers

> . . . so many French people were brought over
> That the English were held of no account.
> And the king let them do as they wished, so that each behaved as a king
> And took the goods of the poor.[19]

Earlier, in his account of the Norman Conquest, he points out that French then became the language that earned social esteem and English the language of 'lowe men'. And England, he adds, is the only country in the world that does not use its own language.[20] In fact, since 1066, the English had suffered under a Norman yoke.

The chronicler, Peter Langtoft, wrote in French verse. Langtoft, an Augustinian canon of Bridlington, writing towards the end of Edward I's reign, celebrated the achievements of Edward I as—so he believed—the conqueror of Scotland as well as Wales. Yet Langtoft's work, too, shows the new importance of English, for he composed some lines in English to lend authenticity to the songs which form part of the work and which he wished his readers to accept as soldiers' songs. Langtoft, moreover, brings us back to the Arthurian romances and to Geoffrey of Monmouth, their disseminator. To the critics of Henry III—and indeed even to some of his admirers—the reign of Edward I opened a new chapter in the history of the British Isles. Here was a king of Arthurian stature, one who might yet fulfil

---

[19] Robert of Gloucester's *Metrical Chronicle*, lines 10,992–5; quoted in T. Turville-Petre, *England the Nation: Language, Literature and National Identity, 1290–1340* (Oxford, 1996), 99 and n.

[20] Robert of Gloucester's *Metrical Chronicle*, lines 7,538–43; quoted in Turville-Petre, *England the Nation*, 95 and n.

the prophecies of Merlin and by his conquests reunite all Albion; and so it seemed to Langtoft:

> Now are the islanders all brought together,
> and Albania is rejoined to its regalities,
> of which King Edward is proclaimed lord;
> Cornwall and Wales are in his power,
> and Ireland the great is at his will.
> There is no longer any king of all the countries
> except King Edward who has thus visited them.
> Arthur had never so fully the feudalities.[21]

Edward was himself deeply conscious of the uses to which he could put Arthurian legend, not least in his relations with Scotland. In his letters to the pope, setting out his claims to overlordship of Scotland, he did not hesitate to borrow from Geoffrey of Monmouth, claiming that Brutus, the Trojan who slew the giants in Albion, gave England to Locrine, his eldest son. Locrine was in turn overlord to his two brothers, Albanact and Camber who were, respectively, the rulers of Scotland and Wales. But the Scots, who articulated their own origin myth in negotiations with the pope at this very time, were also familiar with Geoffrey of Monmouth and the Arthurian romances and made a riposte to the English claim. They pointed out to the pope that Brutus had made his sons equals and that none of them had been subject to another. In any case, the Scots were descended from Scota, daughter of Pharaoh of Egypt, who with the assistance of her husband and son drove the Britons from Scotland. Later, Arthur conquered Scotland—likewise Denmark, France, and Norway—but after his death the realm of Scotland recovered the freedom it had formerly enjoyed. The same legends could help to establish more than one national identity.

[21] Pierre de Langtoft, *Le Règne d'Edouard 1ᵉʳ Chronicle*, ed. J. C. Thiolier (Paris, 1989), 2nd recension, lines 1,167–74; text with translation also in *Thomas Wright's Political Songs in England*, ed. P. Coss (Cambridge, 1996), 308.

New schools and universities

None of the themes so far discussed in this chapter implies that more than a very small proportion of the population of any country in the British Isles could read or write in any language, much less do both. But themes discussed elsewhere in the book do point to a growth in literacy in the course of this period, and in particular to a growth in the relative numbers of people who had at least a basic understanding of Latin. The new bureaucracies in Church and state, for example, depended for their existence on the services of an ever-increasing number of clerks to write the writs and other documents that issued from their chanceries, and seem to have been justified in their assumption that the recipients of the writs, which often required a response, would be able to read these or find someone else to do so without too much difficulty. And if merchants were not to be cheated, they needed at least a pragmatic literacy, enabling them to understand the essentials of the accounts which their clerks prepared for them. In fact, by 1200 most towns of any size probably had a school, and we can be sure that the number of schools in existence at one time or another much exceeded the number known to us. If England did not possess the learned families who, like those recorded in Wales and Ireland, transmitted a fine Latin culture from one generation of a dynasty to the next, its numerous towns were the means of spreading a basic kind of literacy quite widely; and the same is true of south Scotland, where every burgh of any size probably had a school.

For higher studies—that is, for everything not taught in a grammar school—an aspiring student might have to go a long way, and in the twelfth century English scholars who could afford it went abroad. But such an exodus did not constitute a serious brain drain, since many who went also returned. The work of Charles Burnett on the introduction of Arabic learning in England illustrates the complexity of the threads which might draw together scholars from many parts of the world in this period. In 1158, for example, the Jewish scholar Abraham ibn Ezra spent some months in London. Abraham, born in Tudela, had been a visitor to North Africa before leaving home in 1140 to travel to Pisa, Lucca, Beziers, Narbonne, and Dreux, and other places in northern France, and then to England. His astronomical tables and his work on the astrolabe may have been known in the circle of scholars surrounding Henry II. Daniel Morley, an English-man, played a part in the reception of Arabic learning in England a generation and more later than Abraham ibn Ezra. Through his patron, John of Oxford, the curialist bishop of Norwich, if in no other way, Daniel himself had a link with the royal court. He returned to England c.1180 after periods of study in Paris and Toledo, and with some caustic comments to make about the former:

When, some time ago, I went away to study, I stopped a while in Paris. There I saw asses rather than men occupying the Chairs and pretending to be very important. They had desks in front of them heaving under the weight of two or three immovable tomes, painting Roman Law in golden letters. With leaden styluses in their hands they inserted asterisks and obeluses here and there with a grave and reverent air. But because they did not know anything, they were no better than marble statues . . .[22]

When Daniel returned to England, it was with 'a precious multi-tude' of books. His first impressions of English learning were not entirely favourable, either; nevertheless, he and his books stayed, very possibly at Oxford. The books were indeed precious, since they related to Aristotelian works on natural science which were transmitted to western Europe through the medium of Arabic translations.

In the years around 1200, the geography of learning was altered for good, as first Oxford and then, a generation later, Cambridge pulled ahead of their rivals as centres for higher studies. Already, in the 1190s, references to the teaching of theology and of Roman and canon law in Oxford, in addition to the liberal arts, show that its scholars and masters were making the transition from school to university, for these subjects were characteristic of a university curriculum. This process was assisted by the political turn of events in this decade. The war between England and France beginning now, England's sub-sequent loss of Normandy and the battle of Bouvines in 1214 changed for ever the relationship between the two countries and the political and intellectual climate of England. It became more difficult than previously for English students to study in France, and at times impossible for them to do so. Had it not been for the dispersal of

---

[22] C. Burnett, *The Introduction of Arabic Literature into England* (London, 1997), 61 (a translation of *Philosophia*, ed. G. Maurach, in *Mittellateinisches Jahrbuch*, xiv (1979), 204–55, at p. 212).

scholars and masters from Oxford after a violent confrontation between town and gown at the end of 1209, and the decision of some who went to Cambridge to stay there permanently, Cambridge might never have become a university. But the foundation of a Franciscan school here in 1230 is one of the signs we have that it was now of high repute as a centre of academic studies. The next year, Henry III formally recognized that Oxford and Cambridge were both universities—an act which could in itself not make them so but provides a useful indication of the status which each in fact by now enjoyed. Both universities gained enormously from the presence of the friars, and especially the Franciscans and Dominicans, for many of the most distinguished theologians of the period—one in which theology absorbed much of the energy devoted to higher studies—belonged to one or other of these orders.

Until the foundation of a university at Dublin in 1320, these were the only universities in the British Isles. As far as we know, Ireland, Scotland, and Wales between them never contributed more than a tiny proportion of the student population in either place, though their representation was important. In 1270, when the Lord Edward established a peace-keeping force in Cambridge, it included five scholars from the English counties, three each from Scotland and Ireland, and two from Wales. Just occasionally, scholars might join forces against a common enemy—for example at Oxford in 1238, when Cardinal Otto de Monteferrato was staying in Osney Abbey and his cook poured boiling water over an Irish scholar found begging at his doorway—but it was more usual to find them fighting each other, though not on strictly 'national' lines: rather, 'northerners and Scots' took one side, 'southerners, marchers, Irishmen and Welshmen' the other; the dividing line was the River Nene. But none of this ever shook the idea that Oxford and Cambridge were English universities, and furthermore of venerable antiquity. Thus, Edward I, writing to the pope in 1296 about Oxford, could claim that 'according to the evidence of ancient writings, there can be no doubt that the *studium* of France is an offshoot of our schools of England'.[23] It would not be long before credit for the founding of Oxford would go to King Alfred, the king around whom so many myths of English identity would cluster; but that is another story.

[23] T. H. Aston (ed.), *The History of the University of Oxford*, i. *The Early Oxford Schools*, ed. J. I. Catto (Oxford, 1984), 114.

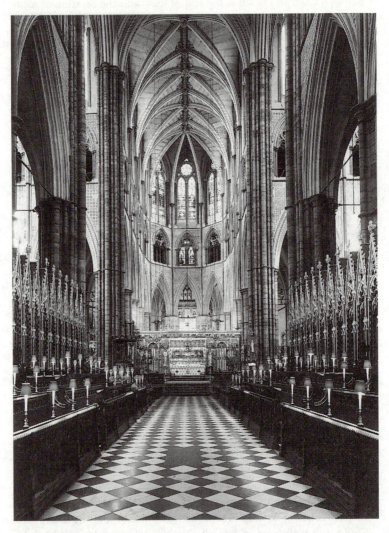

Figure 9 Westminster Abbey: the choir and apse. Built at immense expense by Henry III in the years after 1245, to a design influenced by contemporary French models, Westminster Abbey was conceived as providing an appropriately magnificent setting for a kingship sanctioned and protected by God.

Kingship, government, and political life, *c.*1160–*c.*1280

Henry Summerson

Ruling Britain and Ireland: agencies and aspirations

The accession of Henry II to England in 1154, like that of Malcolm IV to Scotland in the previous year, brought no institutional changes to the government of the country each ruled. Indeed, Henry's determination to restore the state of affairs prevailing at his grandfather's death, nineteen years earlier, implied that such change was not to be expected. But in a wider perspective the accession of a man who was already by inheritance duke of Normandy and count of Anjou, Touraine, and Maine, and by marriage duke of Aquitaine and count of Poitou and Auvergne, was certain to change the balance of power within the British Isles, not least by bringing new preoccupations to English kingship (see Map 14). As long as this continental empire lasted, Henry II and his sons spent years at a time outside England, their demands on the latter realm were constantly shaped by their empire's needs, and their relations with the kingdoms and lesser principalities on the English borders took on a different character.

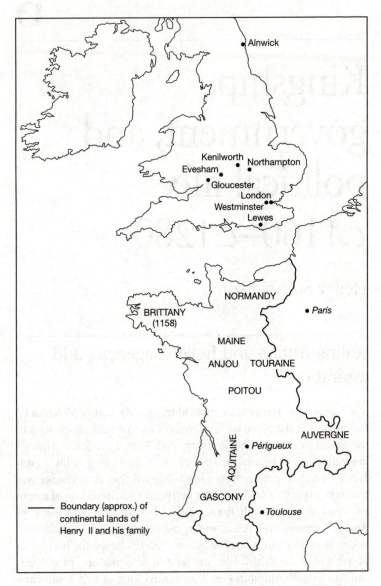

Map 14 England and the Angevin Empire, with places mentioned in the text of Chapter 6

Henry I had cowed and terrorized the rulers of Wales, who to Henry II were little more than a potential distraction from events of greater importance elsewhere. The former sought obedience, the latter was usually content with quiescence. His continental possessions brought the English king wealth, though this has proved difficult to quantify. They certainly brought him prestige, an asset of its nature unquantifiable, but widely attested by contemporary sources, and enhanced by cultural developments which owed little to Henry II, but which he could exploit. The cult of chivalry, based upon the code of conduct of the mounted warrior, now beginning his ascent to aristocracy, owed more to Flanders and northern France than to the lands of the kings of England, where its principal manifestations, namely tournaments, were discouraged where they were not forbidden. The tournament in this period was no carefully regulated single combat, but a great mêlée involving hundreds of knights, mimicking and rehearsing for warfare. Deaths and injuries were commonplace, and brought ecclesiastical condemnation of the violence and wastage of life involved, and also of the encouragement tournaments gave to vanity and pursuit of fame.

But clerical disapproval did not undermine the appeal of chivalric culture, with its glorification of courage, loyalty, and military ability. Tournaments brought men together, in circumstances in which they could hope to attract the attention of rulers needing servants of ability. Knighthood, still an essentially secular honour, gave the entrée to this world, one which provided a means of linking kings with one another and with their own subjects. The young Malcolm IV went to France in 1159 to participate in Henry II's expedition against Toulouse and to receive knighthood at Périgueux. He then celebrated his new honour by conferring it on thirty of his followers. The Church attempted to Christianize chivalry, with some success. But the associations which knighthood developed with refinement and civility owed at least as much to its connections with royal courts. Again, the links thus created could be wide-ranging. When Rhys ap Gruffudd of Deheubarth staged possibly the first eisteddfod at Cardigan in 1176, he may well have been imitating the assemblies of poets and troubadours organized by Queen Eleanor in her duchy of Aquitaine.

The accession of Henry II gave English kingship unprecedentedly wide horizons. The kingdom of Jerusalem was ruled by Henry's cousins, descended from his grandfather, Count Fulk of Anjou; English crusading enthusiasm at the end of the twelfth century owed something to a family connection, though more to religious piety and chivalric ardour. Such a mingling of interests was characteristic of the forces which moved twelfth-century kings and princes. The DNA which gave life to their actions and ambitions was formed by a double helix of lordship and sovereignty, definable respectively as the material and the moral or religious foundations of royal authority. The two were closely interwoven; sometimes in tension, more often they reinforced one another. Justice was perhaps the most important sphere in which these two elements were combined. The centrality of justice to kingship was underlined by the English coronation oath. In 1189 Richard I promised to honour God and the Church, to exercise justice over the people entrusted to him, and to do away with evil customs and maintain rightful ones. It was a misfortune for the twelfth-century rulers of Wales and Ireland that nationwide systems of customary justice had developed there which left relatively little scope for princely involvement, so depriving them of the profits of justice and restricting their opportunities for intervention in the affairs of their leading subjects. Vendetta there remained a principal means of law enforcement, whereas in England and in Scotland it had been increasingly superseded by centrally administered justice, with serious crimes—felonies—reserved for judgment in the king's courts.

Justice had more than one face, however. To a king's humbler subjects it was essentially a manifestation of sovereignty, giving protection against oppression and maintaining order. For the land-owning classes, and especially the nobility, it was inherent in a ruler's lordship as well, and depended upon other links, especially those known as 'feudal'. The validity and usefulness of this term has become a matter of debate. But it can be meaningfully used to define the relationship between a lord and his free tenant (often styled 'vassal'), whereby the latter came to hold a property, or fief (Latin *feodum*), from the former in return for certain services, above all military ones, and in consequence accepted the additional right of his lord to demand his counsel, and to exercise jurisdiction over him. In a looser and more general sense, moreover, the word 'feudal' provides a way of describing connections between rulers and subjects in a society in which the ruler's distribution of power created reciprocal relationships between himself and those upon whom he conferred authority. Such ties, expressed in the ceremony of homage, were not necessarily linked to property rights: they could be extended to people who stood in a relationship with the monarch which was tenurially remote, or even had no tenurial content at all, involving men who either voluntarily or under duress had accepted the latter's superiority. The links between English kings and a number of Welsh and Irish princes would come into this second category. The result was a network of lines of mutual obligation, extending both across and deep into landowning society.

A ruler's most important relationships, however, were with the magnates of his own realm, lay and ecclesiastical. Hereditary descent was accepted throughout the British Isles, but primogeniture was slower to win general acceptance, and all lordships remained vulnerable at the moment of transmission, not least royal and princely ones. In Wales and Ireland disputed successions frequently generated lasting conflict and weakness. In Scotland the deaths of David I and William the Lion were immediately followed by dynastic rebellions. Even Henry II thought it necessary to have his eldest son crowned king in his own lifetime. The fact that feudal tenure commonly served an ostensibly military purpose, that of providing armed men for a lord's host, licensed kings to express their superior lordship by manipulating the descent of feudally held lands. If there was no recognized heir, the lands might revert as escheats to their lord, while if the heir was a minor or a woman, the lord could claim the wardship of the one and the right to grant away the marriage of the other, in order to ensure that the requisite services continued to be performed. Known as feudal incidents, such rights were sources of wealth and power, both for the inherent value of the lands thus disposed of, and for the opportunities for patronage they provided.

Patronage today has heavily pejorative associations, but in the medieval world it enabled rulers to reward service, maintain loyalty, appease enemies, and build up a following. The most sought-after expression of patronage was a grant of land, conferring both wealth and status. In Scotland David I and his successors were able to transform the composition of the country's aristocracy, by encouraging the immigration of men of Anglo-Norman and Flemish origins and endowing them with Scottish lands, while at the same time redefining the terms on which the landowning classes held their estates, through a widespread introduction of feudal tenure. The kings of Scots retained a substantial landed base (an important factor behind the relatively unforceful character of their rule), not least by exploiting their rights as feudal rulers. These enabled them to dispose of the lands of others rather than their own, for instance by marrying newcomers to heiresses. The name of Ness son of William, lord of Leuchars (the site of one of Scotland's finest Romanesque churches; see Figure 10), probably attests the union of a foreign husband with a native wife. In England this type of patronage was taken much further, became, indeed, an essential component of government. Without a whole-hearted exploitation of feudal lordship, to raise money and reward their servants, Henry II and his sons would have found it hard to maintain their rule.

To be a king or prince was to be a leader in war. The defence of the realm, with its associated power to call out all its able-bodied men in its defence, was an essential component of sovereignty, which was itself fully compatible with the lordship empowering a king to summon a feudal host. Success in battle ensured glory and loot for the victor, as well as personal survival. Glory raised his reputation, loot enabled him to reward his followers and recruit more. Chivalry in this context could be an implement of patronage, a fact nowhere more clearly visible than in the remarkable career of William Marshal, the younger son of a minor baron who eventually became regent of England. Having first made his name on the tournament fields of northern France, where he mingled with the leading men of the Angevin world, William had his climb to greatness completed by a striking act of royal generosity, when Richard I gave him the hand of the heiress to the barony of Chepstow, and, with her, lands in the Welsh Marches, Normandy, and Ireland. It was by such means that kings promoted men they had come to trust, and so consolidated their own authority.

No formal career structure existed to regulate the advancement of men like William Marshal. The grant of an heiress which raised him to the baronage was an act of unconstrained royal generosity, underlining the fact that government in Britain and Ireland was still essentially personal. Such institutions as developed, notably the treasury, chancery, and exchequer in England (later followed by Scotland), had by the late twelfth century to some extent developed an ethos of their own, expressed in treatises like *Glanvill* and the *Dialogue of the Exchequer*, but they did not yet aspire to anything like bureaucratic

Figure 10 Leuchars church, Fife, built before 1187, at a time when Scottish lay society was transformed by Anglo-French incomers. The splendid chancel and apse of this small parish church shows English and French influences. The interlaced arcading on the chancel derives ultimately from Durham Cathedral, while the carved corbels have close parallels in churches in north-west Normandy.

independence. No one doubted that just as administration developed to meet the king's needs, so it existed to do his bidding. The same was also apt to be true of justice, which like patronage was all too often a facet of a kingdom's political life. To the nobility both were rights to which they were entitled, but to twelfth-century rulers they were essentially favours they could distribute or withhold. In the resolution of conflicts to which such differences in interest and expectation gave rise, the issue of who gave counsel to kings and princes was one on which the stability of a kingdom might depend. Earls and great lords demanded the right to be consulted on issues affecting the realm as a whole, which they claimed to represent, and expected the king to heed their advice. Rulers acknowledged the principle, while asserting the right to choose their own advisers. Successful rulers were those who won the confidence of the magnates while retaining their own freedom of manoeuvre.

The milieu in which counsel was given was above all that of the court. Every king or prince had one, where he showed his public face, gave ear to petitioners, sat in judgment on important disputes (it is no accident that in Latin, French, and English alike the same word means both law tribunal and seat of royal power), discussed weighty issues, and gave orders for their resolution. In the mid-twelfth century specialization was still rare. To be a courtier, a royal *familiaris*, was to be a man who might be at any time singled out to levy a tax, to govern a shire, to lead a campaign, even to kill the archbishop of Canterbury. The ruler chose whomsoever he wanted to fulfil the task in hand, from the men at his disposal. Not surprisingly in such an atmosphere of favouritism and improvisation, the English court, at least, was regarded as a scene of vice and confusion. Walter Map, himself a clerk in Henry II's service, declared himself unable to define the court, and declared that though it might not be hell, it was certainly a place of punishment.

In the late twelfth century written instruments were known in both native Wales and Gaelic Ireland, especially the former, but neither had anything that could be described as a bureaucracy. In spite of uniformity of law and language, both lands remained politically divided; there was a general tendency towards the formation of a few larger principalities able to dominate the rest, but none of these proved able to absorb or command the others, and the stability of each continued to be threatened by inheritance disputes. In Wales the threat of English invasion and annexation did not impose unity. In Ireland the major kingdoms, Leinster and especially Connacht, came to dispose of impressive military resources, and raised briefly the prospect of an effective high kingship, but English invasions after 1169 destroyed that possibility. In mainland Scotland monarchy itself was old, but the incumbent dynasty of descendants of Malcolm Canmore and Queen Margaret was relatively recently established, and had barely become secure. The Scottish king enjoyed an undisputed regality, but could not otherwise match his English counterpart either in prestige or in resources, enhanced as both were by huge French lordships; nor did he dispose of anything like the sophistication and strength of English government.

By twelfth-century standards that government was remarkable for its ability to use instruments of centralized control—the exchequer's scrutiny of royal revenues, visitations by royal justices, the ability to appoint and dismiss sheriffs, themselves also answerable to the exchequer; all these together gave the king and his agents a penetrative capacity so far-reaching as arguably to nullify the distinction between central and local government. England was a rich country in the late twelfth century, and a hard-working king could exploit its wealth to his own advantage. In a world in which power was assessed primarily in military terms, the English king was pre-eminent among his neighbours. No doubt this perception owes a good deal to the preponderance of English records, narrative and administrative, among those which survive from the twelfth and thirteenth centuries. But the disparity of resources was not one measurable only on parchment. An English ruler had more men at his disposal, whether mercenaries or his own subjects, could arm and equip them better, and could keep his forces together for longer. That his dominance was more often tacitly accepted than physically imposed was due principally to commitments in France. But of his superiority there could be no doubt. Among the movers and shakers in the mid-twelfth-century British Isles the king of England stood out: when he moved, the others prepared to shake.

Henry II, his allies and enemies, 1160–1175

At his coronation Henry II was a formidable young man of 21. The ruler of huge French lordships, who was consequently out of England for long periods, he was simultaneously a man of abundant energy, bold and resolute when occasion demanded, and a master of delaying tactics. Well educated, he understood many languages, though only speaking French and Latin (not English). But for all his intellectual gifts, his kingship was essentially pragmatic. Henry wished to bring back the state of affairs of his grandfather's time, and then to pass on to his successors a restored and augmented inheritance. It could have been said of him, as it was said of his contemporary, the emperor Frederick Barbarossa, that 'he gathered diverse lands into a great mass for the sake of his illustrious progeny'.[1] By a familiar paradox, however, his pursuit of conservative, even reactionary, aims took him down new paths.

Stephen's usurpation and weak rule had opened England to papal authority to an unprecedented extent. Henry II may not have aspired to exclude the influence of Rome, but he certainly wished to control it; in 1168 he was said to have exclaimed that 'now at last he [had] secured the authority of his grandfather, who was king in his own land, papal legate, patriarch, emperor and everything he wished . . .'.[2] It was the pursuit of that authority which led him into his famous dispute with the archbishop of Canterbury, Thomas Becket. But although he had good grounds for claiming that the sixteen Constitutions of Clarendon drawn up in 1164 did indeed embody ancient custom, it was arguably a mistake (as his mother later observed) to set them out in writing. Custom was of its nature flexible, but these clauses had the clarity and rigidity of a political programme, and as such risked proving objectionable under scrutiny. Above all, the context in which Henry II ruled was no longer that of Henry I's day. Even if the English bishops had accepted the king's position on the issue of clerks accused of felony, clauses restricting either papal jurisdiction or

[1] K Leyser, *Communications and Power in Medieval Europe: The Gregorian Revolution and Beyond* (London, 1994), 136.
[2] *Letters of John of Salisbury*, ii, ed. W. J. Millor and C. N. L. Brooke (Oxford Medieval Texts; 1979), 580–1.

access and appeal to Rome would certainly have been unacceptable to a rejuvenated papacy.

The precision of the Constitutions was such as to make compromise difficult. Becket went into exile in France for six years, and when he finally returned to England, it was after an agreement which said nothing about the Constitutions at all. His murder, on 29 December 1170, was occasioned not by a dispute over the relations between lay and clerical power, but by wrangles following the coronation of the king's eldest son. Only when Becket was dead could the issue of ecclesiastical jurisdiction be settled; the archbishop's canonization in 1173 sealed the compromise which his death had made possible. The Church kept control of the trials of criminous clerks, and appeals to Rome continued unabated, but the king retained his influence over elections to abbacies and bishoprics, and continued to receive their revenues during vacancies.

In this last respect, Henry II fared much as did William the Lion, king of Scots, when he too fell out with the papacy over a disputed election in 1178 to the see of St Andrews, in which the king's candidate was one of his own chaplains. The issue was resolved only in 1188, and in the intervening decade William was excommunicated and his kingdom placed under an interdict, while numerous appeals were made to Rome. Yet when the dust finally settled, the new bishop of St Andrews was the king's chancellor. Successive Scottish kings would in future feel obliged to pay more heed to the canonical freedoms now being demanded for the Church, and papal influence was exerted more directly after 1192, when the Scottish Church was placed under the pope's immediate authority, but there was arguably no substantial surrender of royal power. Fearful of Henry II, the papacy was willing to lean lightly on the king of Scots.

The English king certainly had a formidable quality not found in his northern neighbour. When Becket returned to England in 1170 he was greeted by enthusiastic crowds, cheering him for reasons which included his resistance to a government perceived as intrusive and oppressive. All government within the British Isles in this period was predatory, whether through the plundering raids led by Welsh and Irish kings, or the milder rule of Scottish kings maintaining themselves from the food renders of their subjects. The style of government directed by Henry II and his sons was exceptional for its penetrative ability and aggressive quality. English kings constantly wanted money, mostly to meet continental needs. They raised it primarily by an intensive exploitation of the king's rights, both as sovereign and as feudal lord. There were recurrent scutages (payments for the commutation of military service) and tallages (arbitrary levies) on demesnes, which included boroughs. There were the issues of law, particularly of visitations by royal justices. And there was unremitting concentration on feudal incidents, particularly as applied to issues of inheritance.

The pipe rolls on which the exchequer entered details of royal revenue and expenditure reveal the pursuit of royal rights being pushed to the limit. In Devon, for instance, they record the issues of four scutages, seven tallages, and at least fifteen judicial visitations during Henry II's reign, as well as the aid which the king was entitled to demand when he married his eldest daughter (in 1168) and the profits he extracted from the bishopric of Exeter when that fell vacant in 1186—over £250. They also show how the king exploited his rights as feudal lord. It was accepted that a tenant-in-chief should pay a 'relief' to enter his inheritance, but there was no consistency as to the amount due, leading to constant bargaining and bickering between king and magnates. And when it was uncertain who the heir was, or succession was through an heiress whose marriage the king could control, rights in land became still more at the king's disposal. The way the king used his powers, and the personal factors often involved, are perfectly caught in a Hampshire entry from 1188, in which Adam de Port owed £200 as 'fine for his land and his wife's inheritance in Normandy, and that the king may abate his indignation against him and accept his homage'.[3]

It is hard to imagine financial administration more likely to strain relations between government and governed. Sheriffs and their underlings were always apt to be corrupt; pressure from the court and the exchequer made them over-officious as well. Searching nationwide inquests in 1170 simultaneously showed the extent of the maladministration that had resulted, and revealed the length of the government's reach, investigating the conduct not only of royal officials but also of baronial and diocesan ones; only seven sheriffs retained their positions as a result. Then in the following year Henry II engaged in a different form of interventionism. Secular and

[3] *Pipe Roll 32 Henry II* (Pipe Roll Soc., 36; 1914), 173.

ecclesiastical politics interacted to prompt his Irish expedition of 1171. At the beginning of Henry's reign the bull *Laudabiliter* had authorized an English conquest of Ireland, but no action followed. The uproar which followed Becket's murder made it convenient for the king to remove himself to the perimeters of his rule. An added incentive for his expedition was the need to curb the independence of a group of barons from the Anglo-Welsh Marches, led by Richard fitz Gilbert, known as Strongbow, lord of Chepstow, who had become embroiled in Irish dynastic politics. Married to Aoife, daughter of Diarmait Mac Murchadha, king of Leinster, Strongbow was in 1171 preparing to establish himself in his wife's inheritance.

Henry II saw such activities primarily in a Welsh context. Having re-established English supremacy in Wales early in his reign, he was alert to the trouble-making capacity of the Anglo-Welsh marcher lords, habitual warriors by tradition and inclination, whose innate belligerence was encouraged by their developing legal standing; they claimed to hold their lordships by right of conquest, in independence of the English crown. Strongbow was just such a lord, as were several of his followers, and there was an obvious danger that their Irish acquisitions would constitute additional independent lordships, out of King Henry's reach, and so increase their freedom from his control. Even had he not received an appeal for help from some of the Irish kings with whom Strongbow was at war, Henry would probably have intervened.

In October 1171 Henry crossed to Ireland with a substantial force, and stayed for several months. Although he held a reforming church council, his primary concern was secular. Portions of Leinster, notably Dublin and Wexford, were set aside to constitute royal demesne. Otherwise Leinster and Meath became fiefs, held of the English crown by precisely defined knight service by Strongbow and Hugh de Lacy respectively. A number of Irish kings made submission, and some agreed to pay tribute. With regard to the native rulers Henry had created a situation much like that in Wales, whose princes acknowledged the English king's overlordship, and accepted the possibility of his interference, while retaining a good deal of freedom of action. But there would be no marcher lordships in Ireland. The possibility of expansion remained, but the English king could hope to control and direct it. The result was that the Anglo-Norman conquest remained incomplete, usually advancing significantly only when the

English crown was willing to support it. But in 1172 Henry II was content with the establishment of a general overlordship. He left Ireland in April and did not return.

Henry II was soon preoccupied elsewhere. In 1173 the young King Henry, whose coronation had been the immediate cause of Becket's murder, rebelled against his father, abetted by malcontents in many parts of Britain and France, among them William the Lion, king of Scots. Henry II was not the only king in Britain who aspired to restore a grandfather's realm. William never forgot that his brother had been deprived of Cumberland, Westmorland, and Northumberland, and now his determination to recover them led him into an alliance with the English king's enemies. It also led him to disaster. Control of castles and command of a substantial mercenary army gave Henry the military advantage, and his mastery of Britain was finally secured when King William was surprised and captured at Alnwick in July 1174. The Treaty of Falaise of 1175, which compelled William to perform homage to Henry II 'in respect of Scotland and in respect of all his other lands', so acknowledging English overlordship, while five of his main castles were to receive English garrisons, largely drew King William's teeth, and the process was completed when he in turn had to face a major dynastic rebellion, that of Donald Macwilliam, a descendant of Malcolm Canmore's first marriage, one which in 1187 endangered his throne.

King Henry was not a vindictive man. Once the rebellion of 1173–4 was over he tried to make provision for all his sons, and he did not exploit to the uttermost the new dependency of the Scottish king. The English rebels lost their castles, but not their lands. Moreover, he showed some awareness of the oppressive light in which his administration had come to be seen, in 1178 ordering investigation of the excesses alleged against his justices. Henry's reign was of fundamental importance for the development of law in England, and eventually the whole of the British Isles. This was hardly accidental, for he had been concerned with jurisdiction from early in his reign—it was basic to the quarrel with Becket. His innovations may not have been designed in a spirit of conscious hostility to the courts of his tenants-in-chief, but the principle that no one should be compelled to answer for his free tenement except through a royal writ, first formulated in his reign, was bound to undermine them. The king's jurisdiction, by contrast, was exerted in a way that extended it.

The writ was one building block for Henry II's legal reforms. Another was the jury, possibly a continental import, but more probably the refurbishment of a pre-Conquest survival. In 1166 the Assize of Clarendon, bypassing the private accuser who had hitherto been the principal means of criminal prosecution, required local juries to present to the sheriffs, and to the county justices who safeguarded the king's legal rights, the names of those suspected of committing felonies since 1154, so that they should undergo the ordeal which would prove their guilt or innocence. Anyone who came clear might still, if of evil repute, be compelled to leave the country. The assize was probably one more enactment intended to restore order after Stephen's reign. Another was a simultaneous measure against disseisins (forcible seizures of property), inevitably widespread during the civil wars, and a likely cause of disorder and discontent afterwards. Here the presenting jury seems to have been an inadequate substitute for personal prosecution, so that a way had after all to be found to enable the aggrieved to sue for their rights, with the hope of speedy restitution.

The assize of novel disseisin met this need. It did not concern itself with ownership (right), only with possession (seisin), and whether a plaintiff had been recently and unjustly deprived of it. The answer to this question, given by a local jury summoned on the plaintiff's purchase of a writ, settled the issue. If the plaintiff was found to have been disseised, he was reinstated; otherwise the defendant was left in occupation. The writ was capable of indefinite extension; having been used to address one question, it could easily be adapted to settle another. So, for example, in the Assize of Northampton of 1176, another writ was introduced, to deal with disputed inheritances. The presumption of hereditary descent of freehold land, long accepted, was now given legal standing, through the provision of the writ of mort d'ancestor, under which a man denied his inheritance could have a jury summoned to decide whether the land he claimed had been held by his father, and whether he was himself the latter's next heir. If the jurors found he was, he was awarded seisin. Neither assize touched the issue of ultimate right. That could still be raised in further litigation, which might culminate in a judicial duel. But meanwhile potential disputes had been defused.

The Assize of Northampton reflects a renewed assertion of royal authority after the rebellion of 1173–4. The enforcement of the possessory assizes and measures against crime was now entrusted to royal justices, sent out on eyre (from Latin *iter*, a journey) to act as the king's agents. They also investigated the king's rights, notably those feudal incidents which were so important a source of his revenue. Most strikingly of all, it was through his justices that Henry II bypassed the links of homage which in purely feudal terms bound him only to a limited number of his greatest subjects, requiring that all who wished to stay in the realm, not just barons and knights, but all freeholders 'and even villeins', should take oaths of loyalty— fealty—to himself. His sovereignty could not have been more clearly proclaimed.

Angevin apogee and crisis, 1175–1216

The last quarter of the twelfth century saw Angevin kingship at its high-water mark. In the British Isles the Scottish king was in no position to give trouble. In Wales and Ireland efforts were made to channel English influence through native rulers. In Wales Rhys ap Gruffudd, prince of Deheubarth, was in 1172 formally appointed Henry II's justiciar for south Wales, implying that he was the king's official representative there, and as such empowered to check Welsh restiveness with the English king's backing. Rhys's death in 1197 ended the experiment, since Deheubarth then fragmented, and pre-eminence in Wales passed to the geographically remote Gwynedd, whose rulers followed a more independent line. But in the meantime the Welsh princes had benefited from the relative stability born of Rhys's hegemony to apply themselves to the modernization of government, and to the fuller exploitation of their resources. Many built castles in the late twelfth century. Rhys himself was responsible for a codification of Welsh law. In Ireland a similar experiment failed. By the Treaty of Windsor in 1175 Ruaidrí Ua Conchobair, king of Connacht, was recognized as overlord of all the Irish rulers outside Leinster and Meath, in the clear expectation that he would act in Ireland as Rhys did in south Wales, as the agent of Henry II in preserving the stability of a region peripheral to his empire, but still capable of causing trouble. But Ruaidrí proved ineffective in the role allotted to him, and in 1185 Ireland was made into a lordship for

Henry's youngest son, John. This experiment, too, came to nothing, thwarted largely by John's youthful folly, but shows that Henry was still prepared to attempt bold solutions for troublesome problems.

In England itself government remained dynamic, in ways which had a widespread impact. In 1180, for example, the coinage was reformed, with the introduction of the 'Short Cross' penny (deliberately followed by the Scottish mints in 1195). But in the last years of his reign Henry II was mainly concerned with the succession to his principalities. It was one of the few problems which he was unable to solve, and it led directly to his miserable death in 1189, at war with one son and betrayed by another. That personal disaster should not obscure either the effectiveness and creativity of his rule, or the enormous renown throughout western Europe which he enjoyed for most of his reign, Becket's death notwithstanding.

Though Henry II ultimately took the cross, he did not go on crusade. That his successor did was one of the factors which helped to make Richard I little less than a legend in his own lifetime. In many respects Richard deserved his renown. A first-rate soldier in an age when lay society placed military virtues ahead of all others, and when the development of the cult of Christian knighthood (itself owing much to the crusade) had caused the Church to qualify its reservations about the practice of arms, he was dignified, just, and cultivated (he left songs in both French and Provençal), an efficient administrator, and a good judge of men. Like his father, he spent little time in England, which continued to be efficiently governed and very efficiently taxed. English administrative methods and English money, themselves capitalizing on a crusading enthusiasm which touched the Welsh as well as the English (but had little impact at this time on the Scots) were largely responsible for the achievements of the crusade of 1190–2, which failed to recapture Jerusalem, but otherwise enjoyed a remarkable degree of success.

By the end of Richard's reign, there was resentment of the demands of his government, but in its earlier years the only serious malcontent seems to have been Richard's brother John, whose schemes to supplant his absentee brother were encouraged by the French king, though not by either the Welsh princes or the king of Scots. In 1189 King William had taken advantage of Richard's financial needs to buy his freedom from English allegiance for 10,000 marks. It says much for the developing effectiveness of Scottish government that such a sum could be quickly raised, although the abbot of Scone had afterwards to be helped to recover his peasants who had fled rather than contribute. Subsequently, William had nothing to do with John, instead contributing to Richard's ransom. His wisdom became apparent in 1194, when Richard returned to England, and suppressed John's rebellion without difficulty.

Richard soon returned to France, where he spent the rest of his reign, fighting in defence of his inheritance. For most of these five years the government of England was directed by Hubert Walter, archbishop of Canterbury and also successively justiciar and chancellor, holding the latter office until his death in 1205. The safest possible pair of hands, Hubert was also imaginative and innovative in his approach to government. It was while he was chancellor that chancery business began to be recorded on parchment rolls, suggesting that he appreciated the value to administration of precedent and cumulative experience. At the same time Hubert developed the trend, already marked under Henry II, towards non-specialist lay participation in government. In 1194 it was ordered that three knights and a clerk be appointed in every county as 'keepers of the pleas of the crown'—the origin of the coroner's office. By the end of the twelfth century, increasing numbers of the king's subjects were participating in the workings of the king's government. A growth in the ability to read and write among the laity, though impossible to quantify, was a necessary corollary to this involvement (which was also a stimulus to it).

Richard I died on 7 April 1199, mortally wounded in a French siege. His most serious shortcoming as king was his failure to leave either a son or a clearly designated heir, and it was only after some uncertainty that he was succeeded by his youngest brother. John was energetic, clever, and inventive. But he was also cruel, inconsistent, and incurably suspicious, a great taker of hostages; unable to feel trust, he could not inspire it. Above all, his persistent inability to win military success, which earned him the insulting epithet 'softsword', not only resulted in his losing much of his inheritance, but also denied him the prestige which might have offset his personal shortcomings. It is ironic that his tomb effigy should show him brandishing an unsheathed sword. After a good start, John threw away a strong position in France, and in 1204 lost all the Angevin lands north of the Loire. Defeat brought him home, unreconciled to his losses.

Convention required that he recover what amounted to much of his ancestral heritage. But the consequent expense and effort imposed ultimately intolerable strains, as an apparatus evolved to run a great empire was now set to work on England and her British neighbours.

In the years which followed, old sources of income, including feudal incidents, were exploited to the limit, and new sources were found, notably direct taxation on moveable property. The thirteenth of 1207 affected 'every layman of the whole of England, on whosoever fee he be, who has rents and chattels in England'.[4] But though the tax raised the huge sum of over £60,000 (two or three times the sum which could be raised annually by exploiting feudal incidents), it was not repeated by John. Its grant 'by the common counsel and consent of our council' implied a readiness to negotiate, and a consequent sensitivity to the good will of his leading subjects, which were not to John's taste, and he preferred to rely on the methods which had served his father and brother.

Discontent was muted at first. Although there was a crisis at the end of 1204, John's first major dispute was not with the lay barons but with the Church, over Innocent III's appointment in 1207 of Stephen Langton as archbishop of Canterbury, without the king's consent. Against ecclesiastical claims that church offices should be filled without lay intervention stood John's demand for a say in the choice of the English primate. Mutual intransigence led first to England's being placed under an interdict (1208), and then to the king's excommunication (1209), whereupon John was deserted by nearly all the bishops and most of his clerks. John's court increasingly resembled an armed camp, dominated by courtiers and household knights. This was appropriate to his style of kingship, which lent itself easily to shows of strength, as he demonstrated in his dealings with the other rulers in the British Isles. John knew Wales well—his first marriage, to the heiress to the earldom of Gloucester, had made him lord of Glamorgan—and he had made an extended, if unfortunate, visit to Ireland in 1185. But these experiences did nothing to modify the forcefulness with which he subsequently imposed his will on these countries. Between 1209 and 1211 the kings and princes of Scotland, Ireland, and Wales were successively and comprehensively humiliated.

---

[4] *Rotuli Litterarum Patentium, 1201–1216*, ed. T. D. Hardy (Record Commission; 1835), 72.

In Ireland John also showed his constructive side by enacting a formal introduction of the English common law, albeit one which primarily benefited the English settlers there, and followed this up by the dispatch of a register of writs as the basis for litigation. In Wales, Llywelyn ab Iorwerth of Gwynedd had extended his principality at the expense of his neighbours, and in the process established himself as the leader of the native princes in their opposition to the English. Humbled in 1211, Llywelyn led a show of resistance in the following year, only for John to prepare a tremendous display of military power, on a scale sufficient to finish the independence of the Welsh for good and all.

The Welsh expedition never happened, cut short by plots and rumours of plots against a king whose exigent style of government, fatally combining political clumsiness and practical efficiency, was finally beginning to take its toll. Resentment shaded into resistance, starting in the north of England, but not confined to it. Beset on every front, John characteristically sprang a surprise on his opponents, when in 1213 he made peace with the Church, accepted Langton as archbishop, and put himself and his kingdom under the protection of the pope. This unexpected move bought John time to pursue his continental ambitions. But there was to be no let-out when the crushing defeat of his allies at Bouvines, on 27 July 1214, ended his hopes of recovering his lost lands in France. Resistance to a medieval ruler most often took the form of armed rebellion, in the name of another member of the royal family, or perhaps of a dynastic rival. Nevertheless, a charter of liberties was a far from unusual way of resolving disputes between rulers and subjects in western Europe in the years around 1200. In England there was an important precedent, in the charter, rich in promises of good government, which Henry I had granted after his coronation in 1100. By invoking this, the king's enemies conferred respectability on their resistance, taking their stand on a high ground of political morality from which they would be very reluctant to descend. Even after their occupation of London on 17 May 1215 gave them the military advantage, the baronial rebels continued to negotiate with John, in a process which finally culminated in the issue of the great charter (Magna Carta) in the middle of June, probably on the 15th, certainly by the 19th.

Magna Carta's immediate importance lies in its political standing as an attempt to prevent civil war, and in the commentary it provides on sixty years of government by Henry II and his sons. It attests throughout the expanding range and scope of royal administration, and its perceived centralizing thrust. The Charter's penultimate clause, ordering that what the king had granted to the tenants-in-chief should in turn be observed by the latter in their dealings with their tenants, was thus the natural extension of the concern of Henry II and his successors to secure the loyalty and service of all their subjects, and not just of the baronage.

Although they manifested themselves there in concise prescriptions for legal and administrative practice, general issues lay behind many of the Charter's clauses. The Charter expressed acceptance of the judicial reforms and innovations of Henry II's reign, while rejecting the political uses to which the king's extended jurisdiction could be put. Law was still apt to be an agency of government. The famous thirty-ninth clause, promising not to proceed against any free man 'except by the lawful judgement of his peers or by the law of the land', attempted to push them apart. Similarly the following clause, pledging that 'To no one will we sell, to no one will we deny or delay right or justice', aimed to prevent the king's mastery of the processes of justice from serving as an implement of political control. The king's ability to exploit his feudal rights at will was severely restricted when the relief for all baronies was fixed at £100.

Resentment was directed against the king's agents as well as against the king himself. Many were perceived as aliens, hence John's promise to employ as his officers none 'who do not know the law of the land and mean to observe it well', and his undertaking to dismiss his foreign captains and soldiers. Such clauses reflect a growing English self-consciousness, partly expressed in linguistic terms. It had been a criticism in 1191 of William de Longchamp, Richard I's unpopular chief minister, that he knew no English. Other clauses were likewise overtly political in character, for instance the stipulation that all hostages and charters given as security to the king by Englishmen and by the king of Scots (King William in 1209 had been forced to hand over his daughters) and Llywelyn should be given back, that any Welshman disseised by John, his father, or his brother should have his lands restored, and that London should have 'all its ancient liberties and free customs'. But pre-eminent in its political implications was the Charter's penalty clause, ordaining that if John failed to observe his undertakings he was to be forced into compliance by distraint and distress directed by twenty-five barons. No attempt was made to find an external arbiter, consequently the twenty-five would be both a party to and the judge of their own case.

In the short term the Charter solved nothing. John accepted it for just long enough to enable him first to put his enemies in the wrong when they made further demands, and then to secure its annulment by the pope. By September 1215 there was civil war, in which John held the upper hand, until the barons, reverting to an older style of rebellion, called in Louis, son of Philip Augustus of France, as a rival king. Thereafter there was a military stalemate until John died, on the night of 27/8 October 1216. His death did not end the civil war. But increasingly it gave the advantage to the supporters of the 9-year-old Henry III, who was crowned at Gloucester on 18 October 1216. He attracted loyalty as his father's heir, but without his father's enmities, and with the support of the pope. Under the regency of the venerable William Marshal there was a deliberate movement towards reconciliation and political righteousness. Nevertheless, Henry's cause was slow to gain momentum, and it was battle which decided the issue in 1217, the defeat of Louis's forces on land and at sea. Victory was followed by a reissue of Magna Carta, the second of the Minority, but this time accompanied by a separate charter of the forest. Thus quickly did the great charter become what it remained thereafter, both a talisman and a yardstick of constitutional rectitude.

Young kings in England and Scotland, 1216–1234

The Minority regime was a great success. Headed by the justiciar, Hubert de Burgh, after William Marshal's death in 1219, it employed an adroit combination of persuasion, bribery, chicanery, and force to get the kingdom's administrative machinery back into working order with remarkable speed. Between 1217 and 1223 the law courts were reopened and a nationwide judicial eyre held, taxes began once more to be raised, and royal lands and castles were recovered from those who had usurped them. In 1225 the government levied a tax on moveables at the rate of a fifteenth, but took care to show its concern for newly established constitutional proprieties through a definitive

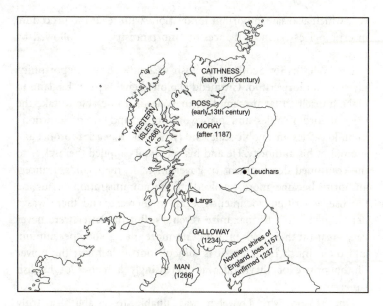

Map 15 The expansion of royal power in Scotland

reissue of the charters. It was still speaking in the young king's name when it declared that the reissue was made 'of our own spontaneous goodwill'.[5] Two years later Henry III came of age and was able to speak for himself.

A young king of Scots was also growing up in these years. Alexander II succeeded his father in 1214, aged 16. Old enough to rule, he exploited John's difficulties to reassert his ancestral claim to the northern shires of England, and was briefly acknowledged as their lord. These gains were quickly lost, and Alexander settled for an English marriage and, in 1237, for the final abandonment of his claim to Cumberland, Westmorland, and Northumberland, in return for English lands worth £200 per annum. But he consolidated his position at home, extending royal power into Caithness and Ross, and above all into Galloway, a show of strength derived from his ability to exploit feudal inheritance law. (See Map 15.) Alexander II was something of an innovator in matters legal: it was during his reign that possessory assizes after the English model were introduced to Scotland, starting with novel disseisin (novel dissasine) in 1230, a

---

[5] *English Historical Documents*, iii, ed. H. Rothwell (London, 1975), 341.

year which also saw important innovations with regard to procedure in criminal cases; mort d'ancestor (mortancestry) had followed by 1253.

For Wales as for Scotland, English weakness meant opportunity. Llywelyn ab Iorwerth of Gwynedd exploited civil wars in England to make himself so far pre-eminent in Wales as to be able to take the titles of 'lord of Wales' and 'prince of Aberffro and lord of Snowdon', to build castles on a noble scale, and (probably) to wear a coronet as a symbol of his authority. He and his successors applied themselves to the continued development of government in their lands. Princely authority became more involved in the administration of justice, the use of written documents began to increase, and there was a determined effort to maximize revenues. But the latter were never very great (at their peak probably no more than £6,000 per annum, and often much less), and it is difficult not to feel that the power of the prince of Gwynedd was increasingly a matter of English sufferance.

One reason why Llywelyn was unable to establish a truly independent authority was that he could be attacked from the west as well as the south and east—it was with the aid of a fleet from Ireland that in 1223 the English recovered Cardigan and Carmarthen castles, lost to Llywelyn in 1215. Although Ireland was far from completely conquered in the early thirteenth century, the native Irish were not yet equipped to counter-attack as the Welsh had done. Indeed, the first two decades of Henry III's reign saw significant English advances at their expense, above all in Connacht, where there were major campaigns in 1228 and 1235. The latter was led by the justiciar, the official head of the king's government in Ireland, and his involvement underlines the importance of royal support for enterprises of conquest. Ireland was prosperous in the early thirteenth century, a fact which stimulated royal interest, and no doubt furthered the development of government along English lines. Most of the institutions found at Westminster also came to be employed at Dublin—exchequer, chancery, centralized courts of law—and there were similar parallels in local government, with the employment of sheriffs and escheators. But the closeness of control implicit in these developments had its dangers for the English settlers, in the power it gave the king to discourage further conquest, or to diminish the chances of a successful campaign by withholding his support.

In the early 1240s a series of deaths put several major Anglo-Irish lordships at Henry III's disposal, through his control of the wardship of minors and the marriage of heiresses. He made the most of the patronage thus fortuitously given him, and a number of new families received Irish baronies. But the incomers were less powerful and wealthy than their predecessors, and less often resident on their lands, while Henry himself remained content to maintain a purely symbolic presence in Ireland, in the form of 'the king and queen sitting with their baronage' which in 1243 he had painted over the dais in the hall of Dublin castle. Without the impetus which strong royal backing could have provided, the English conquest remained incomplete, patchy even in the regions of domination. In County Dublin itself, for instance, the Irish of the Wicklow Mountains were never subdued.

Like his father, Henry III was more interested in the Continent than in other parts of the British Isles. He was reluctant to admit John's loss of his French lands as final, and he also felt the appeal of French artistic culture and of the French monarchy. Louis IX of France, canonized after his death, was in his lifetime a model of chivalry, justice, and piety for western Christendom, at once a rival and an exemplar to the English king. Henry III, though undeniably pious, could also be sharp-tongued and quick-tempered—he is recorded as tearing up the clothes of one of his court jesters, and throwing another into the Thames. But he lacked the cruelty and mean-spiritedness of his father, and also King John's single-mindedness and energy. He wanted to cut a dash on the European stage, but had neither the means nor the personality to support his aspirations. A campaign to Brittany in 1230 was a fiasco, ending with a furious quarrel between Henry and Hubert de Burgh. The latter was dismissed as justiciar in 1232. A new government in which the dominant figure was Peter des Roches, bishop of Winchester, proved too factious to last. An inequitable distribution of patronage and an aggressive policy of resumption provoked rebellion, in which the outstanding figure was Richard Marshal, earl of Pembroke.

The sheer extent of Richard's lands and interests quickly led to an English conflict embracing the whole of the British Isles. There was war on the Welsh March, where the rebels made an alliance with Llywelyn, there appear to have been attempts to form an alliance with the Scots, while it was in Ireland that Richard Marshal met his death in 1234. His removal from the scene led to peace, with des Roches and his followers being dismissed. This was largely organized by the bishops, led by Archbishop Edmund. There is nothing surprising about this. Bishops were of their nature great barons, closely involved in the affairs of the realm, regularly summoned to councils and, later, parliaments. They were also routinely involved with much that would later fall within the remit of secular government, through their concern with such issues as the laws of marriage, the administration of wills, and perjury. Moreover, they often owed their sees to political or administrative services, which they could normally expect to go on performing together with their diocesan duties. In 1234 they helped to establish a peace in England which would last for nearly thirty years.

Contrasts in kingship, 1234–1258

In the wider British dimension, Henry III was content to maintain his own hegemony, usually by peaceful means. In 1237 the Treaty of York finally disposed of Scottish claims to northern England. In 1240 Llywelyn ab Iorwerth died, and at once Henry III set about reasserting English authority in Wales. Llywelyn's son Dafydd lost all the ground which his father had gained. His efforts to gain the pope's protection by becoming a papal vassal were thwarted by English diplomacy, and armed resistence was no more successful. In the war which broke out in 1245, Gwynedd—unprecedentedly—was invaded by land, and Anglesey was ravaged by a force provided by the king of Connacht, acting as Henry III's vassal. But there was no fight to the finish. A comprehensive overlordship in Wales sufficed for Henry, as it did in Ireland. Like his predecessors, he was anxious to promote the interests of his family. When in 1254 he created an apanage for his eldest son, Edward, two of its principal components were the lordship of Ireland and the earldom of Chester, within which was comprised several Welsh lordships.

It was primarily his French ambitions which made King Henry relatively unaggressive in Britain. His marriage in 1236, to Eleanor of Provence, was principally arranged with this consideration in mind. But he seldom had the resources to finance both foreign wars and the ordinary processes of government, not to mention his architectural and artistic undertakings, above all Westminster Abbey (see Figure 9).

The Abbey could serve several purposes. It would give added lustre to the administrative capital of the realm, as Westminster now was, and would do so, moreover, at the expense of London, with which his relations were always uneasy. And it proclaimed the cult of Edward the Confessor, whose name Henry had conferred on his own eldest son in 1239. It was important that the Confessor had also been a king. Westminster Abbey was the traditional coronation church; resplendently transformed, at a cost of well over £40,000, it would glorify kingship in the image which Henry had chosen for himself, one which owed much to the earlier royal saint. It was not a warlike image—no soldier himself, Henry was represented on his second great seal without the ruler's traditional sword—but rather one of a monarch who was wise, peaceful, and generous. Henry's ideas of kingship were undeniably lofty, as he occasionally aired them. But although he might talk as though he had a God-given position above lesser men, a residual common sense usually prevented his acting on these moments of inspiration, which, indeed, usually served to irritate his subjects without adding to his authority. In a dispute over a wardship, the countess of Arundel is reputed to have asked him 'O Lord King, why do you turn your face away from justice? It is impossible now to obtain what is right in your court. You are placed in the midst between God and us, but neither yourself nor us do you rule sanely . . . '.[6]

At a less theoretical level, the king's freedom of action was limited by persistent financial problems. He could very seldom raise money by taxation. He was granted a fortieth in 1232 and a thirtieth in 1237, but was thereafter limited to feudal aids of a traditional kind. In 1245 approval of an aid for the marriage of the king's daughter was obtained from an assembly that can plausibly be described as a parliament, an expression first recorded in an administrative context in 1236. Parliament is not to be too narrowly defined. Primarily a discussion or debate, it took both name and function from the king's need for counsel when the affairs of the realm required it. Important matters, it was felt, needed extensive debate and formal assent. In the 1230s and 1240s, as knights became increasingly

[6] Matthew Paris, *Chronica Majora*, ed. H. R. Luard (7 vols., Rolls Series; 1872–83), v. 336.

involved in government, it is likely that they attended parliaments alongside bishops and barons, perhaps in considerable numbers. It was probably in order to obtain an attendance which would be more manageable, numerically and politically, that in 1254 Henry III ordered that each shire should elect two knights for an assembly which he hoped would grant him an aid. None was forthcoming. But it is significant that Henry believed that the assent of such a gathering would have made taxation possible, and that he did not try to tax without it. Instead he was reduced to raising money as his immediate forebears had done, by ad hoc means.

Some efforts were made to control the growing multitudes of the king's officials in the shires, but to small effect, while very little was done to restrain those of the barons. This was in keeping with Henry III's principal domestic policy from the mid-1230s, which was to remain on good terms with the magnates. If this meant taking an insufficient concern for the fortunes of his humbler subjects, it was a price which he was content the latter should pay. By a clever use of patronage, he managed to win the magnates' acceptance of the kinsmen of his wife, members of the ruling family of Savoy, who had become members of his own circle. The year 1247, however, saw the arrival of a different group of outsiders, members of the Lusignan family from Poitou, sons of Henry III's mother from her second marriage. These newcomers proved far harder to accommodate; the supply of patronage was beginning to dry up, and partly for that reason they quarrelled with the Savoyards and many others.

In 1250 Henry III took the cross. The crusade had retained its appeal to Englishmen (and extended it to Scots). Henry's brother, Richard of Cornwall, and his brother-in-law, Simon de Montfort, went to Palestine in 1240, and perhaps their example, as well as that of Louis IX, who set out in 1248, reinforced King Henry's own strong religious piety, and helped to persuade him that he, too, should fight for the recovery of Christianity's Holy Places. His decision had important repercussions, for as he set about gathering a war-chest, he had less money to give away to friends and favourites. Moreover, Henry added to his difficulties with an expensive expedition to Gascony in 1253/4, and above all with the absurdity of the Sicilian business. To help the pope against the Hohenstaufen, in 1254 Henry accepted the throne of Sicily (nominally a papal fief) for his second son Edmund, undertaking to pay 135,000 marks and provide an army towards this end. The enterprise was utterly beyond Henry's means, and had no hope whatever of success.

The Sicilian scheme on Edmund's behalf was an eccentric manifestation of the desire to provide for his children which in the same year led Henry to create an apanage for his eldest son. Growing up into an arrogant and unruly young man, Edward made a tour of his lands in north-east Wales in 1256 which did much to drive the Welsh into rebellion late in that year. The rising, which was quick to gather support, was led by Llywelyn ap Gruffudd, the grandson of Llywelyn ab Iorwerth, who had been occupied in establishing himself as undisputed ruler of Gwynedd since his uncle Dafydd's death in 1246. Everywhere the English and their Welsh allies were driven back, and in June 1257 an attempted counter-attack was shatteringly defeated in the Tywi valley. Suddenly everything was going wrong for Henry III at once. Also in 1257, the Church would only promise financial assistance on strictly limited terms, while a harvest failure led to deaths from starvation and a crime wave. For most Englishmen, the king's government had become simultaneously oppressive and ineffective, while the magnates, including the Savoyards, were exasperated by the favour being shown to the Lusignans. When quarrels broke out between the latter and their rivals at court, Henry glaringly failed, even refused outright, to do justice. Two strands of discontent finally worked together at the end of April 1258, with a *coup d' état* by the English baronage, demanding both a political purge and administrative reform.

At the same time as the English monarchy was being overwhelmed by its problems, the Scottish one was emerging from a time of troubles resulting from the minority of Alexander III, who had succeeded his father in 1249 at the age of 8. Ten years of political discord had followed, often exacerbated by English interference. But from 1258 Henry III was preoccupied at home, leaving Alexander III, who took control of the government of his realm in 1261, free to respond to the efforts of Haakon IV of Norway to re-establish his overlordship in the Western Isles. In 1263 Haakon brought a substantial fleet to the Hebrides, and thence to the Ayrshire coast, where a small-scale but hard-fought battle took place at Largs on 2 October. The conflict brought neither side a clear-cut victory, but was nevertheless decisive in its results—the Norwegians withdrew, and in 1266

Haakon's son Magnus abandoned his claim to the Western Isles and Man. Resistance on the latter was crushed in 1275.

The Scottish king seldom implemented policy by force of arms, not least because a mercenary army of the sort best able to fight extended campaigns was usually beyond his means. His average annual revenue in the late thirteenth century was about £8,000, derived from a still substantial landed base, from the customs on wool and hides introduced between 1275 and 1282, and from a variety of incidental payments. His finances were controlled by an apparatus which was old-fashioned by English standards, but not therefore unsophisticated—a list of muniments made in 1292 shows that sources of revenue were closely scrutinized and recorded. As in England, the king's council was the highest court in the realm, and was likewise capable of extension into a larger assembly, a parliament or colloquy, when there were important matters to be discussed.

The Scottish king retained the paternal image of an earlier regnal style, and was not yet set apart by crowning and unction from his subjects, who were apt, indeed, to address him in a free and familiar style. Hence the rebuke reportedly given to Alexander III on the night of his death by the manager of the Inverkeithing saltpans—'My lord, what are you doing here in such a storm and such darkness? Often have I tried to persuade you that your nocturnal rambles will bring you no good ... '.[7] The Scottish nobles quarrelled with one another for control of government during a royal minority, but seldom rebelled against their king. The baronial coup of 1258 in England, by contrast, turned into a revolt which led to the king's captivity and could have resulted in his deposition. This was unintended by the barons, whose approach to the task of administrative reform was purposeful and pragmatic, and showed a clear vision of what needed to be done. They believed in the effectiveness of royal government, and since the king could not be trusted to direct it equitably, they took the task upon themselves, acting through councils appointed to wield the king's authority, and enacting that the progress of reform should be reviewed in three parliaments each year. The Lusignans refused to cooperate and were expelled from the realm.

---

[7] *The Chronicle of Lanercost, 1272–1346*, trans. H. Maxwell (Glasgow, 1913), 41.

English travails, Welsh opportunity, 1258–1272

The reforming measures of the baronial movement were embodied above all in the Provisions of Westminster, issued in October 1259. They look back to Magna Carta, sometimes specifically, and likewise provide a commentary on the government they propose to reform. Their range is wide, but they give most attention to the administration of justice and its abuses, both in the king's courts and those of the magnates. Thus, the protection given to the rights of heirs was directed against a 'chief lord' who could have been any lord, not just the king. The justices appointed to investigate malpractices were to inquire into the conduct both of 'the sheriffs and their bailiffs', and also of 'the bailiffs of the great men in the land, and about the great men themselves'.[8] However, the demand for an impartial treatment of abuses was far from universally welcome among the magnates. It split the baronial movement, and allowed the emergence of a new leadership, headed by Simon de Montfort, earl of Leicester. Montfort was the king's brother-in-law, having married Henry's sister Eleanor in 1238, but he was always something of an outsider at court. He was indeed a profoundly unsettling figure, an intense, aggressive, clever, and formidable man, seldom able to suffer fools gladly, or to conceal the fact that he regarded Henry III as one of them. Devout in his religion, he could inspire devotion in others, for whom he was a charismatic leader, but he also aroused fear. The paradox that the strongest protagonist of reform in England was himself French did not go unnoticed by contemporaries. Nevertheless, Montfort repeatedly kept the reform movement going when its former adherents looked like falling back into the king's allegiance, or even did so.

In 1258–9 the king was on the defensive, losing control of government and temporarily estranged from his eldest son. Henry's fortunes started to mend at the end of 1259, when in the Treaty of Paris he finally renounced his claim to the French lands lost by John, but was confirmed in the duchy of Aquitaine, though with the obligation

---

[8] *Documents of the Baronial Movement of Reform and Rebellion, 1258–1267*, ed. R. F. Treharne and I. J. Sanders (Oxford Medieval Texts; 1973), 15.

of doing homage to Louis IX for it. Able now to concentrate on his native realm, Henry took the initiative in his contest with the baronial reformers and in 1261 secured papal absolution from the concessions he had been obliged to make since 1258. Montfort began to lose support among the magnates, but he retained the loyalty of many in the lower ranks of society, not least among knights and gentry unwilling to follow their own immediate lords into the king's camp. The summer of 1263 saw a series of violent attacks on leading 'aliens', foreign-born royalists who stood foremost in the ranks of the reformers' enemies. It was pre-eminently round these men that conflicting attitudes to the important issue of counsel, of the king's freedom to choose his own advisers, had crystallized. It was an issue with a significant bearing on a concept of increasing importance in these years, that of the community of the realm, raising the question of who did or did not belong within it. The treatment of the aliens, and also of the Jews, who suffered a dreadful massacre in London in 1264, shows that there were limits to its inclusiveness.

Ideology as an element in English political life was primarily the creation of Magna Carta, especially through its stress on law, which came to be increasingly regarded as an agent of the greater good. This attitude, which permeates the treatise known as *Bracton*, written *c*.1230, recurs regularly in the propaganda of both sides in the 1260s. There is frequent reference to basic principles, to the king's rights and honour, on one side, to the right of poor men as well as rich to justice, on the other. The *Song of Lewes*, written for the Montfortian cause in the mid-1260s, sets out the basis of the king's claim to select his own counsellors, only to rebut it. The king is placed firmly under the law, and his first duty lies not towards 'his own profit, but his regard for his subjects by whom he is trusted'. The community of the realm has a proper interest in the choice of the king's advisers, who should be neither strangers nor favourites 'who supplant others and the good customs'.[9] A king ought, indeed, to be a Christlike figure, the servant of his subjects, whose interest he should set before his own. Not surprisingly, the baronial movement took on some of the characteristics of a crusade.

Civil war did not come without every effort being made to avert it, as in November 1263, when both sides agreed to submit the dispute to

[9] *English Historical Documents*, iii, ed. Rothwell, 911, 912.

the arbitration of Louis IX. On 23 January 1264, however, Louis quashed the Provisions entirely. Inevitably his award was rejected by Montfort and his followers. Disorder spread, beginning in the Welsh Marches, where Montfort made an alliance with Llywelyn of Gwynedd, and their forces attacked English marcher lords who were the enemies of both. Since 1257 Llywelyn had gone from strength to strength, establishing an unchallenged hegemony within native Wales, and making substantial gains from the marchers. The beginnings of civil war would later be dated to 5 April 1264, when Henry III's army stormed Northampton. But this promising start for the king was soon reversed, for on 14 May he was defeated and captured, along with his brother and eldest son, at Lewes. Henry had no alternative but to swear to observe the Provisions and dismiss his objectionable counsellors, and a council of nine was set up, in effect to govern in his name. This meant more than personal humiliation, it entailed a total surrender of royal power.

Montfort's triumph was illusory, his power insufficient to support his ambitions. The papacy was unfriendly. Ireland was hostile, the Welsh March unsettled, the north of England disordered. In an attempt to broaden the base of his government Montfort had burgesses as well as knights summoned to the January parliament of 1265, but his problem was not one which could be solved by gestures of this kind. As anarchy loomed in all directions, Montfort found that the very completeness of his mastery had nullified the royal authority on which government depended. Hostility to his regime was exacerbated by the violence and greed of some of his supporters, led by his own sons. The deadlock was finally broken by Edward, who on 28 May escaped from captivity. He quickly joined up with the royalists among the marcher lords, and together they overwhelmed and killed Montfort at Evesham on 4 August.

The revolting mutilation of Montfort's corpse is one indication of the passions his career had aroused. Another is the wave of reprisals against his followers after his defeat and death. But Henry III was a peacemaker by temperament, and so was the papal legate, Ottobuono Fieschi, who arrived in England in October 1265. The Dictum of Kenilworth, issued on 31 October 1267, declared Henry III restored to all his previous authority, but also requested him to observe Magna Carta and the charter of the forest. Among the enactments of the years since 1258, it upheld those to which the king had assented 'freely and not under compulsion'. Effectively, it upheld the Provisions which Henry had himself confirmed, in a bid for support, in January 1263, and quashed the rest, as made under duress. Equally important, the Dictum offered rebels deprived of their lands the opportunity of redeeming them, for sums calculated in proportion to their involvement in the rebellion. At first it did not provide that rebels should be reinstated in their lands before they started to pay for their recovery, and it was only in April 1267, after the earl of Gloucester put pressure on the king by occupying London, that this essential concession was granted.

The following year saw two major enactments. The Treaty of Montgomery, concluded on 25 September 1267, was primarily concerned with Llywelyn. Not for the first time, political instability had created opportunities for native Wales. Disunity, arising from internal divisions, had in the past been exacerbated by the deliberate policy of the English crown, intent on preventing the establishment of a hierarchy of command dominated by any single Welsh ruler. Llywelyn hankered after an acknowledged overlordship, giving him authority over lesser lords and making him the arbiter in their disputes, while excluding English influence and capacity for interference. In 1265, shortly before Evesham, a treaty with Montfort, acting in King Henry's name, gave Llywelyn most of what he wanted, and two years later Henry himself was no less amenable. Llywelyn's recent gains, above all in Powys and Builth, were confirmed, and his pre-eminence in Wales was underlined by his being conceded the title of 'prince of Wales', to whom all save one of the lesser Welsh rulers owed homage, as tenants-in-chief to their lord. He himself still owed fealty and homage to the English king, and his position was arguably unstable, derived as it was from English weakness, and bitterly resented by Edward's followers among the marchers who had done so much to overthrow Simon de Montfort. But for the present Llywelyn's position looked secure.

The Statute of Marlborough, issued on 18 November, was England's great peacemaking statement. Embodying much of the Dictum of Kenilworth, and of the Provisions of Westminster concerned with the reform of law and judicial practice, the Statute, like the Dictum, was presented as an act of royal grace. No longer did Henry feel obliged to regard the reforms of 1259 as a threat to his regality. The end of civil war was followed by a good deal of disorder, but the recovery of administrative order was swift enough for Edward to be able to plan a crusade, and for a twentieth levied to pay for it to raise nearly £31,500 in 1269 and 1270.

Henry III presided at the translation of the remains of Edward the Confessor to Westminster Abbey on 13 October 1269, and just over three years later was buried in the abbey after his death on 16 November 1272. Matthew Paris had in 1254 identified him as 'the lynx penetrating all' foretold by Merlin. The likeness was not intended as a compliment, being chosen with reference to the king's indefatigable pursuit of other people's money. Henry's inability to manage his finances had nearly brought him to total disaster, and though he ultimately proved a survivor, later attempts to proclaim him a sanctified king like the Confessor came to nothing. But although his son was still on crusade when Henry died, there was no lapse of the king's peace, and Edward I's reign began just four days later. Probably no English king needed the assurance of an undisputed accession less than Edward I. Aged 33 when his father died, more than anyone else the victor in the civil wars, in the world of aristocratic chivalry he moved as an insider as his father had never done. The self-confidence born of military prowess was reinforced, moreover, by an untroubled faith that the law was always on his side. Sure of himself, certain that he knew what needed to be done, he probably arrived in England for his coronation in 1274 ready to set about recovering lost ground.

Kingship and statecraft in the late thirteenth century: the supremacy of Edward I, 1272–1284

Edward I was a great legislator, and the years after 1275 saw the issue of a remarkable series of statutes. These were commonly enacted in parliament, whose growing importance as an extended agency of counsel made it natural that it should be associated with law-giving, partly because its growing attendance allowed for wider publicity (it became increasingly common for knights and burgesses to attend), and partly because it also became the regular occasion for the presenting of petitions for the redress of grievances. These two functions may be detected in Edward I's statutes. Some statutes dealt with individual issues, for instance with alienations of property to the Church in 1279, and with law enforcement in 1285. Others dealt with a whole series of different points, originating in petitions presented by individuals to parliament, or arising from actions in the courts, or from troublesome incidents which drew attention to particular problems. Even before his first parliament met, Edward I ordered a wide-ranging investigation of government in the shires. Many of the clauses of the first Statute of Westminster, issued on 22 April 1275, dealt with the abuses these inquiries revealed. The government shrank from a root and branch reform, but his concern with official malpractices had the beneficial effect of identifying Edward I with the aims of the baronial reform movement.

Nowhere was Edward I's readiness to innovate more important than in the sphere of finance. In 1275 a customs duty on wool exports, at the rate of 6s. 8d. per sack, was introduced. Quite apart from their value as a source of revenue—about £10,000 per annum—the customs provided the king with a security he could offer against loans, and the means of servicing the interest payments on the debts he was thus enabled to contract. Thanks primarily to the customs, Edward I was able to live on credit, and as a result enjoyed a financial independence, at least in peace time, that his father had never achieved.

Edward I would still need to raise money by taxation to meet the costs of war, a burden he first shouldered in his dealings with Wales. Llywelyn had worked hard to consolidate the position he achieved in 1267, perhaps too hard. Neither his efforts to extend his authority through the supervision of local courts nor his pursuit of revenue by every available means are likely to have made him friends. A collection of articles presented to Edward I in 1283, after the death of Llywelyn, paid tribute to the beneficial qualities of the latter's rule, his generosity and his readiness to pardon fines, but also listed, at far greater length, the complaints of his former subjects against his exactions and usurpations—his disregard of the traditional rights of the native nobility and the multiplication of princely courts and officials resulting from his governance. Handicapped by divisions within his own family, in his dealings with Edward I Llywelyn found that his position under the Treaty of Montgomery was less secure than he had hoped. Llywelyn's claims to the independence granted him in 1267 were countered by Edward's assertions of the overlordship which the treaty had left in being, and in 1277 the prince of Wales was put in his place in a few months by a massive show of military force. His surrender lost for Llywelyn the gains confirmed to him only ten years earlier, and left him at Edward I's mercy.

The latter was always apt to be tempered by legalism. Tension was maintained by disputes over jurisdiction, and also over whether litigation should be conducted under Welsh or English law, and by the insensitivity of English officials. Against a background of growing Welsh resentment, Llywelyn was unable to control his younger brother Dafydd, who in March 1282 launched a revolt. Llywelyn was quick to join it, but with fatal results, for on 11 December he was killed near Builth and his principality swiftly extinguished. It was characteristic of Edward I that he should have regarded a statute, as well as castles, as an appropriate means of settling a newly conquered country. The Statute of Wales of 1284 in its preamble described how the king and his advisers had reviewed the existing state of the Welsh laws, and had 'abolished some of them, allowed some and corrected some'.[10] A large-scale introduction of English administrative and legal procedures provoked serious discontent, and caused a major rebellion in 1294/5, but the settlement which followed the conquest would endure.

In that respect Wales differed from Ireland. Henry III and Edward I regarded Ireland as primarily a source of wealth and patronage, and they had no strong motive for encouraging further conquest. There was also a shortage of settlers who could have made further English occupation effective, while from the 1250s the unconquered Irish began an energetic series of counter-attacks, strengthened by mercenaries from Scotland. The momentum of advance was consequently lost, leaving a series of ragged frontiers for the English lordship. Nevertheless the king's financial interests would encourage the development of government in Ireland along English lines. By 1300 there were eleven shires, leaving only north-west Ireland entirely out of the administrative system thus created. The sheriffs performed much the same duties as their English counterparts, while judicial eyres administered justice, at least for the English settlers. A native Irishman needed an individual grant of English law if he was to enjoy its

---

[10] *English Historical Documents*, iii, ed. Rothwell, 422.

benefits. In the 1270s a group of Irish prelates, perhaps because they were dissatisfied with their native 'Brehon' law, attempted to gain a comprehensive grant of English law for a payment of 7,000 marks. Edward I agreed in principle, observing that 'the laws which the Irish use are detestable to God and so contrary to all law that they ought not to be called laws'.[11] But nothing further happened. The price was probably too high, and the Irish themselves were unenthusiastic.

Edward I never set foot in Ireland. Nor in the mid-1280s was he greatly concerned about Scotland. In March 1286 Alexander III, an exemplary monarch in everything except leaving a male heir, was accidentally killed. That Edward saw nothing in this tragedy to prevent his going to Gascony later that year is perhaps a tribute to the basic stability of the Scottish realm which, like England itself in 1272, was able to function without a resident monarch. Subsequent uncertainties and faction-fighting failed to bring Edward home, and only in the year after his eventual return did he begin to interest himself seriously in Scottish affairs.

Seen in the perspective of the doctrine that history is the study of change over time, the geopolitical map of the British Isles in the mid-1280s was indeed substantially different from that of the 1160s. The intervening period had seen English expansion and settlement over much of Ireland, and the complete disappearance of independent Wales. Conquest in both lands was closely followed by the introduction of English methods of government and justice, also highly influential in Scotland. There, however, a successful native dynasty kept English power at arm's length, in 1237 settling an enduring frontier with its southern neighbour, and like England expanding at the expense of what had once been independent, or near-independent, outliers. But history also needs to take into account resistances to change. Superficially, at least, much in the 1280s was still as it had been 120 years earlier. In both England and Scotland, the body politic continued to be dominated by kings and magnates. In both countries old ideas about the importance of consent to royal action, and the need for counsel before such consent was given, lay behind the development of parliament from the king's council. The expansion of the royal courts, most noteworthy in England, developed from the

---

[11] J. Otway-Ruthven, 'The request of the Irish for English law, 1277–80', *Irish Historical Studies*, 6 (1948–9), 261–70, at p. 262.

ancient concept of the king as the fount of justice. Government extended further and deeper by the end of the thirteenth century, involving more people in its activities, both as agents and subjects, but no new rationale had been proposed for their involvement.

The development of institutional government in the high middle ages has sometimes been described in terms of state formation. Late thirteenth-century England and Scotland certainly possessed centralized institutions which could have justified their being described as states in the modern sense, but there is no reason to suppose that deliberate policy lay behind this development. Rather, the essential dynamic for political and governmental action in both realms continued to be kingship, seeking opportunities for the expression of its regality. As organs of government helped to unify kingdoms, the latter found in their rulers a focus for the developing sense of nationhood which their own actions had helped to create. But they did so in essentially personal terms, as indeed they had to do.

Systems of government came into being to enable kings to achieve their ends. An adult king could ultimately decide policy, and success or failure would largely depend on his own administrative, military, and political skills. In Scotland the stability and expansion of the realm was due above all to a succession of able (and relatively long-lived) kings; in England the importance of a king's personal qualities can be most easily gauged by comparing Edward I with his father and son. The system of government over which Edward I presided was one capable of enabling spectacular demonstrations of royal power, as in the conquest of Wales. But kings had to be restrained in their use of machinery so powerful; it was a recurrent feature of medieval English history that rulers who worked the system too hard provoked resentment and eventually resistance. Llywelyn ap Gruffudd may have erred thus in Wales. Quite possibly as able a man as Edward I, but without the latter's resources, he could not distance himself from the workings of the administration that he tried to establish, and consequently found that he could not trust his own subjects.

It would be centuries before 'the crown' became an effective agency of government, regardless of the qualities of the man who wore it. A sophisticated administrative apparatus was in itself no guarantee of successful rule. Although the English colony in Ireland developed institutions identical with those operating both at Westminster and in the English shires, from the 1260s the settlement was forced onto the defensive by a native Irish *revanche*. In any case, there was still more to kingship than expressions of power, and its effectiveness continued to depend as much on horizontal links between a ruler and his leading subjects as on the creation of vertical chains of command. Parliaments provided opportunities for informal contacts as well as for the airing of grievances and the discussion of taxes. An atmosphere of splendour proclaimed the greatness of kings who staged chivalric assemblies and court ceremonial, without compromising the dignity of the magnates and knights who attended. The ties thus created or strengthened, as much as the dynamic of administrative expansion, helped to draw men of regional and local stature into the workings of government.

The process went furthest in England. The confusion which Walter Map had perceived at the heart of Henry II's government had largely disappeared from the court and government of Edward I, thanks to the mature professionalism of those who now ran the exchequer, organized the armies, and presided in the law courts. Those same people also set standards for the knights and gentry whom successive rulers had recruited to participation in the administration of the country at the level of the shires and below, while attempting at the same time to direct and control their unpaid activities. That in the 1280s, as in the 1160s, the English king was still both a figure of international consequence and the dominant figure in the British Isles was owing largely to the effectiveness of the government developed in his realm in the intervening years, uniting as well as ruling the nation on behalf of its sovereign lord.

Figure 11 The chapel of King Cormac, in Cashel, Tipperary, dating from 1127–34, holds claim to be the first Romanesque building in Ireland. It was a royal foundation, built by Cormac MacCarthy, king of Desmond, a relative of Abbot MacCarthy of Ratisbon, a monastery which has architectural parallels with the chapel. Many other influences, both from Normandy and from the west of England, are also thought to have played their part in the design of this most eclectic of twelfth-century Irish churches.

Conclusion

Barbara Harvey

Did the British Isles possess a history of their own in this period, amounting to more than the sum of the histories of England, Ireland, Scotland, and Wales? Reforming popes, whose authority was demonstrated in the fading away of the archbishop of Canterbury's claim to a hegemony covering both Ireland and Britain, would surely have answered 'no' to this question; and so, for different reasons, must we. The real life of the islands was not in the whole but in the parts. But living with the neighbours provided by the accidents of geography and history was a formative experience for each of the four, and an experience to be explored in the context of the whole archipelago. Much of this book has been about interactions of this kind, and from the late eleventh century to the late thirteenth, England's claim to dominance is a thread running through a great many. A conclusion may appropriately begin here.

English overlordship

Down to the late thirteenth century, few actions on the part of the rulers of England imply a desire to subjugate any of its three neighbours, much less all of them. Indeed, only King John's abortive Welsh campaign in 1212 stands out as an exception. The ambitions and principal interests of England's rulers were focused in France, and wars and the rumours of war nearer home could only interfere with these. Yet in a material sense they enjoyed a degree of success nearer home that often eluded them overseas. By the mid-thirteenth century, the lordship of Ireland was annexed to the English crown, and its institutions were to an appreciable extent becoming self-consciously royal. If, moreover, in north Britain, Lothian was now unequivocally part of Scotland, Cumbria (the counties of Cumberland and Westmorland), including the poor but important diocese of Carlisle, was now, with Northumberland, just as clearly part of England. And from the accession of Henry II onwards, the general tendency of encounters between the ruler of England and other rulers in Britain or Ireland, of whom there were still many, had been to make ever more clear the client status of the latter. The Treaty of Montgomery, although at the time a means of enhancing the status of Llywelyn ap Gruffudd of Gwynedd in Wales, proved to have dire consequences for the whole of native Wales only ten years later. Given the continued 'irrepressibility' of so many of the British and Irish peoples into the late twelfth century and beyond, the king of England may never have felt entirely secure in his dealings with them. Yet with hindsight we can see that the strong undertow of the exchanges was towards the strengthening of English dominance in the islands. David I's successes in the 1130s and 1140s, when he wrested control of substantial parts of northern England from Stephen, is one of a small number of exceptions proving the rule, for, untypically for a ruler of England in this period, Stephen was not secure in his realm.

Contingent circumstances played a part in these developments, most remarkably, perhaps in 1169, when Diarmait Mac Murchadha's appeal to Strongbow for assistance precipitated an intervention on the part of Henry II in Ireland, although papal readiness to legitimize such action some fifteen years ago had evoked no response. Essentially, however, the king of England owed his dominance to the superiority of his resources, and his most important resource, it may be suggested, was a large population. A likely figure for the population of England at the time of the Domesday Survey in 1086 is *c.*2 millions; if so, by 1300, as we have seen, it was probably three times as large. The figure at each of these dates is very large indeed in comparison to the most generous estimate we can make for the population of any of the other three countries, and the former suggests that take-off occurred in England well before the late eleventh century. Of course, to a ruler whose core armies consisted mainly of paid knights and men-at-arms, money was a vital resource, and if the king of England never had enough for his ventures in France, he nevertheless did well. Towards the end of the thirteenth century, his income from the wool custom alone (£10,000 per annum) exceeded the total average cash income (£8,000 per annum) of the king of Scotland from all sources, and it was probably about three times that of Llywelyn ap Gruffudd towards the end of his life. The major recoinages occurring in England in 1180, 1247, and 1279 reflect this economic advantage. Scottish mints in this period followed the sterling standard, and in Wales the great increase now occurring in the use of money in many different kinds of relationships was achieved without a native currency. But the very size of the English king's income itself reflects the populous character of the realm. Justice, for example, a major source of royal income by the end of the twelfth century, could be exploited in this way because a large number of people existed to pay fines and amercements. And down to the early thirteenth century, the kings of England could scarcely have embarked on a military venture without the feudal dues paid by the aristocracy and profits squeezed from time to time from the estates of deceased bishops and abbots. These dues and profits, however, came ultimately from rents collected in a well-settled countryside, where abundant labour to some extent compensated for poor technology. Similarly, the domainial resources of the crown, which must have appeared so impressive to William of Normandy as he came to terms with his new role as king of England, were available because the labour existed to actualize them in the form of renders in cash and kind.

Population change

How was it, then, that England was so populous in comparison to her neighbours, and pulled ahead so early? She had a much greater extent of fertile lowland in relation to total land mass than any of them, and less infertile upland where the prevailing pastoral way of life was incapable of supporting more than a thin scatter of people, and less undrained bog where even this was impossible. But not even the widest expanse of cultivable land was ever sufficient in itself to bring about a high density of population, or early take-off: it represented a potential for cultivation and settlement, but without a human response even the best brown earths would yield no cereal crops.

Migration was an important factor in the population changes of this period, but tends more to underline the existence of a surplus population in parts of England at an early date than to explain how this came about. Immigrants of humble status, many of them from England, helped to people the Marches of Wales in the years around 1100 and the south and east of Ireland a century later—in each case with profound consequences for social as well as economic life. Moreover, the extent to which the vernacular of southern Scotland became Anglicized points to settlement here on a substantial scale by men and women of low status in the course of the twelfth century: it was not only Anglo-Norman lords and their immediate retinues who took advantage of the open door of David I and his successors.

Mortality was a more important factor than migration. It tended to be unpredictable and volatile from year to year and to be characterized by notable peaks: these were normally occasioned by epidemics and harvest failures and often by the two in combination, and the descent of mortality from such a peak could be slow. Chroniclers liked to notice these events, and they identify 1189, for example, as a year of famine and high mortality in Wales and 1194–7 as a sequence of years of a similar kind in England. Yet it seems very likely that in the long term mortality rates declined and that every major part of the British Isles probably experienced this decline.

For a general decline in mortality, a general explanation is called for, and we may find it in earlier themes of this book: the creation of new rural and urban markets and expansion of many old ones, the increasing use of money in interpersonal relationships, improvements in law and order—in sum, the whole bundle of changes that made economic life over large areas of Britain and Ireland more sophisticated and stable by the end of the thirteenth century than it had been at the beginning of the twelfth. In a market economy it is as easy to fall as to rise, but in periods of scarcity and famine, easier to survive within such a system than outside it. If, however, the decline in mortality is to be explained in this way, we can be confident that it occurred at an uneven pace over the British Isles considered as a whole, for this was characteristic of the market economy itself: the latter developed more slowly in Scotland than in England and more slowly in Ireland and Wales than in either of the former two. But in each country we should envisage regions and localities where trends in mortality possessed an idiosyncratic character of their own.

With a similar respect for regional and local variations, we can conclude that fertility rose in this period; indeed, such a rise may well have been the main factor in the overall rise in population. But in the case of fertility as in that of mortality, the new trend seems to show itself first in England and subsequently went further in England than elsewhere. Birth rates, the measure of fertility, are not recorded. Marriage, however, which provided the normal context for the procreation of children, is more accessible to us, but we must, of course, envisage it in the appropriate social setting. Even in Celtic and Gaelic Britain and Gaelic Ireland, where the bonds of kindred were stronger than elsewhere in the British Isles, the typical household was apparently the nuclear one, consisting of parents, their unmarried children, and their servants if any. In England a household of this kind was certainly normal. Marriage, therefore, was normally associated with the acquisition of land as a preliminary to the attainment of an independent livelihood and household by the parties involved. If so, however, the possibility of acquiring land did much to determine the proportion of the population that ever married, and age at marriage. Both these factors influenced fertility. It is the search for land as part of the marriage process that we can still glimpse, even at this distance of time.

Rules of inheritance, which differed regionally, and sometimes even over quite small areas, exerted an influence on the availability of land to those wishing to marry, but probably to a smaller extent than we naturally tend to assume. The principal difference to be taken into account is that between impartible inheritance, giving the entire holding to a sole heir, and partibility, which in principle divided it among all the surviving sons, or among the sons and the daughters. In real life, however, where high mortality rates often ensured that landholders were survived by only one heir, if as many, when the time came, these distinctions were often blurred, with the result that opportunities for marriage were not much affected by the prevailing mode of inheritance.

But whatever the rules of inheritance, opportunities for marrying young were certainly enhanced in colonizing regions, where parties wishing to marry could acquire new land outside family control, and it is at this point that substantial areas of England begin to look unusual in comparison to other parts of Britain and Ireland. They do so even at the beginning of our period. In the medieval countryside a tension always existed between those wishing to appropriate the waste for private use and those accustomed to use the land in question in common, as rough pasture; and among the latter, men and women of free status were more capable of effective resistance than the unfree. Where, however, lordship evolved from the personal relationship between lords and their dependants, which characterized it in the early middle ages, into a tenurial relationship conferring on the former rights in the land occupied by the latter, or tended in this direction, the lord himself acquired an interest in the situation. Exploiting his new position, and with scant respect for rights of common, he might now decide to encourage colonization—and indeed underwrite it with his unrivalled capital resources—in return for welcome new rents. Much land colonized in this way was held by one or other of the free tenures then in existence. Or the lord might decide to take such land into his demesne.

Over much of England, lordship with a strong territorial and tenurial bias was already well developed by 1066, and extensive colonization took place here in the late Anglo-Saxon period. We must also take into account at this point the relative security enjoyed by Anglo-Saxon society, in comparison to most societies elsewhere in the British Isles at this time. Here, it may be suggested, is a weighty combination of reasons for the early growth of population in England. Anglo-Norman lords established the same kind of lordship in the Welsh Marches, although without being minded or able to establish the same degree of security or the same actual pattern of estates, and the push into the waste, involving Flemish as well as English colonists, began here before the end of the eleventh century. In Celtic and Gaelic Britain, however, and in Ireland, lordship was much slower to assume a territorial aspect, and lords were in consequence much slower to assume control of the waste. In Ireland, where written sources of the right kinds are very scarce in this period, and where archaeologists have shown much greater interest in prehistoric sites than in medieval ones, the chronology of medieval colonization and settlement still withholds most of its secrets. Very tentatively, however, we can say that colonization of the boggy lowlands by the indigenous population probably began at an early date. Indeed, without it the mixed farming characteristic of many settlements here which were probably in continuous occupation throughout the twelfth century could not have developed. But a much greater extent was colonized after 1170 than before, as English lords organized their newly acquired estates on principles long familiar to them in England, and with an eye on the developing market for agrarian products. We can assume that in Ireland and the Welsh Marches, as in the case of England after 1066, the indigenous inhabitants found it exceptionally difficult to assert their customary rights of common in the waste in a conquest situation.

Eventually, seignorial wings in England were clipped by the degree of protection given to free tenures by the rapidly developing common law. From the late twelfth century, free tenants, whose ancestors had colonized the waste with the encouragement of their lords, were able to use the new procedures of the royal courts to slow down further colonization in the region in question. If they believed that such colonization would curtail existing rights of common there to a harmful extent, they were no longer obliged to ask the lord's own court to hear their plea, but could sue in the king's court, with correspondingly greater hope of success. For this and other reasons, colonization of the waste apparently slowed down in many parts of England after 1200—the very period when evidence of it begins to accumulate in some other parts of the British Isles for the first time.

The growth of a peasant land market in England—a striking feature of the rural economy there in the thirteenth century—was also helpful to those in search of land as a preliminary to marriage. Of course, this development did not augment the actual supply of land. But it helped to bring about a more rapid circulation of the available amounts than would otherwise have been possible, and did so in the very period when the supply of new land to colonize declined. By a 'market', in this context, we should understand a system of exchanges in which land was transferred from seller to buyer on terms freely negotiated between the two parties, without more than a formal intervention, if as much, by lord or kin in the proceedings. The land market in this sense was most active in the south and south-east of England. Here, it represents a way of obtaining land, in regions where the economy was now highly monetized, that did not develop to the same extent in other parts of the country. Indeed, with the possible exception of English Ireland, this market may have had no parallel in other parts of the British Isles. By the end of the thirteenth century, in the manor of Redgrave, in Suffolk, it was as common for land to change hands in the market as by the mechanism of inheritance, and at Hinderclay, in the same county, more common.

Finally, it is possible that the legal status of women in England had consequences of a positive kind for marriage and fertility that were not replicated elsewhere in Britain or Ireland, except in some Anglicized regions there. In England, by the thirteenth century, the generous apportionment of dower to widows in aristocratic society was, it appears, often mirrored in town and countryside lower down the social scale. In consequence, the widows in question were able to take substantial amounts of property into a new marriage. 'Housbondes at chirche dore she hadde fyve.' In the twelfth and thirteenth centuries, as in the fourteenth, when Chaucer wrote these words of the Wife of Bath, the exchange of vows in a lawful marriage, conducted according to the Church's rites, took place at the church door, before husband and wife, as they now were, entered the church for the nuptial Mass. Gap-toothed, bold in face, and of a ruddy complexion, the Wife was no longer prepossessing in appearance, if she ever had been. Yet she had participated in the ceremony at the church door on no fewer than five occasions, on four of which she must have been a widow. Surely, we may think, she was not merely a skilled cloth-maker—more skilful, Chaucer tells us, than the cloth-makers of Ypres and Ghent—but a rich one too. In English Ireland, wherever English legal systems were well-rooted, propertied and much married women are also in evidence. Dame Alice Kyteler, a wealthy widow, famously tried for heresy in Kilkenny in 1324, had been married four or five times. By contrast, in native Wales and native Ireland the inability of women to inherit or transmit a claim to land may have tended to minimize the likelihood of remarriage there. Yet potentially, remarriage had important consequences for fertility, since it enabled women who were widowed before their child-bearing years were over to complete the fertility cycle of which they were capable.

Even a rudimentary exploration of the reasons underlying England's political dominance in our period leads us, through population change, to the fundamental structures of the societies inhabiting the British Isles, and to some of the most important variables operating there—the market or lack of it, the marriage process and the position of women, and the nature of lordship. Within England, the prevailing form of lordship influenced not only the chronology of colonization but also the subsequent use of land. Common-field husbandry attained a high degree of development in a great swathe of cultivable land, extending almost without a break from the north-east through the central Midlands to the south. Very roughly, we can identify this swathe with the area where lordship possessing highly developed rights over land is most frequently mentioned in our sources. Field-systems of this kind were a means of making land go, in a manner of speaking, further than was possible under less regulated systems: they permitted an increase in the number of families the land would support.

Yet lords, like brown earths, could not in themselves bring about a growth of population. In the last analysis, the varieties of demographic behaviour we find in this period, so profound, if we are right, in their political consequences, represent varieties of human response to the available resources, each conditioned by social and economic factors which more often than not elude our analytical probes. In this respect, as perhaps in many others, the fortunes of the English overlordship, which provide one of the threads holding together the life of the British Isles as an archipelago in this period, retain an element of the unknown and the unknowable.

Political structures

Political structures were enlarged in this period, as the more powerful rulers reduced the less powerful to a subordinate status and innovators like John and Alexander II brought distant parts of their realms within the ambit of royal government, as never before. Moreover, both Llywelyn ab Iorwerth and Llywelyn ap Gruffudd gave form and substance to the idea that the whole of native Wales should properly be regarded as a single political unit. All this was done, it may seem, with remarkably little attention to the natural orientations that are so conspicuous on the map. The kings who controlled the south and east of Ireland had their own power-base in the south and east of England, and the kings of Scotland, whose power-base was in the south and east of *their* country, not content with Alexander's advance into Ross and Caithness, won a significant degree of recognition in the far north and west, from the Hebrides to the Isle of Man. The political map witnesses to the energy and resource with which rulers and their servants and ministers used the, at times, daunting systems of communication at their disposal and to the essential viability of these.

Within the larger units, however, physical geography was often a weighty factor, encouraging rulers to rely less in the provinces in question on the writs and charters, the professional administrators, and their own itineraries, on which the maintenance of their authority often depended in the areas they directly governed, and more on the timely act of patronage to powerful individuals and the ancient tie of fealty. Every kingdom, in fact, contained a core area and a periphery, and these were ruled differently. If fealty counted for little day by day in the currency of political life, it worked effectively in a crisis—as in 1138, when levies from Galloway, a province given to particularism and not yet within the Scottish shrieval system, provided a substantial part of David I's army in the Battle of the Standard. It is noticeable, too, that in distant provinces, where lines of communication were extended, the tension between rulers and the largest landholders among their dependants might be resolved in favour of the landholders. Thus, in English Ireland, some of the 'outer' lordships, including Ulster and Connacht, retained a degree of independence of the normal structure of royal government that was denied to most of the magnates of England after the mid-twelfth century.

The kingly and aristocratic virtues were understood in similar ways over much of Britain and Ireland. But the differences in political life between England and Scotland, on the one hand, and native Wales and Ireland, on the other, were of a fundamental kind. Over much of our period, and with only a little hesitation, we can attribute to England and Anglicized regions outside England, and to Scotland south of the Forth–Clyde line, the quality of 'regnal solidarity'. This memorable phrase, introduced into the vocabulary of historians by Susan Reynolds, denotes the sense of being a community that a kingdom—a people living under a single ruler—may possess but does not necessarily possess. In the thirteenth century, the English often appealed to the idea of such a community and did so at a wide variety of social levels. In practice, the so-called community of the realm in England, like the humbler communities of village and town, was often divided among itself. But it showed its underlying strength precisely in the capacity to survive the political crises which brought the divisions to the surface, not excepting the bruising civil wars of 1215–17 and 1264–5. It showed its strength, too, in the capacity to embrace, however loosely, regions like Cornwall that were culturally distinct from the rest of the country. To William of Malmesbury, the Cornish were 'Britons'; and Gerald of Wales noted that their language resembled that of the Welsh and the inhabitants of Brittany. In the late twelfth century, however, Cornwall was brought within the English shrieval system; and subsequently the king's justices on eyre operated as effectively in this county as in any other. In Scotland, Galloway was only with difficulty brought within the realm by Alexander II and his successors. Yet in the late thirteenth century, Scotland from the Forth–Clyde line to the border with England, excepting Galloway, possessed a sense of community which the English could scarcely rival. The Scots found an acceptable leader in their informal and accessible king, and the presence of enemies to the north and south of the kingdom lent very obvious point to his demands for taxes and military service.

The situation in native Ireland and native Wales was very different. In each, there were normally at any one time many rulers and many dynasties contending for power, and within the typical dynasty often more than one claimant to the position of ruler. Moreover, in twelfth-century Ireland, the ambitions of over-kings tended to outrun their capacity to create a stable hegemony or reconcile lesser rulers to a subordinate position—the very situation that explains the appeal of Diarmait Mac Murchadha to Henry II for help against the encroachments of Ruaidrí Ua Conchobair in 1166. In native Wales in the mid-thirteenth century, the rivalry of Llywelyn ab Iorwerth's sons opened the way for others to destroy Llywelyn's hegemony. Such rivalries, together with the pressures applied from time to time by the English lordships in frontier areas in both Ireland and Wales, made for an unforgiving political context in which kingdoms and lordships waxed and waned in influence, and indeed in their capacity to hold onto existence at all, in a manner outside the experience of any of the successors of Malcolm Canmore in Scotland or William the Conqueror in England.

Despite these differences in the very structures of political life, all four countries were affected in the course of this period by a movement to extend the limits of royal or princely power and intensify its application. A high regard for written law, closely identified with a royal or princely giver, and a dismissive attitude towards custom, centralization in government, and the growth of bureaucracy, hostility towards jurisdictional privileges including those of the Church, and the claim that every subject should, if necessary, offer up part of his goods in taxation for the needs of government—all these things are symptomatic of the trend. Both Llywelyn ap Gruffudd and Henry III, during his personal rule, exemplify the latter. In Scotland Alexander II, who tried to suppress the customs of Galloway, leant hard on the liberties of the Church, and enacted substantive changes in the law, is surely a clear case. Equally, the circuit of a superior lord in Gaelic Ireland, on his way perhaps to the high kingship, and claiming tribute from his dependents which was at once larger and more clearly defined than previously, seems to presage a future attempt on his part to move in the direction already taken by Henry and Llywelyn. It is in fact exceedingly hard to establish the chronology of these developments in rulership and government. By 1280, however, rulers were much more inclined to intervene in their subjects' affairs than their predecessors c.1100 or 1150, and much less inclined than the latter merely to respond to situations as they arose. Yet even this wide chronology must be stretched a little in the case of David I, king of Scots, who, during his annexation of extensive parts of northern England in the 1130s and 1140s, made a sustained attempt to integrate administration there into that of his existing kingdom.

This movement, and in particular the growth of institutional government, is now commonly described by historians of the period as 'state-building'—with, as it appears, the implication, and sometimes the explicit claim, that a new kind of polity was under construction. 'State' is not a term of art. On the contrary, it is a description freely applied to a wide variety of political entities, and perceptions of the essential characteristics of 'states' have varied according to period. In the modern period, for example, possession of clearly defined frontiers and integrated territories has sometimes appeared essential for the fully fledged state. By contrast, in the twelfth and thirteenth centuries dispersed territories were found perfectly acceptable, even by ambitious rulers. And permeable frontiers, where jurisdictions overlapped, and where sorties could easily be attempted from one side or the other, were often found desirable. In this period, however, the growth of institutional government made possible a notable clarification of structures of authority, with important consequences for the capacity of rulers to act effectively, both within the frontiers of their kingdoms and principalities and outside. It makes good sense to associate these developments very closely with the history of the state at this time. But were the rulers involved in these developments actually 'builders', with all the deliberation and planning implied in this description, and, if they were, did they build anything new?

The idea that the whole of native Wales should possess a single political structure—the inspiration for the work of both Llywelyn ab Iorwerth and Llywelyn ap Gruffudd—was indeed new. In general, however, the 'state-builders' of this period, including those of Wales, created new resources for polities that remained firmly within the early medieval tradition of personalized kingly rule. The debates and controversies which ensued whenever institutional government flexed its muscles, as, for example, in England during the reign of Henry III, were about the acceptable limits of royal (or princely) power. Among the rulers who participated in this movement—whatever name we give to it—there were winners and losers, and the personal abilities of the rulers in question played an important part in sorting the one from the other. So, too, did contingent circumstances. In the case of Scotland, for example, the accession of a minor on David I's death in 1153 was one of a series of contingent events which robbed his annexation of a substantial part of northern England of hope of long-term success. But material resources perhaps counted more than anything else, and it was for lack of these that the rulers of thirteenth-century Gwynedd, despite many brilliant successes on the way, were in the end losers. They did not have sufficient resources to meet the continual need to buy friends and win over enemies that a ruler of this period ignored at his peril.

Ecclesiastical structures and Christian life

Christian life also had to come to terms with new structures in this period: with territorial dioceses and networks of parishes, and with religious orders and congregations possessing a degree of organization without precedent in Britain and Ireland, though long exemplified on the Continent in the Cluniac Order. To many Cistercians, it did not seem strange that abbots from distant provinces of the Order should travel to Cîteaux each year to attend its general chapter, there to be disciplined or even removed from office, if thought necessary. Similarly, in the thirteenth century, the peripatetic general chapter of the Franciscan Order regulated matters as central to the life of the local priories as the form and content of the novitiate and where it should be spent. And over all was indeed the pope, whose authority was manifest from the early twelfth century in the appointment of legates and judges-delegate—England, Ireland, Scotland, and Wales had each received at least one legate by 1125. Papal authority was manifest, too, in the work of bishops and archbishops, who slowly adapted their ways to that of the papally directed reform movement of this century and the next. By 1280, the Church in each country had experience of the practice of papal provision, whereby the pope actually nominated candidates to benefices, including from time to time episcopal sees. If the several parts and orders of the Church were not as well articulated as Gilbert of Limerick had envisaged when, in the early twelfth century, he arranged them in the form of a pyramid, the papal headship was nevertheless a reality, affecting the way in which every lesser institution functioned.

The changes occurring in the twelfth and thirteenth centuries greatly enhanced the importance of the secular clergy, and gave them for the first time something approaching parity in this respect with the monastic order. The insistence of the reforming papacy that a monk's proper place was in the cloister, and not in the world outside, even if he was engaged there in the service of the laity, tended to produce the same effect. Yet there were in fact too many clergy for the good of the Church or that of society in general. Since it was not thought necessary that a candidate for ordination should demonstrate that he possessed an adequate livelihood, many more were ordained than could be usefully employed. The number existing at any one time in England in the thirteenth century was perhaps as large as 40,000, a figure representing between 0.5 and 1 per cent of the total population. Even when we have allowed for the many unbeneficed clergy who assisted in parish churches, and taken into account the many chapels needing clergy to serve them, we are left with very large numbers of unemployed. Many of these eked out an existence in the margin of society, and the criminous clerks who achieved notoriety in this period were drawn mainly from their number.

There were too many clergy; but regionally there were too few parishes. In fact even in the thirteenth century, extensive areas, including the Gaelic north and west of Ireland, and much of upland Wales lacked the parochial structure centring on local churches that would have enabled some of the surplus numbers of clergy to be fruitfully deployed. These circumstances explain the important role of the new religious orders in these areas—the Augustinian canons regular and each of the four main orders of friars in Ireland, for example, and the Cistercians in Wales. Around Strata Florida, the Cistercian house founded in Cardigan by the Lord Rhys ap Gruffudd in 1164, all roads and trackways led to the monastery, and we can be confident that the other Cistercian houses founded, like Strata Florida, in native Wales, were also the hub of their local universe. The extent to which the Franciscans and Dominicans were to be found in regions in Ireland that were still essentially rural is noteworthy, since this ran counter to their normal practice, well exemplified in England, of fulfilling their apostolic vocation mainly in towns.

With these circumstances in mind, we may regard appropriation, the assignment of part of the income of the parish church in question to other uses, as both the best of things and the worst of things for the Church in this period. As the supply of land which benefactors felt able to direct towards the Church became a trickle, rather than the flood it had been in the years around 1100, the art of establishing a new religious foundation or shoring up an old one began to consist in large measure of transferring some of the Church's existing possessions from one institution to another. It was in this way that a great deal of tithe and glebe land passed out of the reach of the parish clergy and into the hands of monks and canons regular, and even into those of cathedral chapters. Nuns also benefited. Thus, Amesbury and Nuneaton, two of the four priories of the Fontevraudine Order in England, derived a significant proportion of their income from so-called spiritualities of this kind. Only the Cistercians, forbidden by their statutes to accept such income, remained outside the system, and eventually even their resolution on this point faltered. For the canons regular, spiritualities were an indispensable source of income and essential to their pastoral work. In twelfth-century Galloway, native rulers sympathetic to monastic reform were clearly hoping to kill two birds with one stone when they transferred nearly a dozen parish churches from the control of unreformed communities of secular clergy and gave them to Holyrood Abbey: they were confident that the Augustinians of Holyrood would raise pastoral standards in their province. In fact a genuine desire to distribute, and when necessary redistribute, the Church's endowments in the best possible way underlay many particular acts of appropriation.

But appropriation might take place with a quite inadequate provision for the clergy of the parishes affected by the arrangement, a matter on which the Fourth Lateran Council expressed its concern in 1215. The nearer one was to the bottom of the pile in such a situation, the more precarious the livelihood. By the end of the twelfth century, the monks of Leominster Priory, in Herefordshire, had appropriated the vicarage attached to the Holy Cross altar in their church, together with the chapel of Hope under Dinmore, and the parochial duties for which the vicarage had formerly been endowed were now performed by three chaplains. They were entitled to a penny for every Mass they celebrated, and a penny on principal feasts, the offerings of bread and ale made by the faithful, and a reasonable share of mortuary dues. Daily meals in the priory, to which they were entitled, enabled them to keep body and soul together, perhaps with greater success than some of the parishioners whom they served; and if the Mass pennies did not provide an adequate cash income—an asset one could scarcely do without by the end of the twelfth century—they could perhaps use some of the bread and ale as a medium of exchange. Yet their income was variable and uncertain.

Did the new structures and new initiatives in the religious life enable the Church to engage more effectively with the great mass of the faithful and not-so-faithful than in the past, or at least to keep up with the changes in society itself which made this task ever more difficult? It is unlikely that the religious orders often received men or women of humble status to full profession. In the course of the twelfth century, Benedictine houses abandoned the practice of receiving children as oblates, to be educated in the cloister as a preliminary to profession, and the new orders of this period never adopted it. In houses for men, therefore, it became necessary for recruits to possess the grounding in Latin which they could no longer acquire in the cloister school; and both in these houses and in those for women, entry was restricted by the convention that each recruit would offer a gift in the form of real property or money in lieu. In England, the net result of these expectations was probably to restrict entry in the typical case to the sons and daughters of the knightly class and lesser aristocracy or well-to-do townsmen, and the situation may have been similar elsewhere. Certainly, Stephen of Lexington's insistence at Mellifont in 1228 that entrants to this house and houses affiliated to it should have a knowledge of Latin and French implies that they would come from a social elite. In fact, monastic communities lacked the social heterogeneity of the hermits discussed by Golding, who ranged in status from a baker of Derby to the well-born Christina of Markyate.

However, the establishment of orders for lay brethren, which was characteristic of the new religious orders of the twelfth century, marks a dramatic widening of the monastic vocation to include many who would previously have had no opportunity of living in a religious order under vows of any kind. Some, moreover, including the Gilbertines, and Cistercian houses for women, recruited lay sisters. In the Cistercian Order from the beginning, and in the Gilbertine Order after the early years, both the lay brethren and the sisters were servants, and we have no reason to doubt that many were of extremely humble origin. Gilbert of Sempringham himself testified that he had rescued the family of Ogger, who in 1168 led a revolt of the lay brethren of this order, from destitution and had seen to it that Ogger and one of his brothers learnt the blacksmith's trade and two other brothers that of a carpenter. But in both orders, the lay brethren, in particular, were treated with great harshness, and it is scarcely surprising that, although this group was at first very numerous in proportion to the numbers of monks and canons, it ceased to be so well before the end of our period. In fact, as population increased and labour became cheaper, both orders preferred to rely on hired labour for most of the tasks for which the lay brethren had at first been recruited.

Both the Benedictines and the new monastic orders engaged more successfully and more continuously with men and women who were of some little standing in society than with those who struggled daily for an existence at society's very base. And in the course of the twelfth and thirteenth centuries, as their almsgiving declined, each generation of monks may have had less contact with the so-called naked poor, the utterly destitute, than its predecessors. Among the religious orders, only the friars had a vocation that by its very nature embraced the seriously poor and, indeed, the utterly destitute in the regular course of events. In England, moreover, they not only served the destitute but actually joined them, by establishing their priories, whenever they could, mainly in the towns where the destitute were principally to be found. Similarly, in the Christian life outside the cloister we sometimes glimpse arrangements better suited to the comfortably off than to others. Thus, membership of one of the guilds or fraternities which became common features of the Christian life in towns in this period might require a substantial entry fee as well as many incidental expenses later.

Any account of popular religion in this period must find some room for indifference, if not for the complete ignorance of the Christian religion reported, though only as hearsay, by Gerald of Wales. In the course of his travels in Ireland, Gerald was told by some sailors of their own encounter with two natives of Connacht, who had never heard of the seasons of the Christian year or of Jesus Christ. On a wider view, however, we can only be impressed by the strength of lay enthusiasm in this period and the varied ways in which it was expressed. In Lincolnshire in 1188, the eagerness to take the Cross on the part of many who were in the end too poor to go betrays, not merely an impulsive response to preaching that may have been of a highly emotional kind, but also the anxiety of ordinary people to share in the spiritual benefits of the crusade. And whatever the limitations in other respects of the monastic orders in engaging with the laity, they proved capable of attracting patronage that transcended the national divisions so often conspicuous in other contexts. In Scotland, both Gaelic lords and the Anglo-Normans patronized the new religious orders in the twelfth century, and in Wales and Ireland we find a similar situation: both native lords and the Anglo-Normans and English patronized the Cistercians and Augustinians.

Finally, the absence of organized heresy from the islands is indeed striking. It reflects in part the lack of more than a handful of large cities or towns of the kinds that proved most receptive to heresy on the Continent of Europe, but also perhaps the dedication of many of the parish clergy of this period and their generally inoffensive character in the eyes of the laity. The shortcomings of the clergy were conspicuous, and they included, in Celtic and Gaelic regions, a persistent tendency to marry. But the laity's judgement of its pastors has not always coincided with the priorities of bishops and archdeacons and may not have done so in this period. After all, we may be tempted to think, in keeping many of the clergy poor, appropriation served a useful purpose. On the Continent, and especially in the south of France, the corruption and wealth of many of the clergy proved to be a potent influence on the spread of heresy.

Social change and adaptable aristocracies

Social distinctions were in general more sharply drawn in 1280 than in the mid-eleventh century, and this change was intimately associated with rising standards of living at the higher levels of society and growing pressures on resources at lower levels in the intervening period. By 1280, there were more grounds, and not, of course, only economic grounds, on which distinctions of this kind could be based, and a greater desire than previously to have them. At both dates, it was the interaction of vertical with lateral bonds that gave individuals their place in society. Lordship created powerful vertical bonds; so, too, did kinship, which attached great importance to lineage in the transmission of property. Powerful lateral bonds might be created by membership of the same rural or urban community, or possession of a similar status, as, for example, that of a knight or free man; and kinship also operated laterally. By the late thirteenth century, however, the lateral bonds often had an importance in society, and the institutions they helped to create had a prominence there, that neither possessed anywhere in the British Isles at the earlier date. Knights, free men, townsmen, villagers, the lower clergy and their parishioners, all possessed an identity in 1280 which was different from anything that we find at the earlier date, and in several cases a new capacity for collective action. Bishops now summoned the lower clergy to synods, and popes attempted, not always with success, to tax them. In England, it was sometimes impossible to proceed in a case in the king's court for lack of knights to form a jury. If, moreover, the same designations were in use at each date, they had normally changed their meaning in the interval. Thus by the thirteenth century 'free man' had for the most part lost its earlier association with nobility; and 'knight', by contrast, had acquired a genteel and even aristocratic connotation.

Yet at the end of this period, as at the beginning, the influence of lordship in society was pervasive. Over extensive areas of the British Isles, we still have to ask whether a genuine town life existed, and to our knowledge villages scarcely existed in Scotland, native Wales, and native Ireland: here hamlets and dispersed farmsteads were the characteristic form of rural settlement. As for the kin, even in areas where it had once been important, the scope of its activities was now reduced, and the kin itself was now less in evidence than the nuclear family. Its values often survived, not in the bonds of kinship itself, but in those of lordship, which largely adopted them. In the case of lordship itself we have always to enquire what form it took in the locality in question, whether, for example, it was characteristically personal or territorial, and whether the lordships in which it was embodied were typically large, middling, or small-scale. We need not ask whether it was present, or felt as a presence, by the local inhabitants: we can be sure that it was.

Observing this feature of social relationships, we are brought face to face once again with the French-speaking aristocracy whose exploits so greatly influenced the history of Wales, Scotland, and Ireland, as well as that of England, where these exploits began. Of course, by no means every lord belonged to this aristocracy, or to any of the native elites who were, though in differing degrees, casualties of its success: many operated on too small a scale for this to be entertained as a possibility. But no one in this period could hope to win a place for himself and his family among an aristocratic elite, or retain it, who was not a lord of dependants or lands, or of both; it was not necessary to have a great many of the former or a great extent of the latter, but to be a lord of one or the other, or of both, was essential. In fact the twists and turns of lordship in this period are those of the aristocracies themselves.

Lordship owed its continuing influence in so many different environments to its adaptability, and many were the pressures obliging it to cultivate this characteristic, many the conflicting messages received as it did so. The Church, for example, now forbade lords to receive the homage of clergy, on the grounds that they were laymen, but tried to sacramentalize knighthood and send those who assumed it on crusade. In the twelfth century, economic trends squeezed the incomes of lords, but the conventions of chivalry made it quite essential for many of them to spend more. Ideas about the rights and duties of kings, which were used with such effect in

England in the political disputes of John's reign and those of Henry III, were soon complemented by rather similar ideas about the rights and duties of lords in respect of their tenants; and some of these are indeed enshrined in Magna Carta. In England the distinction between free and unfree became clearer in the course of the twelfth century, and in Wales less clear; but each of these changes had consequences for the lords who depended on the renders and services of the populations in question and, in some cases, possessed estates in each country.

The adaptability of lordship in the face of challenging circumstances is perhaps most clearly displayed in its response to the growth of a monetized economy—a process already well advanced in England by 1066 and one that left scarcely any considerable part of the British Isles untouched in the course of the next two centuries. Lords planted boroughs, granted markets, and commuted into money rents many of the labour services and renders in kind owed by their peasants. In the course of the twelfth and thirteenth centuries, even the lords of native Wales began to realize that a peaceful economic exploitation of their dependent peasantry might be more profitable than a life of plunder along traditional lines. Here, and in Gaelic Ireland and Scotland, where kinship ties were stronger than elsewhere, lords made use of these to create networks of clients or dependants. By the late thirteenth century, however, lords in both England and English Ireland were using cash fees and livery of clothing to create networks of dependants of a kind foreshadowing the more elaborately organized affinities of the later middle ages. Their ancestors had explored and refined forms of lordship that were intimately associated with land. Now they themselves were taking lordship into an apparently new situation—though actually, of course, a very old one—where it could thrive at this level of society independently of tenurial bonds between lord and man.

The aristocracies of the British Isles in this period responded with varying degrees of openness and flexibility when exposed, as they so often were, to alien cultural traditions. Some readily assumed a new cultural identity; others resisted assimilation of this kind. Hence, the all-important contrast noticed earlier in this book between, on the one hand, the French-speaking settlers who became English in England and Scottish in Scotland, and, on the other, those of their number, and that of their descendants, who retained an English identity as settlers in Wales and Ireland. Yet in many other ways, these aristocracies proved themselves to be adaptable, and, indeed, agile. They had a capacity for reinventing themselves when circumstances changed that many aristocracies in different periods and countries might well have envied.

Further reading

Historical studies relating to the British Isles as a whole in this period are still relatively uncommon, but notably exemplified in R. R. Davies, *Domination and Conquest: The Experience of Ireland, Scotland and Wales, 1100–1300* (Cambridge, 1990), and Robin Frame, *The Political Development of the British Isles* (Oxford, revised edn., 1995). Among 'national' histories, R. R. Davies, *The Age of Conquest: Wales, 1063–1415* (Oxford, 1991) and A. A. M. Duncan, *Scotland: The Making of the Kingdom* (London, 1975) are outstanding.

Each of the preceding works is important for the topics discussed in this book. Robert Bartlett, *The Making of Europe: Conquest, Colonization and Cultural Change, 950–1350* (Harmondsworth, 1993) and Bartlett and Angus Mackay (eds.), *Medieval Frontier Societies* (Oxford, 1989) provide the wider context of Christian Europe and its moving frontiers.

In addition, the following books and articles are recommended.

Introduction

Aalen, F. H. A., Whelan, K., and Stout, M., *Atlas of the Irish Rural Landscape* (Cork, 1997).

Davies, R. R., 'The peoples of Britain and Ireland, 1100–1400, i. Identities', *Transactions of the Royal Historical Society*, 6th ser., 4 (1994), 1–20; ii. 'Names, boundaries, and regnal solidarities', ibid. 5 (1995), 1–20; iii. 'Laws and customs', ibid. 6 (1996), 1–23; iv. 'Language and historical mythology', ibid. 7 (1997), 1–24.

Fenton, A., and Stell, G., *Loads and Roads in Scotland and Beyond* (Edinburgh, 1984).

Gerald of Wales, *Expugnatio Hibernica* (*Conquest of Ireland*), ed. and trans. A. B. Scott and F. X. Martin (Dublin, 1978).

—— *The Journey through Wales and The Description of Wales*, trans. L. Thorpe (Harmondsworth, 1978).

—— *The History and Topography of Ireland*, trans. J. J. O'Meara (Harmondsworth, 1982).

Glasscock, R. E., 'Land and people, c.1300', in *A New History of Ireland*, ii: *Medieval Ireland, 1169–1534*, ed. A. Cosgrove (Oxford, 1987), 204–39.

Griffiths, R. A., 'Medieval Severnside: The Welsh connection', in Griffiths, *Conquerors and Conquered in Medieval Wales* (Stroud, 1994), 1–18.

Hindle, B. P., *Medieval Roads and Tracks*, 3rd edn. (Princes Risborough, 1998).

Hutchinson, G., *Medieval Ships and Shipping* (London, 1994).

McNeill, P. G. B., and Hector, L. M., *Atlas of Scottish History to 1707* (Edinburgh, 1996).

Ogilvie, A., and Farmer, G., 'Documenting the medieval climate', in M. Hulme and E. Barrow (eds.), *Climates of the British Isles: Present, Past and Future* (London, 1997), ch. 6.

Rackham, O., *Trees and Woodland in the British Landscape*, revised edn. (London, 1996).

Stenton, F. M., 'The road system of medieval England', in Stenton, *Preparatory to Anglo-Saxon England* (Oxford, 1970), 234–52.

Thomas, C., 'Thirteenth-century farm economies in North Wales', *Agricultural History Review*, 16 (1968), 1–14.

Chapter 1

Barrow, G. W. S., *Feudal Britain: The Completion of the Medieval Kingdoms* (London, 1956, etc.).

—— *Kingship and Unity: Scotland 1000–1306* (London, 1981).

—— *The Anglo-Norman Era in Scottish History* (Oxford, 1980).

Bartlett, R., *Gerald of Wales 1146–1223* (Oxford, 1982).

Carr, A. D., *Medieval Wales* (London, 1995).

Chibnall, M., *Anglo-Norman England 1066–1166* (Oxford, 1986).

Clanchy, M. T., *England and its Rulers, 1066–1272*, revised edn. (Oxford, 1998).

Duffy, S., *Ireland in the Middle Ages* (London, 1997).

Empey, C. A., 'Conquest and settlement: patterns of Anglo-Norman settlement in north Munster and south Leinster', *Irish Economic and Social History*, 13 (1986), 5–31.

Flanagan, M. T., *Irish Society, Anglo-Norman Settlers, Angevin Kingship* (Oxford, 1989).

Gillingham, J., *The English in the Twelfth Century: Imperialism, National Identity and Political Values* (Woodbridge, 2000).

Green, J., *The Aristocracy of Norman England* (Cambridge, 1997).

Griffiths, R. A. (ed.), *The Boroughs of Medieval Wales* (Cardiff, 1978).

Le Patourel, J., *The Norman Empire* (Oxford, 1976).

Lynch, M., *Scotland: A New History* (London, 1991).

Otway-Ruthven, A. J., *A History of Medieval Ireland*, revised edn. (London, 1980).

Stringer, K. J., *Earl David of Huntingdon, 1152–1219: A Study in Anglo-Scottish History* (Edinburgh, 1985).

Warren, W. L., 'The interpretation of twelfth-century Irish history', *Historical*

Studies (Papers read before the Irish Conference of Historians), vii, ed. J. C. Beckett (London, 1969), 1–19.

Williams, A., *The English and the Norman Conquest* (Woodbridge, 1995).

Chapter 2

Barlow, F., *William Rufus* (London, 1983).

Barrow, G. W. S., *Scotland and its Neighbours in the Middle Ages* (London, 1992).

Bates, D., *Normandy before 1066* (London and New York, 1982).

—— 'Normandy and England after 1066', *English Historical Review*, 104 (1989), 851–76.

Clanchy, M. T., *From Memory to Written Record: England, 1066–1307*, 2nd edn. (Oxford, 1993).

Crouch, D., *The Reign of King Stephen* (London and New York, 2000).

Duffy, S., *Ireland in the Middle Ages* (London, 1997).

Gillingham, J., *The English in the Twelfth Century: Imperialism, National Identity and Political Values* (Woodbridge, 2000).

Green, J. A., *The Government of England under Henry I* (Cambridge, 1986).

—— 'Anglo-Scottish relations, 1066–1174', in M. Jones and M. Vale (eds.), *England and her Neighbours, 1066–1453: Essays in Honour of Pierre Chaplais* (London, 1989).

Holt, J. C., *Colonial England, 1066–1215* (London, 1997).

Hudson, J., *The Formation of the English Common Law* (London and New York, 1996).

Ó Cróinín, D., *Early Medieval Ireland, 400–1200* (London and New York, 1995).

Roffe, D., *Domesday: The Inquest and the Book* (Oxford, 2000).

Strickland, M., *War and Chivalry: The Conduct and Perception of War in England and Normandy, 1066–1217* (Cambridge, 1996).

Stringer, K. J., *The Reign of Stephen: Kingship, Warfare and Government in Twelfth-Century England* (London, 1993).

White, G. J., *Restoration and Reform, 1153–1165: Recovery from Civil War in England* (Cambridge, 2000).

Chapter 3

Ault, W. O., *Open-Field Farming in Medieval England: A Study of Village By-Laws* (London, 1972).

Barrow, G. W. S., *The Kingdom of the Scots: Government, Church and Society from the Eleventh to the Fourteenth Century* (London, 1973).

Beresford, M. W., *New Towns of the Middle Ages: Town Plantation in England, Wales and Gascony* (London, 1967).

Bradley, J. (ed.), *Settlement and Society in Medieval Ireland: Studies Presented to F. X. Martin, O. S. A.* (Kilkenny, 1988).

Britnell, R. H., *The Commercialisation of English Society, 1000–1500* (Cambridge, 1993).

Carus-Wilson, E. M., 'The first half-century of the Borough of Stratford-upon-Avon', *Economic History Review*, 2nd ser., 18 (1965), 46–63.

Charles-Edwards, T. M., *Early Irish and Welsh Kinship* (Oxford, 1993).

Dodgshon, R. A., *Land and Society in Early Scotland* (Oxford, 1981).

Faith, R., *The English Peasantry and the Growth of Lordship* (London, 1997).

Kosminsky, E. A., *Studies in the Agrarian History of England in the Thirteenth Century* , ed. R. H. Hilton, trans. R. Kisch (Oxford, 1956).

Lennard, R., *Rural England, 1086–1135: A Study of Social and Agrarian Conditions* (Oxford, 1959).

Owen, D. H., *Settlement and Society in Wales* (Cardiff, 1989).

Pierce, T. Jones, *Medieval Welsh Society: Selected Essays* (Cardiff, 1972).

Razi, Z., and Smith, R. (eds.), *Medieval Society and the Manor Court* (Oxford, 1996).

Reynolds, S., *An Introduction to the History of English Medieval Towns* (Oxford, 1977).

Thirsk, J., 'The common fields', *Past and Present*, 29 (1964), 1–25.

Chapter 4

Barlow, F., *The English Church, 1066–1154* (London, 1979).

Blair, J. (ed.), *Minsters and Parish Churches: The Local Church in Transition 950–1200* (Oxford University Committee for Archaeology, monograph no. 17; 1988).

Brooke, R., *The Coming of the Friars* (London, 1975).

Burton, J., *Monastic and Religious Orders in Britain, 1000–1300* (Cambridge, 1994).

Christina of Markyate, *The Life of Christina of Markyate, a Twelfth Century Recluse*, ed. and trans. C. H. Talbot, revised edn. (Oxford Medieval Texts, 1987; reprinted in paperback by The Medieval Academy of America in association with Oxford Medieval Texts, 1998).

Cowan, I. B., *The Medieval Church in Scotland* (Edinburgh, 1995).

Davies, J. C., *Episcopal Acts and Cognate Documents relating to Welsh Dioceses, 1066–1272* (2 vols; Historical Soc. of the Church in Wales, 1946–8).

Finucane, R. C., *Miracles and Pilgrims: Popular Beliefs in Medieval England* (London, 1977).

Golding, B., *Gilbert of Sempringham and the Gilbertine Order c.1130–c.1300* (Oxford, 1995).

Hugh of Avalon (St Hugh of Lincoln): *The Life of St. Hugh of Lincoln*, ed. and trans. D. L. Douie and H. Farmer (2 vols.; Nelson's Medieval Texts, 1961–2).

Malachy, St, archbishop of Armagh: *St. Bernard of Clairvaux's Life of St. Malachy of Armagh*, trans. H. J. Lawlor (London, 1920).

Matthew Paris, *Life of St. Edmund*, trans., ed., and with a biography, by C. H. Lawrence (Stroud, 1996).

Mayr-Harting, H., 'Functions of a twelfth-century recluse', *History*, 60 (1975), 337–52.

Moorman, J. R. H., *Church Life in England in the Thirteenth Century* (Cambridge, 1955).

Nicholls, K. W., 'Rectory, vicarage and parish in the western Irish dioceses', *Journal of the Royal Society of Antiquaries of Ireland*, 101 (1971), 53–84.

Southern, R. W., *Saint Anselm: A Portrait in a Landscape* (Cambridge, 1990)

Stalley, R., *The Cistercian Monasteries of Ireland: An Account of the History, Art and Architecture of the White Monks in Ireland from 1142 to 1540* (New Haven and London, 1987).

Stringer, K. J., 'Reform monasticism and Celtic Scotland: Galloway, *c.*1140–*c.*1240', in E. J. Cowan and R. A. McDonald (eds.), *Alba: Celtic Scotland in the Middle Ages* (East Linton, 2000), 127–65.

Watt, J., *The Church in Medieval Ireland*, revised edn. (Dublin, 1998).

Chapter 5

Alexander, J., and Binski, P., *Age of Chivalry: Art in Plantagenet England 1200–1400* (London, 1987).

Aston, T. H. (ed.), *The History of the University of Oxford*, i. *The Early Oxford Schools*, ed. J. I. Catto, assisted by R. Evans (Oxford, 1984).

Breeze, A., *Medieval Welsh Literature* (Dublin, 1997).

Bullock-Davies, C., *Professional Interpreters and the Matter of Britain* (Cardiff, 1966).

Burnett, C., *The Introduction of Arabic Learning into England* (London, 1997).

Cobban, A. B., *The Medieval English Universities: Oxford and Cambridge to c.1500* (Berkeley and Los Angeles, 1988).

Davies, R. R., *The Matter of Britain and the Matter of England. An Inaugural*

Lecture Delivered before the University of Oxford on 29 February 1996 (Oxford, 1996).

Eales, R., and Sharpe, R. (eds.), *Canterbury and the Norman Conquest: Churches, Saints and Scholars, 1066–1109* (London, 1995).

Geoffrey of Monmouth, *The History of the Kings of Britain*, trans. L. Thorpe (Harmondsworth, 1966).

Gillingham, J., *The English in the Twelfth Century: Imperialism, National Identity and Political Values* (Woodbridge, 2000).

Gransden, A., *Historical Writing in England, c.500–c.1307* (London, 1974).

Hughes, K., *Early Christian Ireland: Introduction to the Sources* (London, 1972).

Leyser, K., *Communications and Power in Medieval Europe: The Gregorian Revolution and Beyond*, ed. T. Reuter (London, 1994).

Salter, E., *English and International: Studies in the Literature, Art and Patronage of Medieval England*, ed. D. Pearsall and N. Zeeman (Cambridge, 1988).

Schmolke-Hasselmann, B., *The Evolution of Arthurian Romance* (Cambridge, 1998).

Wallace, D. (ed.), *The Cambridge History of Medieval English Literature* (Cambridge, 1999) (discusses writing in the British Isles and not only in England or in English).

Webber, T., 'The diffusion of Augustine's *Confessions* in England during the eleventh and twelfth centuries', in J. Blair and B. Golding (eds.), *The Cloister and the World: Essays in Medieval History Presented to Barbara Harvey* (Oxford, 1996), 29–45.

Wilson, C., *The Gothic Cathedral* (London, 1990).

Zarnecki, G., Holt, J., and Holland, T. (eds.), *English Romanesque Art 1066–1200* (London, 1984)

Chapter 6

Barrow, G. W. S., *Kingship and Unity: Scotland 1000–1306* (London, 1981).

Binski, P., *Westminster Abbey and the Plantagenets: Kingship and the Representation of Power 1200–1400* (New Haven and London, 1995).

Brand, P., *The Making of the Common Law* (London, 1992).

Cam, H. M., *The Hundred and the Hundred Rolls* (Oxford, 1930).

Carpenter, D. A., *The Minority of Henry III* (London, 1990).

Clanchy, M. T., *From Memory to Written Record: England, 1066–1307*, 2nd edn. (Oxford, 1993).

—— *England and its Rulers, 1066–1272*, revised edn. (Oxford, 1998).

Crouch, D. B., *The Image of Aristocracy in Britain, 1000–1300* (London, 1992).

Holt, J. C., *The Northerners: A Study in the Reign of King John* (Oxford, 1961).

—— *Magna Carta*, 2nd edn. (Cambridge, 1992).

Keen, M. H., *Chivalry* (London, 1984).

Maddicott, J. R., *Simon de Montfort* (Cambridge, 1994).

Otway-Ruthven, A. J., *A History of Medieval Ireland*, revised edn. (London, 1980).

Smith, J. Beverley, *Llywelyn ap Gruffudd, Prince of Wales* (Cardiff, 1998).

Stacey, R. C., *Politics, Policy and Finance under Henry III, 1216–1245* (Oxford, 1987).

Warren, W. L., *Henry II* (London, 1973).

—— *The Governance of Norman and Angevin England, 1066–1272* (London, 1987).

Conclusion

Coss, P., *The Knight in Medieval England, 1000–1400* (Stroud, 1993).

Davies, R. R., 'The status of women and the practice of marriage in late-medieval Wales', in D. Jenkins and M. E. Owen (eds.), *The Welsh Law of Women: Studies Presented to Professor Daniel A. Binchy on his Eightieth Birthday, 3 June 1980* (Cardiff, 1980), 93–114.

Faith, R., *The English Peasantry and the Growth of Lordship* (London, 1997).

Golding, B., *Gilbert of Sempringham and the Gilbertine Order, c.1130–c.1300* (Oxford, 1995).

Graham, B. J., and Proudfoot, L. J., *An Historical Geography of Ireland* (London, 1993).

Kerr, B., *Religious Life for Women c.1100–c.1350: Fontevraud in England* (Oxford, 1999).

Reynolds, S., *Kingdoms and Communities in Western Europe, 900–1300*, 2nd edn. (Oxford, 1997).

Roberts, B. K., *The Making of the English Village: A Study in Historical Geography* (London, 1987).

Smith, R. M., 'Demographic developments in rural England, 1300–48: A survey', in B. M. Campbell (ed.), *Before the Black Death: Studies in the Crisis of the Early Fourteenth Century* (Manchester, 1991), 25–78.

—— 'Women's property rights under customary law: some developments in the thirteenth and fourteenth centuries', *Transactions of the Royal Historical Society*, 5th ser., 36 (1986), 165–94.

Chronology

	Rhys ap Tewdwr and Gruffudd ap Cynan defeat Caradog ap Gruffudd ap Rhydderch and other princelings at Battle of Mynydd Carn
1085–6	Proposed expedition to England of Cnut IV of Denmark comes to nothing
1086	Domesday Survey/Inquest
*c.*1086–9	Compilation of Domesday Book
1088	Rebellion of Odo of Bayeux and Robert Curthose against William II
1090s	Building of Westminster Hall
1092	William II establishes castle and settlement at Carlisle
1093	Deaths of Malcolm III and Margaret, queen of Scots
	Death of Rhys ap Tewdwr
	Anselm nominated as archbishop of Canterbury
1093–8	Enlargement of Norman power in Wales and the north of England
1094	With support from William II ('Rufus'), Duncan, son of Malcolm III, supplants Donald Bàn, king of Scots, but for less than a year
1095	Rebellion, led by Robert de Mowbray, earl of Northumberland, against William II
*c.*1095–1123	Eadmer composes *Historia Novorum*
1095–1137	Gruffudd ap Cynan establishes dominance in Gwynedd and over a wider area
1096–9	First Crusade
1097	With support from William Rufus, Edgar, son of Malcolm III, captures Donald Bàn and begins ten-year rule as king of Scots
1098	Magnus of Norway ('Magnus Barelegs') makes agreement with Edgar, king of Scots, and participates in defeat of Normans in north Wales
1100	Death of William II and accession of Henry I
	Henry I marries Edith/Mathilda of Scotland
1101	Henry I defeats Robert Curthose at Battle of Tinchebrai
1102	Arnulf de Montgomery, earl of Pembroke, marries daughter of Muirchertach Ua Briain, king of Munster and high king of Ireland
1102–3	Henry I defeats Montgomeries; Robert de Bellême forfeits lands in England
*c.*1107	Settlement of Flemings in Pembrokeshire

1108	Primatial council at London issues decrees to promote celibacy of clergy
1111	Council of Rathbreasail plans diocesan organization of Irish Church
1113–14	David of Scotland marries Maud (Mathilda), heiress of earldom of Huntingdon
1114/15–41	Orderic Vitalis composes his *Historia Ecclesiastica*
1115	Bernard, chaplain of Henry I, becomes bishop of St Davids
1118	Henry I defeated at Alençon by Fulk, count of Anjou
1120	William, son of Henry I, dies in wreck of White Ship
	David 'the Scot' is consecrated bishop of Bangor at Westminster and acknowledges the authority of Canterbury
	Relics of St Dyfrig are translated from Barsdey to Llandaff
c.1120–30	St Albans Psalter
1124	Accession of David I, king of Scots
	Toirrdelbach Ua Conchobair builds 'castles' in Connacht
c.1124	David I grants Annandale to Robert de Brus
1127	Henry I obtains oaths from leading bishops and barons to accept Mathilda, his daughter and widow of the Emperor Henry V, as his heir
1128	Mathilda marries Geoffrey, count of Anjou
	Cistercians first established in England
1130	David I settles Flemings in Moray, after Moray rising
c.1130	Henry, archdeacon of Huntingdon, completes first version of his *Historia Anglorum*
c.1130–64	Somerled, lord of Argyll, establishes dominance in Argyll and the Western Isles
c.1135	David I begins to associate Henry, his son, with his own authority
1135	Death of Henry I and accession of Stephen
	David I invades northern England
c.1136	Geoffrey of Monmouth's *Historia Regum Britanniae*
1136	Risings by Welsh
	David I begins minting coins in Cumberland
1138	Battle of the Standard
1138–57	Scottish kings control Cumbria (Cumberland and

	Westmorland) and Northumbria as far as R. Tees
1139	Mathilda lands at Arundel; beginning of civil war in England
c.1140	Gratian's *Concordance of Discordant Canons*, or *Decretum*
1141	Stephen is captured at Battle of Lincoln
1146–9	Second Crusade
1149	David I knights Henry, son of Mathilda, the future Henry II, at Carlisle
1152	The future Henry II marries Eleanor of Aquitaine
	Death of Henry, son of David I
	At Council of Kells-Mellifont, papal legate sanctions four archbishoprics in Ireland and effectively brings to an end Canterbury's claim to hegemony there
1153	Death of David I and accession of Malcolm IV
	Rebellion of Somerled, lord of Argyll, and the sons of Malcolm Mac Heth
	Settlement between Stephen and Henry, and recognition of the latter as heir to the English throne, is announced in so-called Treaty of Winchester
1155	Wace's *Roman de Brut*
1155–6	*Laudabiliter*: papal licence to Henry II to enter Ireland
c.1155–60 and	
c.1170–85	Winchester Bible
1157 and 1158	Henry II campaigns in Wales
1159	Malcolm IV serves Henry II at Toulouse and is knighted by him at Périgueux
1160	Rebellion of Fergus, lord of Galloway, and five earls against Malcolm IV
1160–4	Malcolm IV intervenes in Galloway and Argyll
By 1161	Winchester Psalter completed
1161–2	Last levy of geld in England
1163	Henry II campaigns in Wales; Owain Gwynedd and Rhys ap Gruffudd do homage to him
	Malcolm IV does homage to Henry
1164	Constitutions of Clarendon
1165	Henry II campaigns in Wales
1166	A group of Cathar heretics is condemned at a council at Oxford summoned by Henry II

	Assize of Clarendon introduces presentment of suspected criminals by jury in England
	Assize (legal action) of novel disseisin introduced in England
1166–7	Diarmait Mac Murchadha, king of Leinster, flees to Henry II
1168	Owain Gwynedd offers alliance against Henry II to Louis VII of France
1169–70	Troops from south Wales campaign with Diarmait Mac Murchadha in Ireland
1170	Richard de Clare ('Strongbow') in Ireland; capture of Waterford and Dublin
	Inquest of Sheriffs in England
	Murder of Thomas Becket
1171	Henry II traverses south Wales on way to Ireland
1171–2	Henry II in Ireland; submission of most Irish kings; Leinster confirmed to Strongbow; Meath granted to Hugh de Lacy
	Rhys ap Gruffudd made 'justiciar' in Deheubarth
	Council of the Irish Church at Cashel
1172	Pope Alexander III endorses fealty of Irish kings to Henry II
1173	Canonization of St Thomas Becket
1173–4	William the Lion, king of Scots, joins revolt of Henry II's sons and is captured at Alnwick
1174	Choir of Canterbury Cathedral destroyed by fire; rebuilding begins
	Treaty of Falaise between Henry II and William the Lion
1175	Treaty of Windsor between Henry II and Ruaidrí Ua Conchobair
1175 x 1200	Hue de Rotelande's *Ipomedon*
1176	Assize of Northampton introduces assize (legal action) of mort d'ancestor in England
1177	John de Courcy invades eastern Ulster
	Council of Oxford: homage of Rhys ap Gruffudd and Dafydd ab Owain to Henry II; future King John named lord of Ireland; grants of Desmond (Cork) and Thomond (Limerick)
1178	Inquiry into conduct of royal justices in England
1178–88	Dispute between William the Lion and papacy over election to see of St. Andrews

*c.*1179	*Dialogue of the Exchequer*
1180	Coinage of Short Cross pennies in England
1181–2	Scotland under papal interdict
1185	Expedition of John, lord of Ireland, to Ireland
*c.*1185	Royal mint established at Dublin
*c.*1186–94	Gerald of Wales composes his books on Ireland and Wales
1187	Rebellion of Donald Macwilliam against William the Lion ends in his death
1187 x 9	*Glanvill*
1188	Archbishop Baldwin preaches crusade in Wales
1189	Death of Henry II and accession of Richard I
	'Quitclaim of Canterbury' cancels Treaty of Falaise
1190–2	Third Crusade
1190s	Evidence for teaching of theology and canon law at Oxford
1192	Celestine III rules that *ecclesia Scoticana* is independent of York
1194	Appointment of first keepers of crown pleas in England
*c.*1195	Speculative grant of Connacht to William de Burgh
1195	Minting of Short Cross pennies in Scotland
*c.*1195–6	Royal mints established at Waterford and Limerick
1199	Death of Richard I and accession of John
*c.*1200	Llywelyn ab Iorwerth ('the Great') in control of Gwynedd
1200 x 25	Layamon's *Brut*; *Ancrene Wisse*; *Song of Dermot*
1204	Loss of Normandy and Anjou to Philip II
	Llywelyn the Great marries Joan, illegitimate daughter of King John
1207	General levy of thirteenth on moveables in England
1207–13	John's quarrel with the papacy over disputed election to see of Canterbury
	William Marshal, earl of Pembroke and lord of Leinster, mostly in Ireland
1208–13	England under papal interdict
*c.*1209	*Romance of Fergus*
1209	Llywelyn the Great serves John in Scotland
	Treaty between John and William the Lion

	Dispersal of masters and students from Oxford; some go to Cambridge
	John is excommunicated
1210	John campaigns in Ireland; Hugh de Lacy, earl of Ulster, and others forfeit lands
	John confirms that lordship of Ireland is subject to English law
1211	John campaigns in north Wales
1212	Renewed agreement with William the Lion
	John knights the future Alexander II
	John's intended campaign in Wales comes to nothing
1213	John submits to Innocent III
1214	Battle of Bouvines: defeat of John's allies by Philip II of France
	Death of William the Lion and accession of Alexander II
1215	Fourth Lateran Council
	Magna Carta
1215–17	Civil war in England, which is invaded by French and Scots
	Alexander II takes Carlisle
1216	Death of John and accession of Henry III
	Reissue of Magna Carta is transmitted for observance in Ireland
1216–27	Minority of Henry III; regency of William Marshal followed, after an interval, by that of Hubert de Burgh
1217	Reissue of Magna Carta, with separate Forest Charter
1218	Llywelyn the Great's military gains accepted in negotiations at Worcester
1220	Rebuilding of Salisbury Cathedral, on a site in the new town, begins
1220s	Cistercian crisis in Ireland
1221	Dominicans first established in England
1223	Brief English campaign in Wales achieves modest success
1224	Franciscans first established in England; some settle in Oxford
1225	Definitive confirmation of Magna Carta and Forest Charter
1226	Accession of Louis IX in France
1227	Ulster restored to Hugh de Lacy; Connacht granted to

	Richard de Burgh
1228	English campaign in Connacht
*c.*1230	*Bracton*
1230	Henry III campaigns in Brittany
	Assise of novel dissasine introduced in Scotland
	Franciscans establish school in Cambridge
1232	Fall of Hubert de Burgh; forfeiture of Richard de Burgh
1233–4	Rebellion of Richard Marshal, earl of Pembroke; rising of his supporters in West Country, Wales, and Ireland
1234	Marshal fatally wounded in confrontation with royalist forces on Curragh of Kildare
1235	English campaign in Connacht
	Robert Grosseteste elected bishop of Lincoln
1236	Marriage of Henry III and Eleanor of Provence
1237	Henry III retains Chester on death of John of Scotland, earl of Chester and Huntingdon
	Treaty of York between Alexander II and Henry III: abandonment of Scots' claim to northern England
1230s and 1240s	Earliest known summonses of knights to parliaments in England
1240	Death of Llywelyn the Great
1241	Treaty of Gwern Eigron: Dafydd ap Llywelyn surrenders Llywelyn's gains
1242–3	Henry III's campaign in Poitou and Gascony; barons from Ireland participate
1245	Death of last Marshals, followed by partition of their lordships in England, Wales, and Ireland
1245–69	Rebuilding of Westminster Abbey
1247	Partition of north Wales after death of Dafydd ap Llywelyn
1249	Alexander II dies on expedition to Western Isles
	Accession of Alexander III
*c.*1250	*King Horn*
1250	Henry III takes the cross
By 1253	Assize of mortancestry introduced in Scotland
1253–4	Henry III's expedition to Gascony
1254	Gascony, Ireland, Chester, and royal lands in Wales become an apanage for the future Edward I

	Henry III accepts papal grant of throne of Sicily for his son Edmund
1255–6	Llywelyn ap Gruffudd defeats his brothers and reintegrates Snowdonia; he attacks the Four Cantreds, Edward's lands east of River Conwy
1257	Welsh defeat English army under Stephen Bauzan in Tywi valley
1258	Llywelyn ap Gruffudd uses the title 'Prince of Wales'
	Baronial programme of reform initiated in parliament at Oxford
1259	Provisions of Westminster continue programme of reform
	By Treaty of Paris with Louis IX, Henry III abandons claim to lands in France lost in 1204; retains Aquitaine but agrees to do homage to Louis IX for Gascony, hitherto held by Henry in full right
1260	Defeat of Brian Ó Néill 'king of the kings of Ireland' at Downpatrick
1261	Henry III obtains papal absolution from concessions to barons and others in 1258 and subsequently
1263	Lordship of Ulster granted to Walter de Burgh, lord of Connacht
	At Battle of Largs, Scots have the advantage, though not a clear-cut victory, over the Norwegians
	Henry III and Simon de Montfort agree to accept arbitration by Louis IX
1264	Mise of Amiens
	First definitely attested parliament held in Ireland
	Massacre of Jews in London
	Henry III captured at Battle of Lewes
1264–5	Civil war in England
1265	Montfort, in king's name, summons burgesses as well as knights to parliament
	Treaty of Pipton: Montfort recognizes Llywelyn ap Gruffudd as 'Prince of Wales'
	Montfort dies at Battle of Evesham
1265–8	Ottobuono Fieschi, papal legate, in England
1266	Treaty of Perth: Magnus of Norway cedes Western Isles and Man to Alexander III
1267	Dictum of Kenilworth
	Statute of Marlborough

	Treaty of Montgomery: Henry III recognizes Llywelyn ap Gruffudd as 'Prince of Wales'
1269	Translation of St Edward the Confessor to new shrine in Westminster Abbey
1272	Death of Henry III and accession of Edward I
1274	Llywelyn ap Gruffudd refuses to do homage to Edward I
1274–5	Comprehensive inquiry into loss of royal rights in England; the returns are now referred to under the general heading of *Hundred Rolls*
1275	Alexander III suppresses rising on Isle of Man
	Edward I imposes custom on exports of wool and hides from England
1275–90	Edward I's principal statutes enacted
1275 x 82	Alexander III introduces custom on exports of wool and hides from Scotland
1276–7	Edward I defeats Llywelyn ap Gruffudd, who is restored to a truncated Gwynedd in Treaty of Aberconwy
1279–80	Inquiry into landholding, rents, and services, and judicial liberties etc. in England. The returns, like those of 1274–5, are now referred to under the general heading of *Hundred Rolls*
1282	Llywelyn assumes leadership of rising begun by his brother, Dafydd, and is killed
	Edward I conquers north Wales
1284	Statute of Rhuddlan ('Statute of Wales'), legal and administrative settlement of north Wales
1286	Death of Alexander III
1290	Expulsion of Jews from England
c.1300	Chronicle of Robert of Gloucester (*fl. c.*1270) reaches its present form
	Peter Langtoft at work on his chronicle

Glossary

alien priory: a religious house dependent on a foreign monastery and in most cases on a monastery in Normandy. Relationships of this kind were normally created in the decades immediately following the Norman Conquest of England.

antecessor (Latin), a term used in Domesday Book and signifying the pre-Conquest landholder from whom the post-Conquest landholder in question derived his (or, exceptionally, her) title.

apanage: a provision of land for a son or other relative; normally for a younger son.

appropriation: the acquisition, normally in this period by a religious house, of the income of a parish church or the greater part of this, but increasingly confined to acquisition of the glebe and the rector's share of the teind or tithe (q.v.).

arch-lector: see lector (1)

assize: (1) a legal enactment; (2) a form of legal action; (3) the jury summoned in the course of (2); (4) the court hearing the action.

bailiff: (1) a manorial official, sometimes of a superior kind having oversight of several of his lord's manors; (2) one of—normally—two principal officials of a town.

baron: in England and wherever else feudal tenures developed, the holder of a barony: in principle, a tenant-in-chief (q.v.) or an important tenant of a tenant-in-chief. However, eventually, through the fragmentation of feudal estates, landholders with relatively little land could be 'barons'.

barton/berewick: outlying settlement.

berewick: see **barton**

betagh (Irish, *biatach*), a customary tenant, originally rendering food dues to his lord; assimilated to some extent during the thirteenth century to the status of an English villein (q.v.).

bíad (Irish), food-rent.

birth rate: the number of births per 1,000 population.

boll: a measure of capacity for grain and other dry products, varying locally but sometimes equivalent to two bushels.

borough, burgh: a settlement with a market and burgage plots, sometimes possessing additional privileges specified in a charter from the ruler or lord.

brithem (Irish/Gaelic), a local or regional judge; see also *iudex*.

burgess: an inhabitant of a borough or burgh who contributed to its taxes and was entitled to share in its privileges.

burh: a fortified place in Anglo-Saxon England, sometimes, though not invariably, the site of a market.

cáin (Gaelic), *can* (Scots), (1) law or right; (2) a fixed render to a lord, payable traditionally in the produce of the area; (3) a tax.

canons regular: clergy living in common according to a rule, and often engaging in pastoral work as well as the office prescribed by their rule. See also **secular canons**.

cantref, pl. *cantrefi* (Welsh), an administrative district consisting in principle of one hundred farmsteads, and often divided into two commotes (q.v.).

carucate: a unit of land in England, related to the acreage which a team of oxen could plough in a year; used in Domesday Book to indicate the geld-liability of the land in question, and therefore affording only a very rough indication of its actual extent.

castlery: a lordship, often large, focusing on a castle and existing for its defence.

ceann cineil (Gaelic), a head of a kindred; synonymous with *toíseach cloinne* (q.v.).

cenn fine (Irish), a head of a kindred.

chapel: a local church, subordinate to the parish church where this existed, and sometimes privately owned.

chevage: (1) a tax paid by a villein for permission to live away from his native manor; (2) less commonly than (1), a tax levied by the lord of a manor on immigrants of low status; (3) also less common than (1), a tax paid by landless labourers to the lord of their manor.

chief lord: a fief-holder's immediate lord.

clann (Irish and Gaelic), children, descendants.

clas, pl. *clasau* (Welsh), the mother-church of a large district, which was served by the abbot and canons of the church. The district in question was sometimes identical with a *cantref* (q.v.).

cog: a ship with flush-laid and flat bottom, straight stem and stern posts, and clinker-built sides.

coinnmed (Gaelic), *conveth* (Scots), hospitality rent.

common fields/open fields: fields in which the land of the individual cultivator was divided into scattered strips and subject to rules accepted by all cultivators. At their highest pitch of development, the rules regulated rotation courses, including fallowing, and common rights in the arable, meadow, and pasture.

common fine: a fine payable on some manors by adult men to the lord, either on a per capita basis or as a conventionalized lump sum.

commote: an administrative district in native Wales, and by *c.*1200 the most important one.

condominium (Latin), joint rule.

conveth: see *coinnmed*

coracle: a small boat, with wicker-work frame and skin covering.

Cumbria: (1) the former kingdom of Strathclyde; (2) ('English Cumbria'): the counties of Cumberland and Westmorland, formerly the southern part of (1).

cymyd, pl. *cymydau* (Welsh), commote (q.v.).

cynnwys (Welsh), (1) a share granted to a bastard son; (2) the adoption of such offspring into the lineage which such a share implies.

dawnbwyd (Welsh), food render given by bondmen to their lord.

death rate: the number of deaths per 1,000 population.

demesne: (1) the home farm of a manor; (2) that part of an estate which had not been alienated but was under the lord's direct control.

diptych: an altar-piece with two wings.

dispersed farmsteads: see **dispersed settlement**

dispersed settlement: (1) an isolated farmstead (q.v.); (2) a small cluster of farmsteads which had grown haphazardly.

disseisin (Scots **dissasine**), the forcible or unjust dispossession of a free tenant of his property.

Domesday Book, Domesday Survey: terms which are often used interchangeably. In the present volume, however, the latter is the inquest into landholding etc. which took place in 1086, the former, the two volumes, sometimes called Great and Little Domesday, in which the findings of the inquest were distilled over a period ending early in the reign of William II.

double order: a religious order accepting both men and women to profession. The structure of authority varied among such orders, but invariably the men and the women occupied separate quarters.

dower: the bridegroom's gift to the bride at the marriage, of land, chattels, or money.

dún (Irish), fortified dwelling.

escheat: feudally held lands which reverted to the king for lack of heirs or as a result of confiscation or forfeiture.

escheators: officials appointed in England and the lordship of Ireland in the thirteenth century, to keep the king's escheats and wardships and account for them.

eyre: a visitation by royal justices, usually part of a circuit.

familia, familiaris (Latin), household, member of the household, and, by extension, a man dear to his lord. The terms are often used in relation to the king's domestic and military households.

farmstead: a compact farming unit, consisting of a homestead surrounded by, or adjacent to, its own arable and pasture enclosures.

fealty: the loyalty, often sealed by an oath, which a man owed to his lord.

fee, fief (Scots, *feu*), a lord's provision for his vassal, normally of land and normally heritable, in return for homage (q.v.) and services.

feodum, feudum (Latin), fee (q.v.).

fertility rate: birth rate related to relevant features (e.g. age structure) of the population under observation.

feu, see **fee**

feudal incidents: the occasional, as distinct from the regular and recurring, obligations of a fief-holder to his lord, and notably escheat, marriage, relief, and wardship (q.v.). Sometimes called 'casualties'.

forest: land reserved for hunting, other uses being correspondingly restricted.

frankpledge: a system whereby males aged, normally, 12 and over were organized in tithings (q.v.) and provided mutual surety.

galley: a large warship powered by oars.

gavelkind: a custom associated with privileged forms of tenure in Kent. Land so held was partible among all the sons of the previous holder, and among daughters if there was no son; and services owing to the lord were light.

geld: a general land tax in England, levied for the first time on what proved to be a permanent basis *c.*1012, but anticipated in some earlier levies on an occasional basis; levied for the last time in 1161–2. The general tax on the entire English kingdom was often known as 'Danegeld' in the twelfth century. The term 'geld' was also then used to describe other levies on land.

glebe: the land or other kinds of real property forming the endowment of a parish (q.v.).

gwestfa (Welsh), food render owed by freemen to the king.

halmote: a manor court.

hamlet: a cluster of farmsteads or other dwellings, without a nucleus.

homage: the act creating the bond between man and lord in respect of property held by the former of the latter.

hospital: a charitable institution serving a variety of purposes, which might include the care of the transient sick but more often focused on long-term care of the infirm.

hulk: a ship with rounded hull and strakes gathered into the upper edge of the latter.

Hundred Rolls: the name now given to (1) rolls recording returns to an inquiry into the loss of royal rights in England in 1274–5, and (2) rolls recording returns to an inquiry into the lands, rents, and services of landholders, and judicial liberties, in England in 1279–80; in the case of (2), returns survive in whole or in part for only a few counties.

impartibility: a rule of inheritance giving the entire inheritance to a single heir.

infield–outfield system: a field system in which part of the cultivable land (the infield) was cropped regularly, and part (the outfield) in shifts. The rotation course for the infield might or might not include a fallow year; the shifts on the outfield allowed for long periods when no crops were taken.

inland: land belonging to a seignorial estate which was closely supervised by the lord, worked by servile tenants or other forms of servile labour, and in England exempt from geld (q.v.).

intercommoning: the sharing of common rights by the inhabitants of different settlements.

iudex (Latin), in Scotland, a local or regional judge; see also *brithem*.

latimarius, pl. *latimarii* (Latin), a professional interpreter.

lector: (1) one in the Minor Orders having the liturgical duty of reading the Old Testament prophecies and the Epistles; (2) the person appointed to lecture in theology in one of the schools of theology which the friars were permitted to have for their own orders in Oxford and Cambridge.

lineage: the group of freemen descended from a common ancestor to which the heir to land in process of transmission must belong.

literati (Latin), men trained in the skills and culture associated with Latin texts, classical and ecclesiastical.

loan (of land), a lease.

maerdref, pl. *maerdrefi* (Welsh), a demesne estate of a king or other ruler, worked by servile tenants, and adjacent to a court which it provisioned. See **multiple estate** and **shire**.

manor: (1) a unit of estate administration; (2) a unit of lordship.

marriage: a lord's right to grant the marriage of an heiress to land held of him by any of the feudal tenures.

minster: a mother-church from which a community of secular clerks served an area known as a 'parish'; the latter was much larger than the typical parish dependent on a local church which developed over much of Britain and in south and east Ireland in the course of the twelfth and thirteenth centuries. Analogous to the *clas* (q.v.); see also **parish**.

mortality rate: death rate related to other relevant features (e.g. age structure) of the population under observation.

mother-church, see *clas*, **minster**

moveables: chattels, as distinct from real property, used in the assessment of taxes.

multiple estate: a discrete estate, comprising outlying and scattered settlements worked by servile tenants, but focused on a central court or hall to which rents and services were owing. See *maerdref*, and **shire** (1).

murdrum (Latin) **fine**, a sum payable by the hundred in whose district a Norman was killed secretly, but where no suspect was arrested; it could be avoided by proving that the victim was English. The law probably derived from a law of Cnut for the protection of Danes in England.

native Wales/*pura Wallia*: the area of Wales subject to native rule.

nativa, nativus (Latin), a born serf or villein; a neif.

neif, see *nativa, nativus*

new monasticism: a comprehensive description of the new religious orders for men and/or women which made their first foundations in Britain and Ireland in the course of the twelfth century; relates not only to the specifically monastic orders, among which the Cistercians were pre-eminent in influence, but also to the Augustinian and Premonstratensian canons regular and the double orders of Fontevraud and Sempringham, and sometimes to hermits and anchoresses. See **canons regular**.

Northumbria: historically, the ancient kingdom of this name, stretching at its fullest extent from the Humber to the Forth and consisting of the provinces of Bernicia (Forth to Tees) and Deira (Tees to Humber). The name is frequently used by present-day historians of this area in the eleventh and twelfth centuries, when the political allegiance of the northern part was unsettled as between England and Scotland. The disputes principally related to the land between the Cheviot–Tweed line and the Tees, of which the English finally gained control in 1157.

nucleated settlement: a settlement where the dwellings or tofts were clustered either at a particular point or contiguously, along rows.

oblate: a child offered by his parents, to be brought up in the monastery in question, with the intention that he would make his profession there in adolescence. Some traces of a similar, less formal system relating to girls survive. A Benedictine institution, shunned by the new monasticism (q.v.)

and brought to an end among Benedictines themselves by the end of the twelfth century.

open fields, see **common fields**

ordeal: a form of trial representing an appeal to the judgement of God, as evinced in the accused's response to a (normally) physical ordeal; this commonly consisted of carrying a hot iron or plunging a hand into boiling water, guilt or innocence being revealed by the state of the hand after a short period, or of immersion in a pool of water, which, it was believed, would reject the guilty.

papal bull: a document issuing from the papal chancery and sealed with the double-sided, leaden, papal seal known as the *bulla*.

papal provision: the right claimed by the pope to provide a nominee for a benefice and so set aside the customary right of the patron.

parish: the area paying dues to a particular church and dependent upon it for the administration of the sacraments and religious instruction. In the course of the twelfth and thirteenth centuries, the multiplication of local churches and formalization of tithe obligations led to the splitting up of large older parishes over much of Britain, and in south and east Ireland, into smaller new and autonomous ones to which tithe (q.v.) and other dues were assigned.

partibility: a rule of inheritance recognizing more than a sole heir—e.g. all the sons of the deceased landholder—and dividing the inheritance among them.

peasant: a word used variously; in this volume it signifies (1) an inhabitant of the countryside who owned land or held it as a tenant (rarely more than 100 acres and normally less than 40) and himself or herself took part in its exploitation; and (2) rural labourers and artisans and others whose work was essential to the life of the countryside, even if they held no land. In practice, the two groups overlapped.

pencenedl (Welsh), head of a kindred.

pipe roll: the record of the annual accounts presented at the English exchequer or the exchequer in Dublin, by officials obliged to account there.

planctus (Latin), dirge.

planned village: a nucleated settlement (q.v.), where the regularity of the layout, and in some cases the relationship of this to the layout of strips in the common fields/open fields (q.v.), points to preliminary planning.

primogeniture: the rule of inheritance giving all the land or other property to the eldest son of the deceased owner or tenant. If there were no sons, the English custom, probably dating from the later years of Henry I's reign, was to make an equal division among all the daughters.

pura Wallia (Latin), see **native Wales**

reeve: (1) the head man of a vill (q.v.); (2) a manorial official, normally in charge of a single manor, of which he was an unfree tenant.

regent master: a master engaged in teaching in the university in question.

regular clergy: clergy belonging to a religious order; see also **canons regular**.

relief: the sum payable to his lord by a free tenant for the right to succeed to an estate.

reliquary: a receptacle for relics, often made of precious metal, and sometimes in the shape of the relic in question.

rent: a recurring payment owing to a lord or other person for land or other property, assessed in money, labour services, or produce, or a mixture of these.

romanesque: a descriptive term for styles of, respectively, architecture and manuscript decoration created in western Europe in the eleventh century and flowering then and in the twelfth.

scriptorium: the collective name for scribes collaborating to produce books and documents for a monastery; the name is often used by present-day historians of the room or other location where the scribes worked.

scutage: a payment in commutation of the military service owing in respect of a knight's fee.

secular canons: clergy serving, and in principle resident in, a cathedral or other greater church, or a collegiate church, but not otherwise living according to a rule.

secular clergy: clergy not belonging to a religious order.

seisin: possession.

serf: an unfree man or woman, sometimes, but not invariably, a landholder on the manor (q.v.) in question.

sester: a measure of capacity for grain and other dry products, probably equivalent to a quarter.

sheriff: in England, Scotland, and the lordship of Ireland, an official with financial, judicial, and police responsibilities; in England, and to some extent Ireland, his sphere of duty was the shire or county, but in Scotland, the sheriffdom, a province with close links with a royal burgh or burghs.

shire: (1) anciently, in England and south and east Scotland, a royal multiple estate (q.v., and see also *maerdref*); (2) a larger territorial unit, also known as the county, and, as the sphere of duty of the sheriff (q.v.), the most important unit of local government in this period in England. Introduced to some extent in the lordship of Ireland in the thirteenth century.

shout: a large boat with flat bottom, used for carrying heavy loads on large inland waterways.

slave: a rightless person who was legally owned by his or her lord.

soke: (1) jurisdiction; (2) the area over which (1) was exercised.

sokeman: one who acknowledged the jurisdiction of a lord but was otherwise little dependent on him.

sterling: (1) the English currency; (2) a standard referring to the weight of the alloy added to the silver of sterling coins during minting.

synodal legislation: statutes issued by a bishop at a meeting of his diocesan synod.

taeog (Welsh), bondman.

tallage: a tax leviable without consent.

teind: tithe (q.v.).

tenant-in-chief: a landowner holding his estate as a fee (q.v.) directly from the king.

tenement: the total holding, comprising toft, arable, meadow, and other appurtenances, of a free or unfree tenant in England.

teulu (Welsh), a lord's household troop.

thane: in twelfth-century Scotland, the official who sometimes had charge of the royal estate known as a shire (q.v. (1)); formerly this arrangement for shires may have been the universal practice.

tithe: the tenth of produce or income payable to the Church and increasingly, in this period, paid to the local church; the payment served to identify the latter as the parish church of the district in question. In Gaelic Ireland, however, and in Argyll and the Western Isles, tithes were normally divided between the bishop, a sinecure rector, and a vicar, and this arrangement persisted to the end of the period.

tithing: a group of males of 12 years and over, normally ten in number, responsible for one another's good behaviour, and as such forming the basic unit of the frankpledge system (q.v.); (2) a village or hamlet which itself constituted a tithing for all its male inhabitants.

toiseach cloinne (Gaelic), head of a noble kindred.

tonnage: a ship's cargo capacity measured in tuns (q.v.).

tonne: a metric measure of weight, equivalent to 1,000 kilos = *c.*2,200 lbs.

toun: see **township**

township: a settlement, which might be clustered or dispersed, or a number of settlements of either kind, sometimes referred to in England as a vill and in Scotland as a *toun*; in Wales, a *tref*.

transhumance: seasonal droving of swine and cattle to distant pastures.

treenail: a wooden peg used to fasten a ship's or boat's frame to the planks.

tref, pl. *trefi* (Welsh), township (q.v.).

tribute: a payment to a lord that rested on a personal and not a territorial basis.

tun: (1) a cask; (2) a measure of capacity, especially for wine, containing 252 gallons.

vill, see **township**

village: a nucleated settlement (q.v.). See also **planned village.**

villanus, pl. *villani* (Latin), in Domesday Book, an imprecise description signifying inhabitants of a manor who were of low status but not of the lowest. Translated as 'villain'/'villains' in this volume, to distinguish the persons in question from the 'villeins' of the twelfth century and later: these were disadvantaged in more precise ways.

villein: a serf (q.v.).

wapentake: a district in eastern England equivalent to the hundred elsewhere.

wardship: a lord's right to the custody of lands held of him by any of the feudal tenures during the minority of the heir.

waste: (1) land not appropriated for private use but available as common pasture; (2) land or other property which was not yielding its normal dues and profits; (3) devastated land or other property.

wick, see **barton**

Map section

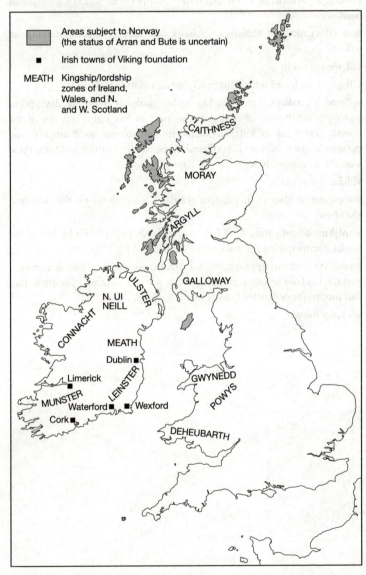

Areas subject to Norway
(the status of Arran and Bute is uncertain)

■ Irish towns of Viking foundation

MEATH Kingship/lordship zones of Ireland, Wales, and N. and W. Scotland

CAITHNESS

MORAY

ARGYLL

GALLOWAY

ULSTER

N. UI NEILL

CONNACHT

MEATH

Dublin ■

Limerick ■

MUNSTER

Waterford ■ ■ Wexford

LEINSTER

Cork ■

GWYNEDD

POWYS

DEHEUBARTH

Map A Changing power structures in north-west Scotland and the Irish Sea zone c.1100

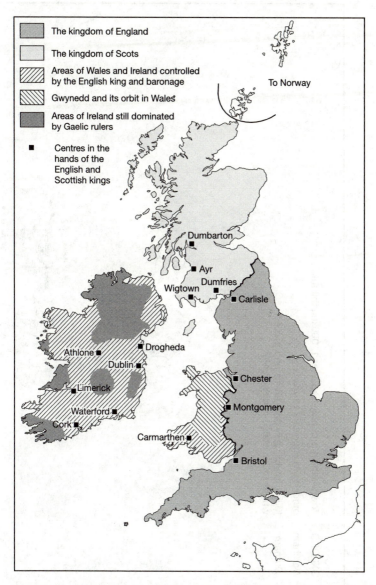

Map B Changing power structures in north-west Scotland and the Irish Sea zone *c.*1270

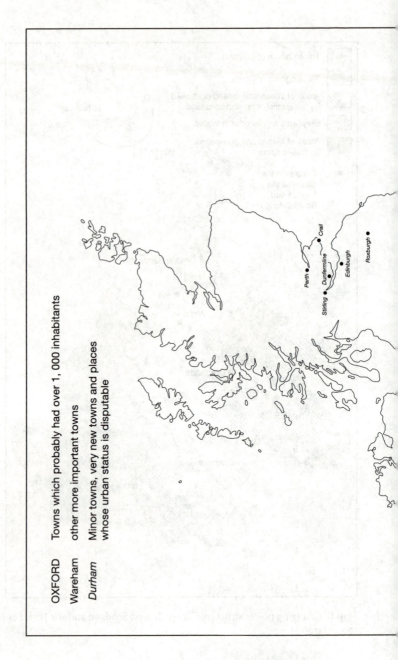

OXFORD   Towns which probably had over 1, 000 inhabitants

Wareham   other more important towns

Durham   Minor towns, very new towns and places
whose urban status is disputable

Map C Towns in the British Isles c.1100

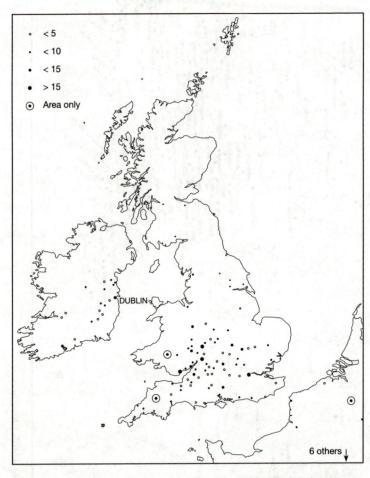

Map D Origins of the burgesses of Dublin. The origins of Dublin's burgesses in the early thirteenth century. The evidence of the personal names from Dublin shows a colonizing pattern; many more burgesses came from England and Wales than from Ireland.

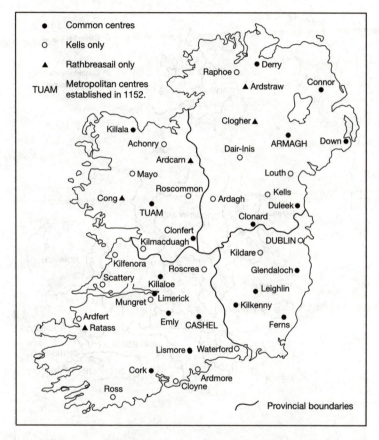

Map E Provinces and diocesan centres in Ireland established at the Council of Kells-Mellifont, 1152

Map F Dioceses in England and Wales *c.*1300

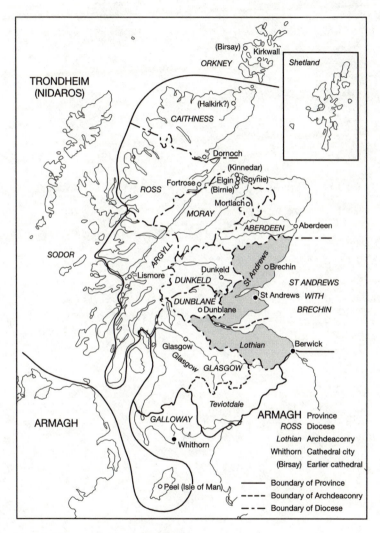

Map G Dioceses in Scotland c.1300

Index